Leading Strategy
Execution

Also by Richard McKnight

Victim, Survivor, or Navigator:
Choosing a Response to Workplace Change

Leading Strategy
Execution

*How to align the senior team,
design a strategy-capable organization,
and get all employees on-board*

by Richard McKnight
with Tom Kaney & Shannon Breuer

Philadelphia

Published by TrueNorth Press, Philadelphia, PA

McKnight, Richard, 1947–; Kaney, Thomas, 1945—; and Breuer, Shannon, 1956—. Leading strategy execution / How to align the senior team, design a strategy-capable organization, and get all employees on-board.
Philadelphia: TrueNorth Press, 2010.
p. 294: ill. ; cm.
Summary: A guide for executives in implementing strategy.
Includes index.
    ISBN: 978-0-9824683-1-9
    Library of Congress Control Number: 2009940358
10 9 8 7 6 5 4 3 2

This book is available at discount when purchased in bulk (15 or more copies). To inquire about discounts, go to TrueNorthPress.com.

*Book design, cover design, typesetting, and illustrations
(unless otherwise noted) by Richard McKnight*

Contents

Foreword

ETURNING FROM ASIA, AFTER A week spent with consultants, human resource and organization development professionals, as well as business leaders from corporations, government agencies, and state enterprises, I reflected on a frustration I've heard around the world: "We have spent much energy and focus on developing a strong strategy, but the organization is not able to execute."

When leaders set strategy, they are indicating that new capabilities are needed. Today, regardless of industry or region, public or private sphere, those capabilities are complex: organic growth through innovation, adding high value solutions to product and service offerings, managing the web of global and local decision-making, and gaining the advantages of scale without sacrificing speed. Building such capabilities requires changes in decision rights, processes, skills, and communication patterns.

Orchestrating the alignment of the organization to build new capabilities is the task of leadership. McKnight, Kaney, and Breuer have produced a valuable guide to creating this alignment and, in the process, of creating an organization capable of strategy execution. *Leading Strategy Execution* complements the literature on business strategy by providing a sound model by which to create strategy with execution in mind, a means of bringing the rational and socio-emotive aspects of the organization into alignment, and by showing how strategy execution requires designing and building organizational capabilities.

Taking a holistic perspective, this book blends a belief in the power of individuals with a commitment to creating organizational forms that bring out the best in those people. In doing so, this book does several things for business leaders who will otherwise struggle to implement their strategy. It...

• Outlines the characteristics of an executable strategy

• Identifies the "Four Jobs of Strategy Execution"

• Provides guidance in designing an organization capable of delivering on the strategy

• Offers valuable counsel for leaders who have to enlist the support of employees, and sustain their energy even when strategy calls for dislocation

In this book, you will find a summary and application of the work of Jay Galbraith, myself, and others in the field of organization design. You will also find the integration of thought leaders in the fields of leadership, change, and human resources brought together into a clear and actionable framework. For example, the authors take the concept of the Balanced Scorecard—a powerful concept that many leadership teams struggle to implement successfully—and turn it into an easy to use strategy map that makes absolutely clear the relationship between capabilities and results.

These authors' many years working as organizational consultants (combined with Richard McKnight's photographer's eye for the telling detail) enable many insights into the workings of organizational life. *Leading Strategy Execution* is infused with a humanity not often found in business writing.

This wise, easy-to-read, and very helpful book will provide concrete guidance in getting the strategic results you seek.

—Amy Kates
Co-author, with Jay R. Galbraith, of
Designing Your Organization

Acknowledgements

First and foremost, we thank our clients who have allowed us to get in the trenches with them and fight the good fight, especially Art, Dan, Diane, Janet, Jim, Terry, Todd, and Sharon.

Hadley Williams, organization designer *extraordinaire,* helped us untangle many theoretical knots, provided insightful guidance on the Action Learning pieces, and encouraged us to use his ideas as our own. Thank you for your uncommonly generous support.

We are grateful (and every reader should be, too!) for the help of Miryam Roddy, our editor, who rooted out countless typos and many other problemz. (Sorry, Miryam, had to do that!)

Numerous colleagues contributed exceptionally valuable feedback on early drafts. They responded promptly to our request for critical evaluation and took pains to be kind. They include Linda Ackerman Anderson, Dave Bolz, Mario DiCioccio, Melody Evans, Megan Gilason, Cindy Howes, Karen Fanta Love, Todd Kleinman, Ron McKnight, Mike Taylor, Chris Sam, Irv Stern, Mary Vila, Dick Watson, and Zak Zaklad.

Portions of this book were adapted from the following,
all by Richard McKnight

"Top Team Alignment: The Epicenter of Strategy Execution." *OD Practitioner,* April, 2009.

"Deconstructing Obama Mania: Lessons for Business Leaders from the Obama Victory." Unpublished, 2009.

"HR's Role in Strategy Implementation." *Business Canada,* 2007.

"Business Literacy: What it is, How to Get it, and Why You Need it." *OD Practitioner,* 2004.

"The Social Side of the Supply Chain." *Industrial Engineer,* February, 2004. (with others)

"Moving the Rock: Transforming Prudential Through Whole System Change." *Proceedings,* OD Network, Vancouver, BC, 2002.

"One Prudential Exchange: the Insurance Giant's Business Literacy and Alignment Platform." *Human Resource Management Journal,* Fall, 2002.

"Balancing the HR Scorecard: A Review of The HR Scorecard," *Human Resource Planning,* December, 2001 (with Alan Zaklad, Ph.D.)

"The Four Jobs of Strategy Implementation." *OD Practitioner,* Fall, 2001.

"White Collar Blues." (Book Review), *PRODN Network News,* November, 1995.

Leading Strategy Execution

Chapter One

Execution is Everything

Strategy is important. Execution is everything.
—JP Garnier, former CEO, GlaxoSmithKline

MOST LEADERS FAIL TO EXECUTE their strategies. Decades of research into the subject reveals that well over half of America's business leaders go to bed at night frustrated that their achievements are falling far short of their aims. Even the most celebrated executives, i.e., those possessing intellectual brilliance, position power, and access to the best strategy-creating consultants money can buy, often struggle to live up to the promises they've made to their shareholders (London Business School, 2010).

This book explains what contributes to those failures, but while this is important to understand, we will devote only five percent or so of the book to those causes. More importantly, we will allocate 95 percent of the book to very practical guidance that any manager or executive can use to close the gap between current reality and future intentions. If you wish to get far better at achieving your strategic objectives, you've picked up the right book.

At its most basic level, a strategy is a plan that spells out how you intend to make your way from one place to another. It's a kind of navigation plan: today, we're here, tomorrow, we wish to go there. Here's how we will do so. Making your way from one position to a more favorable one requires four things, *each* of which is addressed in this book:

- You need to know where you are now
- You need to know where you're going
- You need to take relevant action
- You need to learn

The last item on this list tends to get overlooked in almost all books on strategy-making. As businesspeople, we love to plan, and we love taking action, but we seem to be far less interested in doing the learning that is required the minute we trot out our plan and make an attempt to implement it.

For nonscientific evidence of this, go to amazon.com's search box and enter the term "strategic planning." You are likely, as we did, to see over 47,000 titles listed. On the other hand, if you enter the phrase, "strategy implementation," only 7-8,000 will return. Far fewer titles will show up if you type in "strategy execution." In fact, the ratio of books on strategic planning, to those on strategy execution and strategy implementation combined, is 5:1. For every one book on the *"How"* of strategy, there are five on the *"What"* of strategy.

Underscoring the importance of learning in the process of strategy execution, a famous military quotation says, "No battle plan survives contact with the enemy." We have seen this quote attributed to everyone from Dwight Eisenhower to Colin Powell, but according to Wikipedia.com (2010), it was first uttered by one Helmuth von Moltke the Elder, a Prussian field Marshall (1800-1891).

In searching for the origin of this quote, we came across some additional lines about strategy and strategy execution that are clever variations of Murphy's Law. You will recall that Murphy's Law states, "If something can go wrong, it will go wrong." Here are four of the "Murphy's Laws of Combat" that we thought have the most to say to would-be strategy implementers:

- *The easy way is always mined.*
- *The easy way generally gets you killed.*

- *The law of the bayonet says the man with the bullet wins.*

- *The only terrain that is truly controlled is the terrain upon which you're standing.*

These maxims counsel against complacency and smugness and are in complete accord with the view that strategy cannot be divorced from action and learning.

To improve your game at strategy execution, your learning has to start early, i.e., while you're creating your strategy. This is because two of the most virulent causes of strategy execution failure, invisible to the unschooled and lying in wait like dormant anthrax spores, can doom your best intentions. One is employing a bureaucratic, top-down approach to creating strategy. The other is failing to effect alignment among the group of leaders. In this book, we tell you how to do both.

Along with some relatively familiar ones like employee engagement, organization design, and alignment, this book introduces some new terms, most notably:

- The executable strategy

- The strategy-capable organization

- The Four Jobs of Strategy Execution

Importantly, we also explore the idea that not all strategies are equal when it come to execution. We will clarify what makes a strategy executable in this chapter and later in the book will tell how to fit an organization to a strategy so that the organizational apparatus can shape, support, and direct the human energy necessary to deliver the desired future. We will also show how doing the Four Jobs of Strategy Execution enables you to win the hearts, minds, and hands of every employee in every work unit, top to bottom, side to side.

Our Aims

This book is for any organizational leader who has a strategic vision and wishes to manifest it, but whose aspirations require the support of others. Our aim is to offer a book that is useful to anyone who has responsibility for turning an organizational vision into a reality, whether their role is the head of a large, complex corporation or that of a manager in a small social service agency.

Thus, if you are a manager, a director, *or* if you carry a "Chief..." title, *Leading Strategy Execution* is tailor-made for you. You will also find this book valuable if you are an organizational consultant, an HR professional, and/or have responsibilities for helping managers and executives be more strategic in their thinking and behavior. But fair warning: If you're an individual contributor whose role does not position you as an advisor to someone who leads others, our guidance may frustrate you. You will see what should be done but you may not have access to the levers of influence required to use what you're learning.

To help you decide if this book will be useful, here's the core thesis: Most approaches to strategy implementation fail because strategy is created at one level (the top) and handed off to another (the middle and bottom). We believe that to improve strategy implementation, you have to involve employees extensively in *creating* the strategy, and senior managers have to become involved in *executing*—as well as formulating—the strategy. Our aim is to help you do both in ways that honor role expectations and align with job responsibilities and accountabilities.

Thus, this is the book for you if you're an organizational leader who believes there is huge untapped potential in most organizations and you want to unleash it, but, if you admire the traditional top-down, command-control management style or if the idea of involving lower-level employees in creating and executing on parts of the strategy seems inadvisable, this book will challenge you to rethink your approach.

As we said at the opening of this chapter, over half of the strategic plans created each year fail utterly to deliver the results expected from them. We promise you: By applying these ideas, you will beat those odds and simultaneously put practices in place that attract and retain the best talent in your industry. Many executives struggle to do the work of leadership, i.e., to fire people up, engage employees as willing partners, and create efficient organizations that produce needed results over time. This book will help you do all of this. We will explore what others have done to get the results their company or department needs while improving their leadership skills.

What Kind of Leader are You?

Bearing in mind that leaders are those who envision the future and pave the way for it, this is a book for people who wish to be better at the craft. We believe that if you wish to be a better leader of strategy execution, you need to begin with knowing what your assumptions about organizations and organizational change are. Every organizational leader operates from a theory—usually unconscious—about the best way to produce business results. Those theories were summarized in one of the best books we have ever read on the subject of leading organizational change: *Breaking the Code of Change: Resolving the Tension between Theory E, and O of Change* (Beer & Nohria, 2000). This gem came out of a most unusual project.

A few years back, Professors Michael Beer and Nitin Nohria hosted a conference at Harvard Business School to discuss organizational change, inviting an all-star cast of academics, consultants, and business leaders who had credentials in driving successful organizational transformation. The purpose of the conference was, in the authors' words, "to identify the key considerations in choosing among different change strategies in the transformation of large underperforming companies."

Beer and Nohria paired the participants and asked them to debate points of view about organizational change along the lines of the purpose of change, how to lead the change process, and how to leverage change. In summarizing the results of the convocation, Beer and Nohria concluded that most consultants and executives employ one of two approaches to organizational change. They called those approaches Theory E and Theory O, summarized in Figure 1-1.

Which theory do you espouse?

Theory E devotees pay relatively little attention to people's feel-

Is Your Strategy Executable?
Not all strategies are!

A strategy describes a set of interrelated actions (causes) that are calculated to lead to a given set of results (effects).

An *executable strategy* is a narrative, not a set of bullet points. That narrative tells a comprehensive story of aspirations, of how value is created and how change will unfold, what steps will be taken and why, and how those steps lead one to another.

That narrative includes the following:

1. The goals the strategy is intended to achieve, with particular emphasis on customer benefits, and how those results will lead to financial gain.

2. The value discipline to which the organization is committed (i.e., product innovation, operational excellence, or customer-intimacy).

3. Why achieving those goals is important, the rationale behind the strategy.

4. How and why taking these steps is crucial NOW.

5. The steps required in four organization design arenas, and how taking those steps will lead to results for customers, and thus for shareholders:

   • The structure of the organization; the lines and boxes.
   • The key business processes and how they contribute to results, noting which need improvement, development, etc.
   • The organization's reward and performance tracking system.
   • The organization's people practices.

ings and to cultural issues. Instead, the powerful levers of organizational structure, IT systems, business processes, and the like are their focus. If we change these, Theory E adherents argue, financial performance improves, we all retain employment, and therefore, the shareholders are happy. And who drives Theory E change efforts? A few highly placed senior executives along with a squad of high-priced advisors from well-known external consulting firms.

Theory E	Theory O
Purpose of organizational change: Create shareholder value	Purpose of organizational change: Develop human assets
Focus: Formal structure and systems, "hardware"	Focus: Culture, people, "software"
Leadership: Tightly held by the top	Leadership: Distributed, participative
Incentives: Tangible, chiefly money	Incentives: Intangible, chiefly camaraderie

Figure 1-1: Beer and Nohria's Theories E & O

As an extreme example of Theory E, Beer and Nohria offer Al Dunlop at Scott Paper. You may recall Dunlop's nickname: "Chain Saw Al," a moniker obtained when he eliminated 11,000 jobs at Scott paper, selling off Scott businesses, moving its headquarters to Florida from Pennsylvania, and for taking other draconian actions to improve shareholder returns.

Theory O practitioners take a contrary view, holding that only when employees become emotionally devoted to the firm's success can a firm thrive in the long-run. Large-scale cut backs are counterproductive, Theory O defenders maintain, unless the firm takes countervailing measures to sustain employee goodwill and engagement. According to Theory O, the solution to nearly every organizational problem can be extracted from within the firm itself, i.e., if the cultural conditions are right. Those conditions are participative leadership, high levels of employee engagement, and so forth. The Theory O practitioner may acknowledge the contributions organizational structure or other systems and processes make to performance, but instead of bringing in powerful outsiders to identify and drive change in these realms, the Theory O practitioner will set up change processes that bring forth solutions from *within* the organization.

Beer and Nohria conclude that, "The arguments for E and O change are equally persuasive," observing that they approach the matter of organizational change from different "but equally legitimate perspectives." In an urgent situation, Theory E may be exactly the tough medicine required. But if your goal is organizational health over time, they conclude, "Theory E change must be combined with Theory O." They also declare that this "and/also" approach is the hardest to pull off and a clumsy, halfhearted attempt to combine the two may set up gridlock and confusion. The ideas in this book will help you take this type of "and/also" approach.

Throughout *Leading Strategy Execution,* we say that those who successfully lead strategy execution do what we will call the Four Jobs of Strategy Execution. They:

- Educate employees about the strategy
- Get them excited about the strategy
- Conform local effort to the strategy
- Align all organizational systems to the strategy

Doing the Four Jobs requires taking the best from Theory E *and* from Theory O: keeping the need to be financially successful uppermost *and* understanding that winning requires fully engaging employees. In our view, when added together, E + O spells LEADER, a person capable of creating a community of learning, service, and contribution.

What does this look like? We think the phrase, "A community of learners with high spirits" sums it up pretty well. Does this phrase describe your workplace? Odds are, it does not.

Noting that a majority of workers are sick with stories of workplace greed and of celebrity CEOs feathering their own beds, *BusinessWeek* presented what it called "25 Ideas for a Changing World." The first suggestion offered was, "Have CEOs remake their companies into paragons of corporate responsibility, luring investors via their virtue." When the article appeared, we were a bit skeptical this would happen. We are glad we did not hold our breath: this was in 2002 and look what's happened since (Nussbaum, 2002).

Going back even further, Studs Terkel (1997) once interviewed hundreds of people about their work and wrote a book called *Working: People Talk About What They Do All Day and How They Feel About What They Do.* His conclusion in 1974 when it was published? "Most people have work that is too small for their spirits." Terkel found that most people come to work, hover there in a state of numb disengagement, and can't wait to go home again.

Can a workplace feel like a home for people's spirits, or is this just some starry-eyed, unrealistic dream? This is a reasonable question since, as we will explore in Chapter Two, statistics from 2008-2009 Corporate Executive Board research show employee engagement at all-time lows—and declining.

A home to the spirit. Does meeting this qualification mean anything when it comes to financial performance? You will learn in this book, if you are not already familiar with the research in this area, that workplaces *can* feel like home and that when they do, they tend to be much more financially successful than when they do not.

Why Should You Listen to (More) Consultants?

We are consultants, so we know that consultants are often very persuasive and that their advice can bewilder as often as enlighten. Like listening to the proverbial blind men describe the elephant, each consultant has his or her own perspective. For instance, strategy-creation consultants emphasize that the right market positioning or breakthrough business concept will win out while technical process improvement consultants see deliverance in process mapping and Six Sigma approaches. And then there are the Enterprise Resource Planning consultants who tout IT and standardized business processes as the pathway to success. And behind them are coaching gurus who argue for more and better leadership throughout the organization, and behind them HR colleagues intone about the virtues of talent management and competency models.

Each of these perspectives has something to offer. But consultants of all of these persuasions tend to think their perspective is *the* solution to organizational performance problems. As the saying goes, "If your only tool is a hammer, everything looks like a nail." And ultimately, what gets "pounded" is the client organization.

In writing *Leading Strategy Execution,* we have taken the view that when change is complex (and sometimes even when it isn't!), *many* kinds of expertise will be necessary.

Even though you might need temporary external support to achieve your strategic ambitions, our view is that most of the information, expertise, knowledge, and wisdom necessary to transform your organization is almost certainly already present: in the form of the people who live in that system day in and day out, i.e., your employees at all levels. We believe, based on over 60 years of combined experience, that when employees are brought into the process of creating something larger than themselves, their energy, commitment, and creativity goes up and up and their willingness to take responsibility goes through the roof.

The Holy Grail of strategy execution for most senior leaders is getting everyone in the organization to understand, feel enthusiastic about, and take action in alignment with the company's strategy. They know that when people comprehend the big picture, they make better decisions concerning their own piece of the action. Our aim here is to help you accomplish *all* of this.

Finally, in rounding out our approach to strategy execution, we believe that when people come to work each day, they do so as whole people: They bring their entire self to work, i.e., their bodies, minds, and spirits. People have needs in each of these domains. When organizations fail to engage the whole of their employees, the organization's performance invariably suffers, but when leaders create organizations that attend to those needs, the sky is the limit. We will show you how others have done this and how you can, too.

How the Book is Organized

Underlying this book is a systems view of strategy execution. By this, we mean that three aspects of an organization need to be addressed while executing strategy. Each is important and makes a contribution. And importantly, once needs in one area are addressed, those gains enable even more potent gains in other arenas. Those three domains are:

- Informed, skilled, and committed *individuals*

- Strategy-focused *work groups*

- A strategy-capable *organization* with structures, processes, and capabilities that foster those individual skills and coordinate that unit performance

Skilled individuals, aligned work groups, and organizational systems that bring out everyone's best: each are important. Thus, we will focus on each level of the value-delivering system. The boxes on the next two pages summarize the book's key concepts and tools. Note that there are nine assessment tools listed (they are in italics) which permit you to diagnose causes of strategy failure and to get your implementation plans on track. Use these tools to drive discussion among the parties that are key to execution in your organization.

At heart, we are educators who are passionate about enabling others to learn and grow. We have studied the learning process and know that unless applied, newly acquired knowledge dissipates rapidly. When a learner, on the other hand, employs new concepts and tools to their own situation and experience, especially in concert with others, learning endures and can be profound.

For this reason, we have included action learning exercises at the end of most chapters. "Action learning," as we'll use it here, is a term that refers to a process of applying what you're reading about. In most cases, the exercises will direct you, if possible, to join with others to answer questions about your organization and to compare your experiences about its effectiveness, all within the context of the material addressed in the chapter. You certainly can do the exercises by yourself, but you will derive maximum value as you read the book with others and do the exercises together. We urge you to modify the exercises to suit your circumstances. As you do what is recommended, your competency as strategy executors will sharpen immeasurably.

Personally, we value books that are down-to-earth yet erudite, practical, yet illuminating. We hope you agree that this book fits that description.

Chapter	Content/Tools
One *Execution is Everything*	Theory E/O Executable strategy *Is Your Strategy Executable?*
Two *Change or Die*	Strategy defined Three drivers of value in a business organization Problems with strategic planning Essential truths about strategy execution *First Things First* (identify your strategic planning problems)
Three *The Human Side of Strategy*	*Strategy Land Mines (pinpoint execution problems)* The Four Jobs of Strategy Execution A formula for strategy execution
Four *Job One:* *Winning Minds*	Business literacy defined Six prescriptions for increasing business literacy
Five *Job Two:* *Winning Hearts*	Common causes of resistance to change Eight guidelines for leaders seeking buy-in
Six *Job Three:* *Aligning Local Effort*	Strategy execution roles: Who does what? Work Unit Meetings The Five Questions Employees Have During Change *JumpStart Assessment* *Work Unit Meeting Assessment*

Chapter	Content/Tools
Seven *Job Four:* *Creating Organiza-* *tional* *Capabilities*	Organization design Organization design criteria Value discipline Star Model *Assess your Organization Design*
Eight *Strategy Maps:* *The Strategy Execu-* *tion Flight Plan*	Strategy maps Leading/lagging measures
Nine *Aligning the Senior* *Team*	Top team alignment defined *Five Sub-Optimal But Common Senior Teams* Model of team development *Senior Team Assessment*
Ten *HR's Role in Strategy* *Execution*	HR deliverables for strategy execution *HR Strategic Partner Assessment* Guidelines for HR during challenging times
Eleven *Right People, Right* *Place, Doing the* *Right Things*	Fitting talent to strategy Talent management in tough times Roles: Strategic, core, requisite, non-core
Twelve *Leading Strategy* *Execution*	A summary of the work of strategy execution

Action Learning

In this chapter, we laid out a definition of an "executable strategy," observing that many, if not most, organizations do not have such a strategy. Obtain the most recent example of your organization's strategy and evaluate it against the definition on page 18, "Is Your Strategy Executable?"

• Where does your strategy meet these criteria?

- Where does your strategy fall short?

- How would I/we change the authors' definition of an executable strategy—if at all?

Best wishes as you learn to move your organization to greatness! Our web site is filled with resources that support the ideas in this book. Avail yourself of them. Let us know what you're up against and share your victories. We'd love to hear from you.

www.MKBpartners.com

Chapter Two

Change or Die

Hope is not a strategy.
—Anonymous

However beautiful the strategy,
you should occasionally look at the results.
—Winston Churchill

WE THOUGHT WE WERE CLEVER when we created a slide
for a presentation about strategy execution that displayed pictures of hands: one showed hands in prayer,
another showed a pair of fingers crossed in fervent hope, and the
third was a "thumbs up" sign.

Showing the slide, we asked our audience, "Which picture reflects how your company executes its strategy?" Someone in the
back was more clever than we were. Prompting gales of laughter,
he shot back, "I can think of a hand signal that would reflect my
company's approach better than any I see up there!"

It was a good joke, but executing strategy successfully is not a laughing matter for most CEOs. We recently asked a dozen executive clients what they would prefer for their organizations: a brilliant strategy poorly implemented, or a fair strategy brilliantly implemented. Ten of the 12 went for brilliant implementation. Why? Because they want results and they know their job depends on getting them!

We've been in the business of strategy execution for a long time, both as senior leaders with responsibility for executing strategy and as consultants coaching and guiding other business leaders as they strive for high organizational performance. We're excited by this work, in part because we've discovered that lower- and middle-level employees are just as concerned about implementing strategy as executives are—when the conditions are right. Why wouldn't they be: their livelihood depends on it. In addition, they have to live in organizations that too often frustrate them, anger them, worry them, and squander their talents. Most employees care about the future of their company but usually have very little understanding of the strategy that they are expected to fulfill. We have found that most employees will jump at the opportunity for meaningful involvement in pursuit of strategic results. But fair warning: You have to go beyond simply *telling* people about the strategy; you have to *involve* them in both its creation and its pursuit.

What is a Strategy?

This is a book about strategy execution, what it takes to turn business intentions into reality. Before going too far, though, it is important also to say what this book is not. This is not a book on how to *create* a strategy per se. As we've said, there are hundreds of other books and countless articles that address that subject. We will, however, help you assess whether or not your strategy is actually *executable* and, if it's not, to make it so.

If you are casual about how you define strategy, your approach to its execution will probably also be casual—and almost certainly ineffective. The word strategy is used in many different ways—and this is part of the strategy execution problem. For instance, Mc-

Gill University business school's Henry Mintzberg, summarized the various uses of the word strategy in business, observing that businesspeople use the word strategy in at least five different ways (Mintzberg, 1994). In its most common usage, a strategy is a PLAN, but many people use the term also to refer to a PATTERN of organizational behavior, a competitive POSITION, a PERSPECTIVE on what it takes to succeed in a given marketplace, and a set of PLOYS or stratagems that one uses to gain competitive advantage. Sheesh! No wonder we struggle!

Consulting Wikipedia (2010), we find that the word strategy comes from the Greek and has military origins. Indeed, the word emerges from the Greek word *strateg*, which means military commander. In popular usage, strategy most often means the set of actions (causes) that are calculated to lead to a given result (effect).

Wikipedia is also helpful in distinguishing strategy from tactics:

In military terms, "tactics" is concerned with the conduct of an engagement while "strategy" is concerned with how different engagements are linked. In other words, how a battle is fought is a matter of tactics: whether it should be fought at all is a matter of strategy.

We are astonished at the number of strategy statements we encounter that are nothing more than a PowerPoint deck of platitudes and objectives. Other statements consist of a simple list of "To Do's," or a vague set of aspirations or values. Is it any wonder that leaders are not seeing the results they need to see? Thirty years ago, when just being in the market meant you could expect returns in many industries, perhaps this was acceptable. It is certainly not today.

We have raised our standards considerably as to what constitutes a strategy because most implementation problems begin there. We now believe that to succeed, an organization must have what we refer to as an *executable strategy*, one that takes into account financial results, the customer results that will lead to them, and a set of organizational capabilities that each requires. A strategy does not exist in a vacuum. It must reflect the nature of the system that has to carry it out and that system—the organization—must manifest the intentions behind the strategy. Thus, a strategy—at least an *executable strategy*—states both what the organizational leaders intend *and* how they will go about realizing their intentions. Making this one alteration to strategy alone would make some organizations many times as likely to reach their goals than at present. Our definition of "executable strategy" appears in the box on "Is Your Strategy Executable?" on page 18.

As you will learn, we employ a multiplicity of instruments and concepts in our work with clients, but primary among them are two tools, each of which contribute immeasurably to the creation of executable strategies: strategy maps, invented by Robert Kaplan and David Norton, and principles of organization design as articulated by Amy Kates and Jay R. Galbraith. Using these two tools calls forth the intellectual discipline required of a rigorous planning and execution process. We will tell you how to use both tools.

While the military, so far as we know, does not use the term "executable strategy," you might find it interesting to learn, as we did, that strategy execution is built into the best practices of military leadership. The conscientious officer knows, for example, that issuing a simple set of bullet points is anything but sufficient preparation for battle. Best practices in military settings require an officer to write out orders that include both the rationale behind the mission and the steps required to reach its objectives. But that's not all: Once verbal and written orders are given, the commanding officer will then ask for a "brief back," by saying, "Now you tell me what I've told you, so that we can both be assured that we're on the same page."

Why Strategy Execution Matters

The marketplace has always punished companies that dawdle in manifesting the promise of their strategic intentions, but today, those beatings come faster than ever. This is evident, in part, in the rate of CEO turnover, increasing at ever-faster rates until quite recently.

CEO turnover is attributable primarily to poor company financial performance relative to industry performance norms. According to Challenger Gray & Christmas (2009), a firm that tracks these data, in the interval between 1992 and 2005, turnover for CEOs increased by 14.9 percent. In the first nine months of 2008, CEO turnover hit an all-time high. In fact, on every work day in America in 2008, six CEOs turned over! Given the economic meltdown of late 2008, the 2009 statistics have improved: Boards are loathe to toss out CEOs in the middle of an economic crisis.

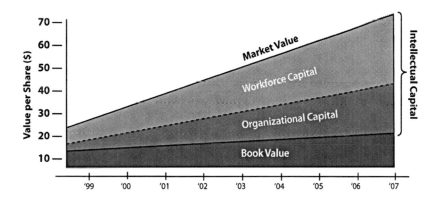

Figure 2-1: A company's market value is made up of three sets of assets. (Data: S&P 500, Russell 2000.)

Let's take a look at what drives company financial performance, the ultimate scorecard by which CEOs are judged. By doing so, we touch on the only real reason why CEOs or *anyone* should care about disciplined strategy execution: because the effort put into it might pay off in the creation of sustainable market value.

A firm's value, as defined by stock price, is made up of three components. They are depicted in Figure 2-1. The least of a company's worth is determined by the *book value* of its assets, the bottommost component of the chart. Book value represents the capital invested since the firm's inception, minus all liabilities, i.e., essentially what could be derived from a sale of its plants, equipment, other tangible property, plus its accounts receivable. Book value tends to grow slightly over time as business activity grows, but typically at a snail's pace compared to the growth driven by organizational and workforce capital.

By *organizational capital* we refer to the innovations the firm's

First Things First

Does the Process You use to Create Your Strategic Plan Impede Execution?

Check all that apply in your organization

❏ Those at the top create the strategy then hand it off to middle-level managers for implementation, failing to involve those at the middle and lower levels in planning. Thus, the strategy-making process is disenfranchising and de-energizing for most employees.

❏ Because the strategy is created exclusively at the top, it must be "driven down through the organization," to use an worn out phrase. Thus, the message gets diluted at every step. It's a kind of "whisper down the lane" phenomenon.

❏ People at lower levels of the organization don't know what the strategy calls for and/or what they *do* know doesn't excite them and there is no system by which to include them in either planning *or* execution.

❏ The strategy is long on financial details and objectives, but short on the story regarding what needs to change in the human system, i.e., the organization and its design and capabilities—to achieve the promise made to customers and shareholders.

❏ At the conclusion of the planning process, the plan emerges as fixed and changeless. There is no process in place to revisit and refine the plan except to start the whole process all over again. Learning and change are not built into the process.

workforce has created over time, innovations that enable it to operate profitably—for example, business processes that permit efficient design, development, and production of goods. This term also encompasses the relationships the company has developed with its suppliers and customers, and signifies the design of the organization, a term we will come back to later (in Chapter Seven). By design, we mean the firm's business processes, reward systems, people practices, and other institutional elements that enable it to create and deliver value.

Importantly, organizational capital results from *workforce capital,* the most potent driver of value. This term, to us, speaks to the resourcefulness and inventiveness of the people in the firm. As our colleague, Hadley Williams, puts it, "It is the sum of energy, commitment, and 'know how' employees apply to the work of the firm. In well managed firms, today's workforce capital is tomorrow's organizational capital."

It is always easier—by far—to quantify the contribution of tangible assets to a company's share price than it is to state with any kind of precision the contribution of intangible assets like workforce and organizational capital. This is why the dotted line between the two appears in Figure 2-1. But there is no doubt that intangible organizational assets make up the lion's share of any organization's value. In this book, we are concerned primarily with those assets and making the most of them. Differences in how these assets are managed and deployed explain why two companies in the same industry, possessing roughly the same strategy and with the same earnings, can vary hugely with respect to stock price and market capitalization.

The value of these intangible assets are identical for entire economies. Countries that invest wisely in systems to support and enable productivity do far better than those that do not. This explains why some oil-rich extractive economies like Venezuela, Russia, Iran, and Saudi Arabia, whose natural resources wealth is staggering, but who do not invest wisely in human resources, often have high levels of unemployment and a host of other social ills.

Good Strategies Gone Bad: A Checklist of Problems

Strategy *execution* remains elusive for some companies because they rely on an approach to *planning* that is based on faulty assumptions. Ironically, this approach can—and very often does—generate a strategy that is doomed to fail on the day it's created even though the strategy might call for the very business results that could make the company great.

The approach we're talking about was invented over 35 years ago by the Boston Consulting Group. That approach, first called "long range planning" then "strategic planning," became wildly popular when it seemed to explain GE's phenomenal success under then CEO Reginald Jones. But Jack Welch, who was forced to participate in that process, knew better: GE was succeeding *despite*, not *because of,* its highly centralized, detail-oriented approach to planning. When Welch took over as Chairman of GE in 1984, there were nearly 200 professionals in planning roles throughout the company, and 55 at corporate headquarters alone! (Mintzberg, 2001). Noting the downside, a *Fortune* writer said in 1984, while "strategic planning was the gospel" at GE, its "stock traded at about the same moribund level all through the seventies, with the PE gradually declining" (Walter Kiechel, quoted in Mintzberg, 2001).

The laborious process of strategic planning that GE created and first used is still widely admired today in corporate America, and indeed, all over the world. This is true even though a case can be made—and Jack Welch made it in the mid-1980s—that the traditional approach to strategic planning itself might be the genesis of most companies' strategy implementation problems. With its emphasis on quantification, analysis, forms, scenario-building, forecasting, endless iterations and cross-checking by staff people, strategic planning has become, for many companies, an annual rite that gives the illusion of control but accomplishes little in the way of actual accomplishment.

As one of his first official acts, Welch slashed the planning function to the bone. He did so, in part, because he was frustrated with a process that required him, like all other GE executives, to spend inordinate time each year creating thick volumes documenting their plans. When he became CEO, Welch would accept a plan that went to only a maximum of five pages. If a business leader couldn't explain a business and its strategy in five pages, Welch believed, the executive probably didn't really understand it and certainly couldn't explain it succinctly.

What follows is a checklist of five problems associated with this traditional model of strategic planning. We invite you to check each problem that exists in your organization.

❏ *Those at the top create the strategy then hand it off to middle-level managers for implementation, failing to involve those at the middle and lower levels in planning. Thus, the strategy-making process is disenfranchising and de-energizing for most employees.*

Everyone who comes to work in the morning—executives, managers, non-managers—is a human being with human yearnings. And among the most basic of those desires is that of a rational world functioning in predictable order. No wonder that businesspeople gravitate to a view of strategy formation and implementation in which there exists omniscient gods atop the organization, acting only in the most rational, deliberate way, to make the most elegant decisions based only on tested fact. It is comforting to believe that the fruits of the "great ones'" decisions will then manifest magically.

Today, executives across America have generally retaken responsibility for planning by taking it out of the hands of staff planners, but they have not changed the basic nature of the approach they use. They have substituted themselves as the problem; they have not solved it.

❏ *Because strategy-creation takes place primarily at the top, all attempts to communicate it—to "drive it down through the organization"—take too long and get diluted at every step.*

Even though it's a common syndrome, many serious problems occur when executives "own" the plan and then try to "drive it down" (an oft-heard corporate phrase) through the organization. Employees—who had no part in creating the plan—are simply not committed to its fulfillment like those are who were actually involved in creating it. Creating a strategy, then handing it over to "subordinates" inherently limits ownership *and* learning. Without dialogue and partnership, there is little or no feedback running back up the pipeline. Communication problems abound as word of the strategy drips slowly—if at all—through the organization. The rationale behind the plan gets distorted or misunderstood, and the intent and urgency behind the plan is either overlooked entirely or misconstrued. In Chapter Six, we will describe the part that employees at every level can play in creating and interpreting strategy.

In a classic study, Charles Heckscher, professor at Rutgers University's School of Management and Labor Relations, conducted an in-depth study of ignorance of corporate strategy among middle-management, concluding that most middle managers in underperforming companies are actually "motivated *not* to understand the strategy" (our italics, 1995). Heckscher found that in many companies—and not just under-performing companies—middle managers so strongly believe that those at the top should create strategy and that those below should carry it out, that they feel their own ignorance about the strategy is justified!

A second execution problem usually accompanies this one. Because the plan is presented as finished and complete, those below the executive level expect it to tell the whole story, i.e., to state not only what should be accomplished by whom, how, and on what schedule. When employees below the executive suite do not find this detail, they become inert, waiting around for "marching orders" instead of discerning the action called for by the strategy at their level. In fact, no leadership group, especially those atop a large, complex organization, could possibly—or should even attempt to—spell all this out.

❏ *People at lower levels of the organization don't know what the strategy calls for, and/or what they do know doesn't excite them and there is no system by which to include them in either planning or execution.*

In today's fast-paced business world, employee ignorance of the strategy is unacceptable. Some executives are doing everything they can think of to communicate the organization's strategic imperatives effectively. Yet every businessperson we know smiles with rueful recognition when we describe this common business scene:

> *There stands the CEO with laser pointer in hand, before a "Town Meeting" of employees, going over the PowerPoint presentation that summarizes the strategy. Eyes glaze throughout the dim room. An hour or more later, the words, "Any questions?" are followed by awkward silence. Perhaps someone asks a safe question, to which the CEO gives a long, detailed answer that no one, including the questioner, really has much interest in. The meeting ends with a predictable pep talk by the CEO about how good the company is and how much confidence he has in his employees.*

> *Confused, the CEO watches as everyone shuffles out with no greater clarity about the strategy, no greater commitment to making the changes needed to achieve it, no understanding of what they should do, and with no increase in confidence that this—or any other strategy—will redeem the company.*

The usual bureaucratic approach—those at the top plan, then expect the others to implement—sets up a classic paradox of bureaucracy: employees below the executive level become passive, waiting to be told what to do, only to become resistant the moment they are directed because they don't feel a personal stake in the outcome and because they feel no one should tell them how to do their jobs.

Our colleague Jim Haudan, President of Root Learning, Inc., touches on this phenomenon when he speaks to his clients about the "Three Lies of Corporate America." According to Haudan, the three "lies" are: 1) we have a strategy; 2) everyone understands and believes in it; and 3) we have data to prove it. In most cases the strategy is lacking, employees don't understand or believe in it, and no one has bothered to find out who knows what.

The tendency of employees to ignore or tune out communication about the strategy is especially pronounced at the lower levels of organizations. Managers need to do more to influence these employees to align their efforts with the strategy: These employees, after all, often know more about the customer than anyone else in the company.

When coaxed to speak about their company's strategy, a disturbing percentage of nonmanagerial employees are almost completely ignorant of it, often despite presentations by the senior staff, articles in company publications, and "All Hands Meetings." A line operator in a manufacturing plant once said to us, "I have no idea what our strategy is. They don't pay me enough to know that." This is not only pathetic, it's costly and avoidable, too.

❏ *The strategy is long on financial details and objectives, but short on the human story, i.e., what needs to change in the organization to achieve the promise made to customers and shareholders.*

Ultimately, successful strategy implementation requires getting three things right: the social system, the technical system, and the business process system. Some organizations get some systems right, some organizations get other systems right. You have to get them *all* right.

When making strategic shifts in their organizations, most executive teams tend to do a far better job of bringing business processes into line with their new strategy and identifying the benefits of new technology, than they do aligning the social system with the strategy and actually getting the benefits of their technology spend.

David Norton (in Becker, et al., 2001), co-creator with Robert Kaplan of the Balanced Scorecard concept, observes that while human capital is the foundation for creating value in the new economy, human assets are the least understood by most business leaders and therefore, the least effectively managed. Most executives today lack the leadership ability required for four critical strategy implementation tasks:

• Informing and educating employees of the need for change

• Motivating employees to do what's required to effect that change

• Putting into place the arrangements that get mission-critical work units to realign their work with the new strategy and with one another.

- Building organizational capabilities called for by the strategy.

When we consult with organizations, the very first thing we do is examine the strategy and interview the senior leaders who have to execute it. Here is what we find:

- Most plans say almost nothing about how the organization must change to meet the objectives set out in the plan.

- The senior-most executives describe the plan in fundamentally different ways, often reflecting an appalling lack of alignment as to which strategic objectives are more important and which less.

- The plan itself, 90 percent of the time, is unclear, is not measurable, and does not state a competitive advantage or value proposition.

To the degree that a strategy departs from the business's current goals or model, the organization itself must change. Consequently, the strategy-making process must include plans to ensure that the organization is capable of enacting it. Beyond a formal, top-down restructuring, this occurs all too rarely.

In Chapter Seven, we will tell you how our client, the leader in its class of software, decided it could make as much money by selling consulting services related to its software as it could through selling products. The executive team appreciated that they would need to cultivate the ability to assess, select, and acquire a different kind of talent than ever before. But the leaders did not quite grasp that the shift from a products to a services business was monumental, and consequently, that the organizational structure, reward system, and business processes would *all* have to change. In addition, the executive team would have to find a way to get their employees to think that doing all this was good, too.

❑ *At the conclusion of the planning process, the plan emerges as fixed and changeless. There is no process in place to revisit and refine the plan except to start the whole process all over again. Learning and change are not built into the process.*

It is a supremely comforting thought: To create a strategic plan, all you must do is break down the strategic plan into discrete steps, put due dates on those steps, inform middle-level managers of what they're expected to accomplish over the next 12 months, and submit the whole thing to a regular, yearly update process. This approach might have rational appeal, but ultimately, it is worse than fruitless: not simply because it doesn't work, but also because it fosters dependency and eliminates the opportunity for learning and flexibility. What ought to be a dynamic and creative process of breakthrough thinking becomes a bureaucratic ritual where planning is approached in a routinized, mind-numbing way.

A victim of this process, a former client who headed up international operations for a pharmaceutical firm, described his company's planning process as "an annual rite." Lifting a thick binder from a shelf, he shook it and explained, "This is the *instruction manual* for the planning process we follow!" Anticipating our question, he said, "Of course it doesn't work. But the better question is, 'Why do we do it?' I'll tell you why: We do it because we do it!"

A final comment: Be careful what you read about strategic planning. One of the best-selling books on the subject of strategic planning urges taking 54 separate steps to create a strategic plan! Do you *really* have a year to create yours?

Things Haven't Changed Much

If you take the perspective, as many business leaders do, that middle- and lower-level employees should not be involved in the strategic planning process and you do not, therefore, engage them as partners in achieving your strategic objectives, you are not making the most of your human assets.

We began writing this book in the fall of 2009, during the worst recession since the Great Depression. Gallup surveys on their site (Gallup.com) at the time indicated that American workers do not feel engaged, far from it:

- More than three-quarters of Americans feel the economy is bad and getting worse.

- Most Americans feel it's a bad time to get a good job—the worst ever in Gallup's survey.

- Most Americans do not trust their senior leaders. They place the blame for the current economic troubles on the backs of executives.

As a consequence of this and other factors, employee discretionary effort is declining dramatically. Discretionary effort, defined by the Corporate Executive Board (2008) as, "An employee's willingness to go above and beyond the call of duty," is the energy an employee might put forth in going beyond basic job requirements, for example in helping a coworker solve a problem, devoting extra hours to helping a client, or taking the time required to polish an important presentation one more time. According to a CEB study published in late 2008, "The number of employees exhibiting high levels of discretionary effort has decreased by 53 percent since 2005."

Let's look a little closer at this study. It describes four other disturbing trends:

- Employee performance is declining dramatically at the very time our economy needs high levels of productivity.

- Disengagement is showing up at all levels: In 2008 only 13 percent of senior executives reported that they put forth high levels of discretionary effort, compared to 29 percent in the second half of 2006.

- Disengaged employees are digging in. Disengaged employees—who are less productive than engaged employees—are significantly less likely to quit today and move to another job than they were in years past.

- The most talented and valuable employees want to leave. According to this report, 25 percent of a company's most valued talent intends to quit in the next 12 months.

This study is not an anomaly. A survey of 5,000 U.S. households conducted for The Conference Board in 2010, discovered that "only 45 percent of those surveyed say they are satisfied with their jobs, down from 61.1 percent in 1987, the first year in which the survey was conducted" (Conference Board, 2010).

To us, these statistics are woeful because they are so avoidable. Business leaders can, and indeed must, do better. These statistics reveal that many employees are living in a state of quiet desperation—and many of their leaders seem to be, too.

We are not pointing out these inadequacies because we like playing a "blame game." The truth—at least in our experience—is that most corporate leaders *want* to do well by their constituents; they just don't know how to formulate and execute a strategy that takes modern concepts of engagement and organization design into account. If you are one of them, hopefully you'll agree that this book helps you do just this.

Essential Truths About Strategy Execution

If you made even one check mark in the box "First Things First" on page 32, your organization has some important work to do. In the remainder of this book we will show you how to do that work. But fair warning: doing it is not easy. As the fortune cookie on the next pages promises, the future can hold big things for your company, but *only* if you do everything right!

The antidotes to the problems we explored relating to the strategic planning process, we believe, are found in seven principles that have been the cornerstones of every consulting project we've undertaken in the past 20 years.

Successful strategy execution requires high levels of coordination and alignment at the top.

Ultimately, strategy implementation is *everyone's* work, but the leadership of the effort clearly belongs to the executive or management group who will be held accountable for results. If these people are not working effectively together, successful implementation is a remote possibility. Unproductive competition across business lines, functions, or divisions almost inevitably reflects a failure of those at the top to work collaboratively. Also, the top of the organization controls the resources needed to mount a serious strategy implementation effort. If you want to implement strategy creatively and brilliantly, top team alignment is crucial. (Chapter Nine is devoted to this topic.)

Big things coming in future—if you do everything right.

Employees can only support what they understand.

No strategy can succeed if the people who have to implement it don't understand it. If kept in the dark, employees are but passengers along for the ride. Having said this, it's astonishing how few executives make sure that employees understand the business, how it works, the factors critical for winning or, indeed, the strategy itself. In fact, we can name on one hand the number of companies we have worked with that have made a concerted effort to inform and educate employees and to help them become knowledgeable business partners.

People go the extra mile only when their passions are engaged.

As important as cognitive understanding is, strategy implementation requires more; it requires employee commitment. Employees may understand the logic of reorganizing along customer segment lines, for example, and they may conceptually see the point of layoffs, but that does not mean they feel moved to support either. Understanding, while necessary, is not sufficient. Even where layoffs are not involved, nearly every strategic shift involves dislocations of some kind, inconveniences, and hassles. If people do not believe the benefits are worth enduring the pain involved, they will resist change.

People support what they've helped to create.

Plainly put, if you want people to support your strategy, you'd better let them at least participate in the decisions about how to implement it, perhaps to critique and fine-tune the strategy, and— gasp!—probably even to help define what it means at their level. Most executives like to think of themselves as leaders, but in truth, many cannot do what fine leaders do: fire people up and connect their passions to a cause they believe in. Employee participation is the fastest pathway to this end. Delivering the future envisioned by many strategies will, in most cases, require executives first to become much more effective as leaders. While it's probably true that "too many cooks spoil the broth," there are ways to sensibly involve nearly everyone in the formulation of some aspect of the strategy, and to make meaningful decisions about how to implement it.

Strategy implementation requires change in the way work is done *and* what work is done.

So far, we've been speaking of the need for individual employees to understand and support the new direction. But even if executives are specimens of leadership, and even if all employees are thoroughly business literate, the strategy implementation work is not complete. Ultimately all of that understanding and motivation by individual employees needs to turn into action and results— by entire *work units,* not just by enthusiastic *individuals.* Strategic change really begins to be noticeable in an organization when every work unit realigns its work with the strategy, eliminating all off-strategy work and beginning any new work required by the shift in focus.

To execute well, entire units have to align more effectively with other units.

To effect most strategic change, work units have to work more effectively with other work units. For example, it is a step in the right direction if a work unit in an insurance company develops a new product called for by the new strategy. But introducing it may cause more problems than it solves if the customer service center is not made aware of the many questions customers are likely to have as the product is introduced and if the sales force isn't trained to sell it. Strategy implementation almost always requires cross-system collaboration. And usually, because of the competitiveness that exists across "silos," this is the most challenging work of all.

No measurement, no change.

Organizations that implement strategy well identify the markers of implementation effectiveness before rolling out a new strategy. They then take periodic soundings to determine whether or not the implementation plan is on track and where the plan is off track, and they take steps to close the gap. A sophisticated approach to measurement yields far more than a report card; the best measurement approach uses the data collected to bring additional resources to bear where the plan is not delivering as hoped. In other words, the measurement is for the purpose of learning and deciding on next steps.

An effective implementation measurement system will address questions like these:

- *"Do employees understand the strategy and the business case behind it?"*

- *"How do employees feel about the company and our new direction?"*

- *"To what extent are our work units realigning their efforts to align with the new strategy?"*

- *"To what degree is the cross-system alignment we need actually occurring?"*

Action Learning

Journalist and curmudgeon H.L. Mencken once said, "There is always an easy solution to every human problem—neat, plausible, and wrong." Nowhere is this more true than in the realm of strategic planning. In this chapter, we explored how the neat, plausible, traditional approach to planning—those at the top plan, everyone else executes—cripples every subsequent undertaking. It's a dream that satisfies the rational, bureaucratic mind, but always disappoints once the results are tallied.

Leaders persist in shopworn approaches to strategy execution at the cost of waste: mostly of human energy and productivity, but also of time and capital. When leaders fail to create good strategy or, worse, when they create brilliant strategies but fail to execute them wisely, they squander resources and create the kind of situation many businesses find themselves in today: employee engagement at all-time lows. We hope to show you a way out of the thicket in subsequent chapters that will revitalize your workplace, delight your customers, and enrich your shareholders.

Exercise: Evaluate your planning process.

By yourself, or preferably with your co-leaders of strategy implementation, reflect on the way your organization creates strategy today. Ask yourself the questions in the box below. Better yet, as a team, ask 10-12 employees at various levels the same questions and then compare the results.

Considering our strategic planning process...		
What works well?	What has questionable value?	What does not work well?

Chapter Three

The Human Side of Strategy

*If there is one generalization we can make about
leadership and change it is this:
No change can occur without
willing and committed followers.*
—Warren Bennis

ANYONE WHO SETS OUT TO help an organization get better at
implementing strategy should ask, "What gets in the way
of execution in this organization *today*?" In part, strategy
implementation is a process of overcoming specific resistances to
change, or at least finessing them. It helps to know what and where
those barriers are.

The truth is that there are barriers facing *every* strategy, even
when everyone agrees that change is completely necessary because
of organizational inertia. Additionally, the more a strategy takes
the organization in a new direction, the more barriers there will
be to its implementation and the more inertia there will be. Identify and limit the impediments to your strategy, and you're at least
underway. Eliminate them, and you are well on your way. Most
likely, those barriers are in the human system—in the form of an

inadequate organizational structure, perhaps, or in the lack of individual motivation, or in an antiquated reward system, or in the lack of teamwork at the top—not in the technical system, i.e., the IT systems or problems in plants, equipment, or processes.

In the last chapter, we explained how your organizations's approach to strategic planning might be contributing to your strategy execution woes. If your organization has some of those problems, any number of second-order difficulties emerge. We call them the "land mines of strategy execution."

Our experience tells us there are predictable land mines or barriers in the human system laying in wait to foil almost every strategic plan. You can see most of them in the box, "Strategy Execution Land Mines" on page 49. These strategy land mines, derived empirically from our many years of organizational consulting, are consistent with a list of six "silent killers" of strategy reported in a study conducted by Michael Beer and Russell A. Eisenstat of Sloan Management School (2000). The term "silent killer," borrowed from the language of cardiology, is an apt one; just as undiagnosed high cholesterol, when unaddressed, can cause catastrophic heart failure, these strategy impediments can annihilate strategy implementation without anyone knowing what happened. In the organizations Beer and Eisenstat studied, the "killers" most often mentioned were:

- An ineffective management team (100 percent of the cases they studied)

- Poor vertical communication (83 percent)

- Top-down or laissez-faire senior management style (75 percent)

- Unclear strategy and conflicting priorities (75 percent)

- Poor coordination across functions, businesses, or borders (75 percent)

- Inadequate down-the-line leadership skills and development (66 percent)

Underlying most lists of impediments to strategy execution is a kind of "meta impediment." It's subtle, but it explains why man-

Strategy Execution Land Mines

Check as many as apply in your organization

Set 1

1. _____ Employees do not understand what change the strategy calls for or why.

2. _____ Employees think the responsibility for strategy execution belongs only to those at the top of the organization.

3. _____ To most employees, the strategy, if they are aware of it at all, is a simple list of business objectives.

Set 2

4. _____ Employees do not feel committed to or excited about fulfilling the strategy.

5. _____ Employees do not feel a sense of urgency to execute the strategy.

6. _____ Employees do not view themselves or their effort as essential to winning in the marketplace.

Set 3

7. _____ Managers are not refocusing the efforts of their work units to conform to the strategy.

8. _____ Managers fail to engage employees as enthusiastic partners in executing the strategy.

9. _____ In mission-critical areas, work proceeds as usual even though the strategy has changed significantly.

Set 4

10. _____ The strategy doesn't communicate specifically how the organization has to change or how those changes will be made.

11. _____ The strategy calls for collaboration across operating and/or functional areas, but there are no mechanisms in place to work through the walls between the silos.

12. _____ Lack of teamwork among executives blocks the cross-system collaboration the strategy requires.

agement fails so frequently to include employees as partners in the strategy execution process. We're referring to patriarchy, the social form in which powerful elders reserve all decisions of consequence for themselves. Where this practice is prevalent in an organization, employees are kept in the dark about strategic objectives and employee participation in strategy execution is almost nonexistent.

It's probably obvious by now that we do not subscribe to this view. Our objection to it is not so much political as it is practical: Patriarchy just doesn't work, especially in an age where most employees have been hired to think for a living. Organizations that limit decision making principally to top executives, that keep employees in the dark and marginalize middle-level managers also fail to attract the best talent, do not get the most value from the talent they do have, respond sluggishly to market opportunities, have retention problems, and tend not to be leaders in their industries.

Identify Your Organization's Land Mines

Check as many of the statements in the box on "Strategy Execution Land Mines" on page 49 as apply to your situation. It is a list of statements describing organizational realities and circumstances that can get in the way of strategy execution.

Now, let's interpret that pattern of check marks. The items fall into four arenas:

Set 1: Employees Don't Understand the Strategy

1. Employees do not understand what change the strategy calls for or why.
2. Employees think the responsibility for strategy execution belongs only to those at the top of the organization.
3. To most employees, the strategy, if they are aware of it at all, is a simple list of business objectives.

How can anyone who does not understand an organization's strategy possibly take steps to execute it? The answer, of course, is they can't. Most studies on the subject show that very high percentages of employees do not understand their company's strategy, with some claiming that up to 95 percent do not (Kaplan & Norton, 1996). Obviously, if your employees do not understand your strategy or think it's someone else's problem, they are not going to do what's necessary to execute it.

Set 2: Employees Aren't Motivated to Fulfill the Strategy

4. Employees do not feel committed to or excited about fulfilling the strategy.
5. Employees do not feel a sense of urgency to execute the strategy.
6. Employees do not view themselves or their effort as essential to winning in the marketplace.

Suppose your employees do understand the strategy and the rationale behind it. What percentage feel some kind of commitment to fulfilling it? Again, this is usually not a high number. Generating the energy necessary to execute a strategy is a key leadership task. Failing to do so creates a land mine.

Set 3: Insufficient Change at the Work Unit Level

7. Managers are not refocusing the efforts of their work units to conform to the strategy.
8. Managers fail to engage employees as enthusiastic partners in executing the strategy.
9. In mission-critical areas, work proceeds as usual even though the strategy has changed significantly.

Here is the plain truth about a strategy: It creates no value whatsoever if no one implements it. And by this, we mean if managers fail to engage employees in pursuing it, continuing to do off-strategy work or not enough on-strategy work, those lofty strategic ambitions will remain elusive.

Set 4: Inadequate Organization Alignment

10. The strategy doesn't communicate specifically how the organization has to change or how those changes will be made.
11. The strategy calls for collaboration across operating and/or

functional areas, but there are no mechanisms in place to work through the walls between the silos.

12. Lack of teamwork among executives blocks the cross-system collaboration the strategy requires.

It is bad enough when employees do not understand the strategy, do not feel committed to implementing it, and work units are not conforming their efforts to the strategy. Success is even more remote when the organizational machinery itself impedes strategy execution. Three common problems are touched on here: the strategy fails to make clear how the organization itself has to change, turf wars hold back progress, and in-fighting among the leaders of the organization blocks cooperative effort.

The Four Jobs of Strategy Execution

For many years, we have been employing a simple model of strategy execution that maintains to successfully execute the company's strategy, the senior team must accomplish four things. We call them the Four Jobs of Strategy Execution. They are summarized in Figure 3-1. While not strictly sequential, each Job tends to build upon the other. As each Job yields results, readiness for subsequent work results.

Pertaining to Job One, employees need to understand not only their company's strategic direction, but also the rationale behind the strategy and the metrics associated with it. If employees don't understand the game, they don't play it very well. We employ a rule of thumb: *Every employee should understand the strategy as least as well as a well-informed shareholder.* Chapter Four offers guidance as to how to accomplish Job One.

Because strategic shifts cause dislocations, employees have to feel impelled (meaning: be motivated from within) to go the extra mile to fulfill the strategy, to turn it into reality. Employees have to believe that the net result of fulfilling the strategy, despite the pain involved in executing it, will have been worth the effort and sacrifice it probably calls for. This is the work of Job Two and how to accomplish it is addressed in Chapter Five.

The Four Jobs of Strategy Execution

Job One: Make sure all employees understand the strategy, i.e., get the "heads" involved.

Job Two: Engender enthusiasm for the strategy, i.e., get the "hearts" involved.

Job Three: Support all work units in taking action called for by the strategy, i.e., get the "hands" involved.

Job Four: Build all organizational capabilities required by the strategy, i.e., ensure that the organization is strategy-capable: supportive systems are in place and alignment exists "across the silos."

Figure 3-1: The Four Jobs of Strategy Execution

Although these are essential and laudable accomplishments, it is not quite time for high-fives when the entire employee population understands the strategy and feels good about it (Jobs One and Two). A strategy calls for change in actual work production. Job Three, then, calls for all off-strategy work to cease and for additional on-strategy work either to begin or to be continued. Chapter Six is devoted to this work.

Job Four—the most challenging of all—is where the implementation magic really starts to happen. Job Four involves making systemic organizational changes called for by the strategy. This can mean changing the reward system (often a problem), altering the vertical structure, building or enhancing business processes, and more. We devote two chapters—Seven and Eight—to Job Four.

Figure 3-1 is a summary of the Four Jobs. Read the descriptions over and ask yourself which of them your organization does well today and which it neglects or does poorly. Run-of-the-mill companies don't do *any* of the Jobs very well, while market leaders tend to do most or all very well.

Figure 3-2 shows that as you go along, accomplishing each Job gets harder. Thus, it is easier—although hardly "easy"—to ensure that employees understand the strategy—Job One—than it is to create a harmonious and smoothly integrated organizational "machine" in which all processes and components work well together and bring about best effort—Job Four. No wonder strategy execution is challenging: There is a lot to do and accomplishing one thing means you're only free then to tackle something more challenging!

Easier to accomplish◄————————►Harder to accomplish

Job One	Job Two	Job Three	Job Four
Inform Employees	**Enlist Employees**	**Align Work Units with Strategy**	**Build Supporting Organizational Systems**
Tools & Processes • Communications • Business literacy efforts • Strategy maps • Training	**Tools & Processes** • Interactive Town Hall meetings • Rewards/recognition • Strategy-related stretch goals	**Tools & Processes** • Continuous improvement • Lean Sigma • Goal cascading	**Tools & Processes** • Organization design • Top team development • Participative strategic planning • Reward system redesign

Figure 3-2: The relative difficulty of the Four Jobs of Strategy Execution

Figure 3-3 is a metaphor that may help you grasp what we're talking about: a bridge. As a strategy leader, you want people to cross the bridge—in their thinking and behavior—to another way of working, to new objectives, to a new era, and so forth. To do so, you have to get them to *want* to do this and you have to build the bridge so that they *can* do this.

The most potent levers of strategy execution come in the form of creating organizational arrangements—structures, business processes, reward systems, and so forth that enable your most expensive assets—usually people—to function at their best. Companies at the peak of their game do not get there automatically; they do so by working arduously at the individual level, the work unit level, *and* at the organizational system level.

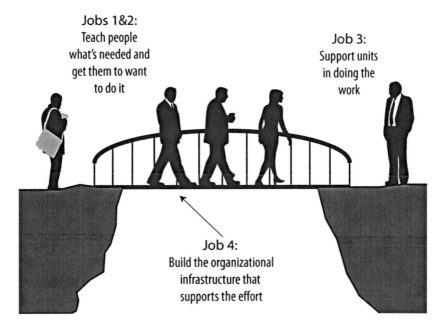

Jobs 1&2:
Teach people
what's needed and
get them to want
to do it

Job 3:
Support units
in doing the
work

Job 4:
Build the organizational
infrastructure that
supports the effort

Figure 3-3: Doing the Four Jobs entails building a bridge to success.

The Four Jobs in Action: An Illustration

This section describes in an anecdotal way how to use the Four Jobs model to guide strategy implementation. We have chosen an example that involves one segment of a company—a pharmaceutical manufacturing operation—but keep in mind that the model applies equally as well to implementing the strategy across an entire, global enterprise. The example is a composite drawn from several consulting experiences with several pharmaceutical companies.

First, some contextual information concerning pharmaceutical manufacturing. In the view of most Wall Street analysts, the future of a pharmaceutical company is in the hands of research scientists who have the power to make the next blockbuster drug. But it is just as true that the well-being of a drug manufacturer is in the hands of its lowest level manufacturing employees, because these employees can either be the first line of defense against troubles with the Food and Drug Administration (FDA) *or* the cause of them. If FDA warnings pile up over time, the FDA can and will shut down your entire operation.

When the FDA does crack down, everyone in manufacturing works exhaustively through a long list of demanded changes, sucking up every spare minute and every spare dollar as a host of technical consultants invade. Pharmaceutical manufacturing environments, notoriously command-and-control oriented, become even more so as employees scurry to make dozens of technical changes to procedures and systems demanded by the FDA. Everyone is working overtime and personnel changes proliferate as persons thought to be responsible for the infractions are forced out. Almost invariably, underlying problems in the social system that may have contributed heavily to compliance problems go unaddressed. As a result, no one is really confident that any of this is going to get to the bottom of things. This includes the FDA, which becomes even more watchful. Generally, production employees are not kept informed of what is going on and their fear about the company's viability is sky-high.

Suppose you're the head of operations where the FDA has shut down a key plant. What is your objective? Obviously, it is to get your plant into compliance and back online. But if this is your objective, what is your strategy? It depends, partly, on the nature of the FDA citings, each of which must be addressed. But again, usually these are technical, not people or organizational matters.

Sooner or later, however, you will realize that a comprehensive response calls for fundamental improvements in the social system as well as in the technical system. Several weeks after your plant has been shut down, you'll be lying awake at night and it will come to you: Your employees, not your new equipment or processes—and certainly not your consultants!—will be your deliverance if anything is. In short, if employees don't use the new technology or procedures or fail to do so wisely and properly, nothing will be different. Somehow, the whole culture has to change. But if you are a typical pharmaceutical executive, you will have no real idea how to make that happen.

In many situations like this we've witnessed remarkable employee indifference towards compliance improvement, supervision so poor that workers are not invited nor encouraged to report compliance problems, and antagonistic working relationships between departments that enable and sustain compliance problems. An imperative for management can be summed up in the question, "How do we get our employees to make compliance their #1 priority—just as we now do—and to take action daily to improve compliance?"

Job One: Ensure That Employees Understand the Strategy

Due to the bunker mentality that often arises among management after FDA troubles, a comprehensive strategy to improve compliance is slow to emerge as management deals piecemeal with FDA demands. The FDA usually requires a comprehensive compliance improvement plan, but often management lacks creativity in sharing it with employees. Doing so effectively is the Job One of strategy implementation.

Employees must, at the very least, know what the compliance improvement strategy consists of. Most companies will inform them, but only through one-way print communications such as newsletters or in large meetings driven by PowerPoint slides. Obviously, this does not truly engage employees.

Educational sessions characterized by discovery learning processes and two-way dialogue with executives is called for here. For example, instead of telling employees that failure to comply will mean dire consequences, why not ask the employees what they think those troubles might be? Even simple table discussions can be effective in getting employees to wrestle with the same issues that management has been struggling with. With even a modicum of facilitation, frank discussions can enable everyone to understand what needs to change and why.

Job Two: Increase Employee Commitment to the Strategy

Employees must both understand the improvement strategy and feel impelled to fulfill it. This work can—and should—begin while educating employees about the new strategy, i.e., while doing Job One. This is so, because employees who are deeply aware and *cognizant* of the problems, especially when that learning takes place in a safe learning environment, tend to be motivated to *solve* those problems.

In this example, the goal of Job Two is to get employees to see the manufacturing organization's success as *their* success. If they do, they will go the extra mile in making sure it is.

If you're a hard-nosed pharmaceutical manufacturing manager, for whom talk of motivation and commitment tends to sound like so much psychobabble, how do you motivate shop floor employees to go the extra mile as partners with you? Again, the simple answer is to engage them in honest and genuine dialogue about the compliance problems and involve them, as appropriate, as parties in the problem-solving process. Listening to shop floor people does not mean you have to solicit their ideas about every needed change or that you need to get their permission to redesign the validation process. Shop floor people can—and usually wish to—play meaningful, but more modest day-to-day roles in identifying and resolving real and potential compliance problems. And they will do so if they feel respected and valued by their supervisors and managers.

Job Three: Improve Performance at the Work Unit Level

Successful strategy implementation requires every work unit to stop all off-strategy activities and to pursue on-strategy results. If the strategy in question is improving the rate of compliance, this means that in the future, every job must be done correctly, all of the time, according to a rigidly fixed procedure and sequence. For instance, if your job is to clean the room where vials are filled with antibiotics, there is a document describing in vivid detail which walls you must wash first, whether those walls should be washed from the top down or bottom up, what should be done with the cleaning equipment afterwards, and so on. Finally, the document will tell you which papers have to be filed to document that you did your work properly. The possibilities for error, in short, are enormous.

In a regulated environment, staying infraction-free calls for an employee population that wants to follow procedures. It also requires active management support for those employees in bringing procedural variances to the attention of those who can intervene when things go wrong. This is best done as a group effort, because when employees discuss among themselves where actual and potential compliance problems exist, they support one another in staying in compliance and can devise useful improvements to work routines.

Job Four: Build a Strategy-Capable Organization

If individual work units are left with the sole responsibility for compliance improvement, strategic change will never occur. Individual departments will have to work differently with one another, some of which may perceive their work as antagonistic to the aims of manufacturing. In this example, the Quality Assurance department, which functions as a kind of quality auditor in pharmaceutical manufacturing environments, comes to mind. When FDA troubles emerge, manufacturing and Quality Assurance often point the finger at each other as the cause of the current problems: On the one hand, manufacturing was careless, and on the other, Quality Assurance allowed manufacturing to do things that got the company into trouble. To effect meaningful, long-lasting change, each must find a way to work cooperatively with one another even though their roles will never be completely compatible.

Those responsible for driving strategy execution will have to identify all the forces that restrain the supply chain from full compliance, then will have to find ways to make the systemic modifications necessary to reduce or eliminate those forces. This includes not only manufacturing and Quality Assurance, but usually includes sales, distribution, and perhaps other departments as well, including HR. Organization improvement methodology that makes use of large groups of employees working together (we share some examples in later chapters) can help significantly to accomplish Job Four. Cross-system issues tend to be complex. The more brainpower applied to them, the better, assuming the process is well managed.

While this is crucial, Job Four is more than ensuring coordination of efforts across organizational boundaries. Job Four also entails process improvement within organizational units, i.e., taking steps to maximize efficiency, predictability, and economy as value gets created by each unit.

The Four Jobs are not Equal

Figure 3-4 shows that each of the Jobs is essential, but by itself, each lower-level Job counts for less than the next, higher-level Job. It's hard to know how, for example, you could have a winning business when employees are ignorant of the strategy or its rationale (Job One), but unless employees are also motivated to fulfill the strategy (Job Two), you don't have much to work with. Still more important is Job Three, because if employees are informed and motivated but are not taking action in concert with others to execute it, understanding and motivation are of little consequence. Of ultimate importance is Job Four, which calls for working out the cross-system issues that otherwise will thwart all strategic hopes. GE's celebrated "Work-Out" process (described in Chapter Six) is an example of how to do this work.

Note that by this formula, each Job has a payoff, but the business benefit of each is less than that of the benefits acquired by doing it *and* the Jobs that follow. If the effort applied to one of the Jobs falls to zero, the entire effort collapses. In truth, the benefits of Jobs One through Three decay rapidly if the implementation work stops when each is accomplished. *You must do all four Jobs!* No wonder strategy execution is so challenging!

There is another way of looking at the Four Jobs: through a systems lens. Think of a bull's-eye (see Figure 3-5). When you set out to execute strategy, you "get points," so to speak, when you create change in individuals, i.e., help them understand and feel motivated by a strategy, and you get more "points" as you help them effect change in their work units. But you don't win the game if you stop there: the actual bull's-eye is change in the organization itself.

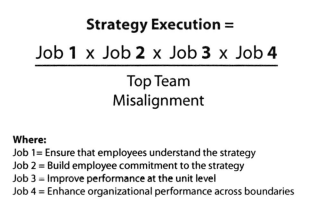

Strategy Execution =

Job **1** x Job **2** x Job **3** x Job **4**

Top Team
Misalignment

Where:
Job 1= Ensure that employees understand the strategy
Job 2 = Build employee commitment to the strategy
Job 3 = Improve performance at the unit level
Job 4 = Enhance organizational performance across boundaries

Figure 3-4: Not all of the Four Jobs are equal in effect over time; you must do them in combination.

Having noted that while none of the work of strategy execution is never easy and that it gets more challenging as you go along, we will help you accomplish each of the Four Jobs. Subsequent chapters focus on each Job and two chapters address the challenging work of Job Four, our "bull's-eye."

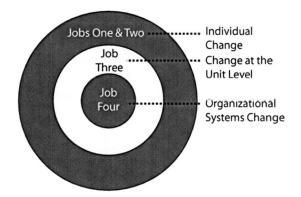

Figure 3-5: The relative importance of the Four Jobs

The Jobs group conceptually into two different kinds of results, as in Figure 3-6. Jobs One and Two have to do with *mobilizing* human energy, i.e., activating it, catalyzing it, readying it for action.

Jobs Three and Four have to do with *putting that energy to work.*

Whether your strategy centers on new product development, installing a new order-entry system, or opening international markets, the work required to implement it, at some level, is the same: You have to get people on their feet, get them excited about the work to be done, point them in the right direction, and pull the systemic barriers out of the way.

Theme	Strategy Execution Work
Mobilizing Energy	**Jobs 1 & 2** • Increase understanding of the strategy • Increase motivation to work toward fulfilling the promise of the strategy
Employing Energy	**Jobs 3 & 4** • Align local effort • Align cross-boundary effort

Figure 3-6: The Four Jobs encompass two themes.

If you are serious about implementing a shiny new strategy—or even an old one!—you should ask yourself, "What gets in the way of executing anything in our organization?" Most people who work in an organization can easily rattle off a half dozen impediments, in part because every strategy meets some opposition, even in the most change-capable companies and even when everyone agrees that change is completely necessary. In truth, however, while most people resist change to some degree, employee reluctance to cooperate with management is nowhere near the most telling impediment to strategy implementation; one or more of the Four Jobs is.

Whose Work Is the Four Jobs?

If doing Jobs One through Four is the essential work of strategy implementation, whose work *is* it? The CEO's? The line's? HR's? We believe that HR will prove its worth as it helps the organization understand and address each of these jobs. Thus, in Chapter Ten, we provide guidance to the HR leaders regarding how to go about this. But HR should not delude itself into thinking it can do all these jobs *for* the organization because it can't.

We believe that ultimately, responsibility for doing the work of the Four Jobs belongs to the senior-most group. Having said this, let us be clear: that senior group might be a Division head or the executive in charge of Asian sales or the head of IT in North America. It does not have to be the CEO and his or her directs. Chapter Nine provides guidance for this senior leadership group, whomever it is, in carrying out the Four Jobs. As we will say again in Chapter Nine, the senior team has responsibility for this, but only an *aligned* senior team can accomplish it. Such a group is aligned when its members:

- Have a common understanding of the strategic objectives. (This is far less common than one would think by reading the Annual Report!)

- Agree that the strategic objectives are worth achieving and are willing to make sacrifices to accomplish them.

- Share a common view about what parts of the organization have to change, why, and how, in order to implement the strategy.

- Commit to a systematic plan of employee engagement, management support, cross-system dialogue, and organization design that will foster efficient strategy execution, i.e., doing the Four Jobs of strategy execution.

Action Learning

Vastly more has been written about how to create a strategy than what to do once it's been created, reflecting the American bias for action over planning and process. The model presented here speaks to closing that gap and tells what is required.

The impediments to execution—what we have called "land mines"—fall into four areas. When employees do not understand the strategy, when they do not feel motivated to fulfill it, when there is insufficient change at the work unit level, and when there is insufficient cross-functional collaboration or inadequate organizational capabilities, strategies—and sometimes entire companies—get blown away. Doing the Four Jobs of Strategy Execution gets heads, hearts, and hands involved, and builds an organization that can make the most of the effort of every asset.

Exercise: Identify your Strategy Land Mines

Ask your direct reports, and your HR business partner if you have one, to fill out the checklist on page 49. Have someone tabulate the results. Discuss the implications for your organization if any of the following are true. What steps could you take to address these strategy land mines if they exist in your organization?

1. Your employees do not understand the strategy.

2. Your employees do not feel enthusiastic about executing the strategy.

3. Work units are failing to conform their efforts to the strategy.

4. Organization capabilities either don't exist or are unaligned with the strategy.

5. Your executive team is misaligned.

Chapter Four

Job One:
Winning Minds

Any company trying to compete
. . .must figure out a way to
engage the mind of every employee.
—Jack Welch,
former CEO, General Electric

Management by objectives works—
if you know the objectives.
Ninety percent of the time you don't.
—Peter Drucker

A FEW YEARS AGO, ONE of our clients, the CEO of a large financial services company, gathered his top 150 executives to provide additional detail about the company's strategy. After speaking for over 30 minutes, he called for questions. Someone in the audience rose and said, "I appreciate the perspective you've given us about our financial targets and the new customer segments we'll pursue. But I still don't understand what the strategy means for my part of the business." Similar comments expressed by others revealed that this questioner wasn't the only one in the room who didn't understand the action implications of the new direction the company was taking.

Afterwards in private, the CEO was sputtering with frustration. Following the advice of his HR and Communications departments, he had devoted enormous energy to communications related to the strategy. He had, for example, been speaking throughout the company for weeks trying to make the strategy clear. He also commissioned a video detailing it, had granted interviews to internal and external publications on the subject, and even commissioned the printing of wallet-size cards bearing the strategy that were distributed to all employees. "How could it be," he asked us in frustration, "that after all this, they—THEY!—don't understand what the hell I've been talking about?"

His experience is not unique. Consultants, HR professionals, and internal communications departments have been haranguing top executives for a long time to share their strategy with employees and many have earnestly tried to follow the advice. Despite this cajoling, most employees—often even very highly paid ones—still have only a vague idea of the strategic aims of their company. Robert Kaplan and David Norton (1996), originators of the Balanced Scorecard, conducted research revealing that 95 percent of employees in their client organizations did not understand the strategy when they started working with the organization.

Strategy is a story that tells what it will take to win in a marketplace. In our view, employees in the strategy-capable organization not only must understand the strategy at a high level, they must also understand the steps the company intends to take in achieving the strategy and what the leading and lagging indicators of success are. In short, the employees must be "business literate."

This chapter defines *business literacy,* the term we use to describe "the state of being knowledgeable, in an action-capable way" about the strategy of one's company. We will pass along numerous suggestions for getting business knowledge quickly spread throughout the workforce, whether yours is a small department, a division, or an international enterprise.

Central to the story of this chapter will be how Prudential Financial "cracked the code" on enhancing business literacy on a grand scale a few years ago, increasing employee knowledge about the business over 300 percent. We will touch on numerous other examples drawn from other organizations, as well. Earlier, we made the case that strategy implementation stalls out immediately when employees do not understand the strategy. The good news is that most employees can easily learn what they need to know if given a chance—that is as long as a few guidelines are followed. In this chapter, we will spell out those guidelines.

What Is Business Literacy?

Management theorists as diverse as Gary Hamel, Tom Peters, Ken Blanchard, and Peter Drucker agree: Employees should understand the strategy of their company. Each of these theorists points out the obvious: No strategic plan can spell out every step to gaining and maintaining advantage in the marketplace. Employees, therefore, need to comprehend the strategy—and the objectives behind it—so they can make the decisions required to implement it at their level.

This is easier said than done, especially if you buy into the standard we use for business literacy. It is based on hundreds of interviews with top executives of whom we have asked, "What must employees at your company know about your business to ensure competitiveness in your marketplace?" Most said that employees must understand the following:

- The company's overall strategy; its key objectives and where those objectives will lead

- The rationale behind the strategy, i.e., the business case it entails, which usually involves an understanding of changing markets, customer preferences, under-performing assets, and so forth

- The key changes the company will undergo to achieve its strategic objectives and any new structures and systems the company will put in place along the way.

- The financial targets for the enterprise as a whole and for the specific business of which they are a part

- Key metrics the company will use to track progress related to the strategy—overall and in their area (i.e., metrics), expressed both as financial and customer results

- The role employees are expected to play in the strategy implementation process

Does this list seem daunting? Is the standard too high? One way of looking at this list is that employees are business literate if they know as much about the strategy as a very well-informed (nonemployee) shareholder. Yes, it is a high standard and it is daunting, partly because you can't force people to learn this kind of material. Like the proverbial horse, you can lead employees to the learning trough, but you can't make them learn. When and where employees become business literate, leaders in their company have made becoming so fun, interesting, and useful. In this chapter, we'll tell you how best-in-class organizations cause employees to want to learn about things like ROI, capital markets, customer buying patterns, and even the effects, if relevant, of economic events in other countries and how they impact the marketplace in which they operate.

A Typical Approach to Business Literacy

All too often, once an executive group formulates a fresh strategy, some senior leader summons the corporate communications people to begin disseminating the strategy throughout the organization.

The resulting business literacy efforts usually take two forms— print and meetings—although larger companies often use video productions as well. The larger the company, the more varied and rich this campaign tends to be. Larger companies use Intranet sites, closed-circuit TV, posters, and in-house employee publications. None of this is bad; it just doesn't work very well because it's all about pushing information at people. Most people have heard that the most compelling part of a message is carried on the nonverbal plane, yet you wouldn't know it by the business literacy efforts in most organizations.

Figure 4-1 graphically displays the truth about communication channels, i.e., various ways to convey a message and the resulting impact of that message. While the most common channels of communication in most businesses are the written and spoken word, both are the two least effective communication modes.

Over many years of interviewing employees at all levels about their understanding of the business, we've found that nearly all employees tune out printed material and even some of the video. The lower in the hierarchy, the more this is true.

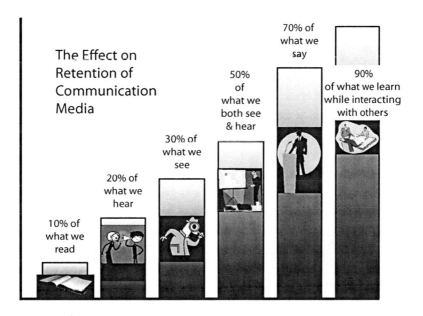

The Effect on Retention of Communication Media

10% of what we read

20% of what we hear

30% of what we see

50% of what we both see & hear

70% of what we say

90% of what we learn while interacting with others

Figure 4-1: Retention by communication channels (Source: RootLearning, Inc.)

Why? For three reasons: because these employees don't feel that information about the strategy has anything to do with them, because strategy-related information is often presented in a way that makes it hard to understand, and because of the media used to convey it is so ubiquitous, the information becomes a kind of background hum without message value.

Please do not misinterpret what we're saying. If you are attempting to educate your employees about any aspect of your business through print or any other mechanism, you get "points" with us; you are doing more than many do. We just want to urge you to be creative because *the typical corporate communications messages do not communicate!* The famous communications guru Marshall

McLuhan once distinguished between "hot" and "cold" media. Hot media—like face-to-face dialogue—compels your involvement and attention. Cold media—like email from a corporate leader sent to all employees or a boring PowerPoint presentation—gets overlooked. Print and one-way communication are both cool, if not cold, media.

Communication, true communication, the kind that leads to learning, needs to be a two-way street: a message is put forth and feedback returns saying whether or not the message has been received. Then, depending on the feedback, the original message is restated, changed, delayed, and so on; it's an iterative process.

In organizational life, if *two-way* communication is a good thing, *multiple-way* communication is better still. That's why so many Town Hall meetings are held these days. Ironically, however, the one-way communication problem is aggravated, not resolved in most such meetings; these meetings may create a certain kind of efficiency of broadcasting, but employees often walk away uninspired and still unengaged.

Here is a description of how a Town Meeting typically unfolds. This is an account of an actual meeting we had the opportunity to sit in on at a client organization. The executive was giving what he surely hoped would be an inspiring speech to a group of about one hundred employees. We have experienced this scene many times, both as consultants and as employees. We call it "Talking Heads, Inc."

In the situation we're about to describe, the lights were dimmed so that the PowerPoint presentation would be easier to see. And there were a lot of slides—over 50, and each laden with words and numbers. The executive assured people that there would be plenty of time at the end of the talk for questions. He literally said these words: "Shame on you if you don't ask any questions." The executive launched into the slides by acknowledging that the business was under-performing. He spoke earnestly about the need to do things differently in order to improve the company's performance. He then talked of competition heating up and about the lack of consumer confidence, all things the employees needed to know. He said "new tricks" would be necessary and that all employees would need to "work together as a team." He made clear to his audience that "every one of you have to embrace change," and implied that holdouts would face unpleasant consequences.

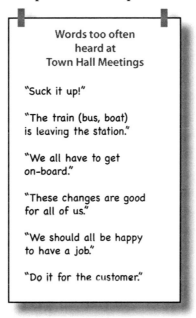

Words too often
heard at
Town Hall Meetings

"Suck it up!"

"The train (bus, boat)
is leaving the station."

"We all have to get
on-board."

"These changes are good
for all of us."

"We should all be happy
to have a job."

"Do it for the customer."

At no point did the executive describe what employee actions would enable the company to win, nor what winning would look like—both essential aspects of a complete story about a strategy. And there was no mention of what benefits would result from the extra effort he was implying would be necessary, except that disaster might be averted and jobs saved. He could have emphasized, for example, the pride they would all have from pulling together to meet the challenge—or that their customers would be delighted with the extra effort, or that they would all learn new skills.

After 90 minutes, the executive called for a five-minute break. People fled to the bathrooms. After literally five minutes (we are not exaggerating), he began again, repeating his, "Shame on you if you don't ask questions" remark. Only half of the participants had returned to their seats; the rest were on cell phones and/or in bathroom lines. He spoke for an additional 60 minutes.

Finally, he asked, "Who has questions?" There were precisely *two* questions. Answering them took three minutes.

Everyone seemed to leave the meeting with heightened anxiety but clueless as to how to help.

More than anything else, this particular executive seemed to relish being the center of attention. Not every executive is so narcissistic of course, but most of us have witnessed this same basic speech many times before, told in the same non-engaging way, with the same numbing effect. Finally, the lights come up and everyone shuffles out. Talking Heads, Inc.

In most cases, we believe business leaders conduct meetings like this not because they're self-centered, but because they don't know of alternative ways to conduct meetings. We provide some better ideas later in this chapter.

If winning minds is more than simply talking *at* people about the company's plans and aspirations, what is it?

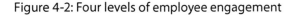

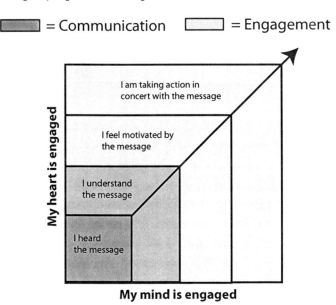

Figure 4-2: Four levels of employee engagement

When an executive steps before a group of employees, he or she has an opportunity to accomplish several objectives related to strategy execution. The model in Figure 4-2 articulates a progression of possibilities. The model is instructive in that it makes a distinction between mere communication—the transmission of information—and meaningful influence. The result of good communication is that a listener can say, "I hear you," *and* "I understand you." In this sense, the mind is engaged. But surely, it is preferable to go beyond this to true engagement in which an employee's basic motivations are affected and the heart is engaged. We discuss this in detail in the next chapter. We like the distinction between communication and the mind, on the one hand, and engagement and the heart on the other. An effective effort to convey a strategy to employees will not merely make people *aware* of the strategy; it will also enable employees to act on it. Obviously, this entails considerably more than delivering a spiel full of facts and figures.

Grab Their Attention

Once, one of us was waiting for a coaching client, the President of an energy company. When he arrived, the client looked rushed and was red in the face, almost as if someone had embarrassed him. "Sorry I'm late," he said. "My previous meeting ended early, but I wanted to meet with my staff afterwards."

We mentioned that he seemed stressed. "Oh, do I? Actually, I'm more confused than anything. I just told an all-employee meeting that we are shifting our business strategy and that this might involve selling off some assets. It was the oddest thing, though," he said. "I spoke for over 45 minutes then asked for questions. No one asked a single question. They just sat there."

We inquired about the agenda of the meeting. "You say you spoke for 45 minutes about a subject that, for most, is anxiety-provoking. Was there an opportunity afterwards for people to talk among themselves and formulate questions? If a person wanted to ask a question, was there a way to do so anonymously?" we inquired. Clearly, our client missed an opportunity and we respectfully said so.

Do you want to get more interaction at your employee meetings? Do you want more questions to come out? Do you really want to know how employees are receiving your messages, and what sense they're making of them? Then follow this sequence. It works every time.

Limit your remarks.

Speak for no more than 20 minutes. Any longer, and people tune out. They won't be able to recall what you said early in your remarks. Consider speaking without PowerPoint slides, and speak from the heart instead. Eliminating slides means you'll say only the most important things and do so in a more engaging way.

Give your audience a task to do while you're speaking.

Before you get rolling, tell the audience members what you'd like them to do while you talk. Tell them to keep track of their questions, their reactions, and the key messages in your remarks as they will be expected to compare notes with others later. Tell them what will happen after you speak, i.e., you will ask them to cluster in small groups to share what they heard, what their reactions were, and what questions they have.

Form informal discussion groups.

When you finish, say something like, "I'd like you to form into groups of 5 to 6 people. Choose someone to keep the conversation on track and to make sure everyone gets heard. (Wait until they do this.) Now say, "First, share among yourselves what you just heard me say. Some will have heard one thing, others will have heard something else. Then, share your reactions to what you've heard: do you like it, does it make you feel angry or anxious, or does it provoke another feeling? Finally, have someone in the group record all the questions that come up about the subjects we've been discussing. That person will act as the spokesperson for the group later, and we'll surface as many questions as we have time for." Let the groups go to work for 15 minutes or so.

Harvest the fruits of the small group discussions.

Reassemble the multitude and go topic by topic, first letting the groups tell you what they heard, then tell about their reactions, and finally, tell you what questions they have. Hear from as many groups as possible during each round. Spend the longest time on the reactions part, as this is where your audience tells you how your message is "going down." Answer any lingering questions.

Ask for feedback on the process.

Finally, ask your group, "How did this format work? Should we employ this way of conversing with one another in future meetings?" We'll bet 10:1 they will clamor for more interaction like this!

Get Them to Come to Your Conclusions

We were asked to help a pharmaceutical firm "increase the level of teamwork" in its largest plant. But we were wary; often when clients go looking for consultants, they have already concluded what will solve the problem. So in this instance, we responded to the request by respectfully asking the client about the mechanics of its business: how the company makes money, what gets in the way, market forces that help and hinder, etc. We wanted to make our own determination as to whether or not teams would help solve the problems.

Because a major competitor had dropped out of this company's market, the firm was in the enviable position of being able to sell—at a handsome margin—every unit of product that could be made. The problem, for which teams were perceived to be the solution, was that the plant was running at over 100 percent capacity, and partially as a consequence, everyone was getting sloppy: They were throwing nearly one-third of what they were making in the trash due to errors at various points in the production cycle. Running flat out was contributing to the major problem, which was waste, not a lack of teamwork.

The result of inefficiency, in financial terms, was lost revenue and dramatic overtime costs. And the waste they were creating was catching the attention of FDA officials who were wondering if the plant was reliable. And on the human side, employees were burning out. Nearly all employees were regularly working a 50-hour week and were often scheduled for even more overtime.

On learning all of this, we said to the client, "Better teamwork is almost always a good thing, but the real need here is to stop throwing product in the trash. If you solve the right problem," we argued, "you can cure a host of ills at once."

We then asked the plant director, "*You* know how much waste there is. Your strategy targets waste reduction. But do *your employees* know how much waste there is?"

"Not everyone," was the reply.

"Fair enough," we rejoined. "Where employees do understand the extent of the waste, do they understand how waste leads to mandatory overtime or diminishes their 401k plans?" The candid answer suggested we were hitting pay dirt: "Most of our employees have no real idea how our company makes money at all, or how what they do on a daily basis makes a difference on *any* performance measure." The plant director went on, "This is true even though we've been telling our employees these things at every All-Hands meeting for the last three years."

And what were those meetings like? You guessed it: Talking Heads, Inc.!

Learning that one of these meetings was coming up, we suggested a completely fresh approach. Instead of auditorium seating, we recommended table seating for the 600 people attending. Instead of hour-long lectures, we limited each speaker to 15 minutes. Each talk was followed by a table discussion of 20 minutes and centered on the three questions outlined above: What did we hear? What are our reactions to what we heard? What questions do we still have?

Then, facilitators with microphones sampled answers from as many tables as possible. This was beneficial in itself, but the real innovation came in the form of a custom-designed, business literacy exercise we created. It was designed to pop eyes open about the need to reduce waste—and it worked. It was based on the principles underlying "learning maps" marketed by companies such as Root Learning, Inc. and Paradigm Learning. (Root calls them "RootMaps," Paradigm calls them "Discovery Maps.")

An artist created a big, colorful poster (see Figure 4-3, "Learning Poster for a Vaccines Company"). We placed one on each table. The participants had a guided discussion about the business, then wrote their answers to several questions on the poster. Finally, each person at the table signed the poster, symbolizing their commitment to reduce waste.

Figure 4-3: Learning Poster for a Vaccines Company

The sequence of discussion followed these lines: First, the employees celebrated the year's accomplishments. Then, they reviewed the company's goals, one of which included saving the lives of children. They wrote the goals on the chart. Next, they were asked to estimate the percentage of product lost each year to waste, and to check their answer with someone at the table who had been provided with the data. Only one-quarter of the tables got the number right. They wrote the actual percentage of lost product on the chart.

After that, the learning experiences provided information that permitted the employees to calculate the number of additional lives that could be saved if they could produce additional product. Finally, they discussed the potential gains in terms of quality of work life for themselves if productivity increased. Almost on cue, across the entire room of 500 employees, people began saying to one another, "I had no idea we produced this much waste. We have to change this!" The employees in that plant finally understood the problem and simultaneously began to feel a shared responsibility to solve it.

This learning experience permitted the employees to "discover" the problem and led them to want to change it. Was it manipulative? It certainly elicited and perhaps even engineered an intense response. But if you were to ask the participants if the process was manipulative—as we did—they would say no. Summing up most of the responses we heard was that of a long-term employee who said to us, "This was the best annual meeting we've ever had. I finally understand this business and feel a part of it. I hope we have more of these meetings, more frequently."

The signed posters created in that meeting hung throughout the plant for six months as visual reminders of the employees' commitment to change. We worked separately with managers and supervisors in the production area to apply improvement tools to various processes. The levels of cooperation exhibited by both leaders and hourly workers were unmatched. Waste levels dropped by 67 percent over the next year.

Business Literacy on a Grand Scale

The plant experience involved 600 employees, a large but manageable challenge. But how do you cause over 55,000 employees, spread over 12 cities, to understand a bold new strategy quickly, to feel good about the direction in which the company is moving, and then to take action towards implementing the strategy in their own areas?

This was the task given to his direct reports and consultants by Art Ryan, then chairman and CEO of Prudential Financial when it was changing its status from a mutual company to a publicly-traded company in 2000. The resulting response, known to Prudential's employees as "One Prudential Exchange" (OPX), stands as one of the largest business literacy and alignment processes ever mounted in corporate America.

At the outset, Art Ryan was clear about his goals for OPX. The way he put it was, "We have to do more than create business literacy and increase employee satisfaction in this effort. These are both critically important and I'm sure we'll achieve these results. But this is not why we're going to do this. We're going to do this to get business results—in every work unit, at every level, in every business—or we aren't going to do it at all." At the end, Ryan saw these work unit meetings as, to use his word, "institutionalizing" a new way of working at Prudential.

Ultimately, OPX had four explicit goals:

- Prepare Prudential's 55,000 employees for the company's future by deepening their knowledge of the strategy and the basics of Prudential's businesses.

- Dramatically improve employee morale, attitudes about the company, and employee commitment to the company and its new direction.

- Effect better alignment of the work of every unit throughout Prudential with the company's new strategy.

- Create a platform for learning, dialogue, and communication that could be used over and over to focus the attention and coordinate the work of all employees and their managers.

For Art Ryan, successful execution of Prudential's strategy would require business-literate employees at every level. Only then, he felt, could employees knowledgeably effect change in their own areas of responsibility. If they had this knowledge, they would be vastly more likely to cease off-strategy work and to initiate new work that would further the strategy. He realized that to achieve his aim of turning a sluggish and bureaucratic institution into a dynamic, modern organization would require every Prudential employee at every level to think and act like an educated businessperson.

Achieving this goal required a massive commitment of resources: not just money but also executive time, manager time, and the commitment on the part of organization to help people learn. But Ryan got this and more through a combination of large, mixed-level employee meetings, work unit meetings, and facilitated dialogue.

Figure 4-4, "The Architecture of OPX," portrays the major elements of this initiative. It began with a series of 225 meetings of 300 employees, held in 12 cities over nine months to lay the case for change. These meetings were followed by smaller meetings in each and every work unit that produced measurable business results and led to significant gains in employee morale and commitment.

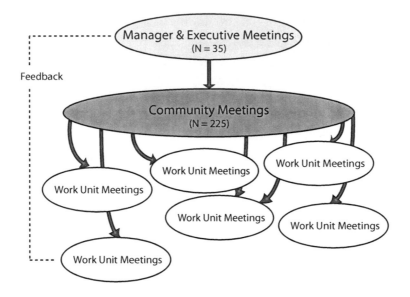

Figure 4-4: Architecture of Prudential's employee engagement intervention

One of the authors of this book was the lead consultant on the Prudential project. He assembled a team of 25 facilitators who, in turn, worked in pairs with two Prudential executives to conduct each meeting. Before each meeting, the executive-facilitator team met to review the agenda and agree on roles. The facilitators taught the executives ways to draw the meeting participants into dialogue—and to make sure the meetings would not devolve into "Talking Heads, Inc."

Described below is the process by which this architecture was rolled out and measured, using the Four Jobs model as an organizing concept.

Job One: Enhance Business Literacy. All executives and managers participated in a 1½-day meeting to prepare to play their part in the process. Every manager at Prudential not only experienced his or her own large business literacy meeting ("Manager & Executive Meetings") but also went on to play a supportive role in two or three "Community Meetings" attended by up to 300 nonmanagerial employees. These meetings featured learning maps similar to those used in the vaccines company example, mentioned earlier.

Job Two: Increase Employee Commitment. The Manager and Community Meetings were dialogue-rich. Executives permitted employees to say exactly what was on their minds, and were coached to respond in a way that deepened the candor. Employee survey data showed that employee attitudes about the company began to shift early and progressively in a positive direction as the meetings rolled out. Not only did employees understand the strategy better, they also felt more motivated to fulfill it and committed to the company and its success. Morale soared.

Job Three: Align Work At The Unit Level. Meetings at every Prudential work site followed the large meetings, each run by managers and supervisors in all Prudential locations. The OPX team provided a simple design for these meetings, which were designed to forge greater strategic alignment at the work unit level. The work unit meetings produced both specific business process improvements and further gains in employee morale and commitment. Over 3,500 work unit meetings were held in the first round. Managers were asked to run at least one such meeting every quarter to ensure alignment over time.

Job Four: Effect Cross-System Alignment. Because each work unit meeting was documented by means of a report filed by the manager, Prudential executives began to form a vivid picture of where there were systemic impediments to strategy implementation. (Chapter Six gives details of how these meetings worked and provides assessment forms, as well.) Prudential found a multitude of ways to use that data to enhance cross-system alignment. For instance, multiple Action-Learning teams had been composed to address the enterprise-wide issues getting in the way of cross-selling. Some businesses found ways to bring key stakeholders into dialogue sessions with them as solutions were sought.

Did all of this effort pay off? Some of the results of the Prudential effort are listed below. It is important to keep in mind that these gains were obtained despite the fact that during this intervention, significant layoffs occurred. After two years:

• Employee knowledge about Prudential's strategy increased by over 300 percent.

- Gains were observed on 38 of the 39 measures of employee morale and commitment.

- Overall, employee commitment to the company and its mission and strategy increased 38 percent.

- 70 percent of leaders continued to hold regular work unit meetings.

- 70 percent of those meetings resulted in action plans.

- 90 percent of all action plans led to improved business results.

Long after those large OPX meetings were held, we asked Art Ryan what results were most significant in the last analysis. He emphasized the important role that business literacy played, and how it helped drive actions at the work unit level. But he also spoke about the value of the whole effort to those at the top, the chief strategists. Here is what he said:

> OPX was really valuable for me and my directs in clarifying our thinking around strategy. At 40,000 feet, strategy is fairly easy to articulate. In the very early stages [of the turnaround], we found that we were articulating strategy around product. We would say things like we're in the insurance, investment, health care, real estate, mortgage businesses. Looking back, we were simply listing what we do, not articulating the strategy. We got away with this at 40,000 feet, because we said we were in the financial services business. Well, anything fits in the financial services business. This forced us, at the senior level, to clarify our thinking and our commitments. As we rolled out the meetings, we were called upon to communicate what our strategy required everyone to do, but was also effective in telling us what we should not be doing. (Source: Interview with the authors.)

To an alert observer, it may look like a flaw in our Four Jobs model: doing Job One well, i.e., educating and informing people about the strategy and its rationale creates a result that is not distinct from Job Two when *it* is done well, i.e., increasing employee motivation and commitment to change. In fact, Jobs One and Two *are* highly correlated. Benjamin Franklin once said, "Those things that hurt, instruct." There is nothing like knowledge of negative consequences to get people's attention. But you don't do it to hurt people but to get them to open up to learning.

When speculating on what made One Prudential Exchange so effective, a Prudential executive said that, for her, it was simple: "We gave all employees the same information senior management had. Like it did us, this information scared them. They came away motivated to turn the company around."

Partly in recognition of his turnaround of Prudential, in 2009 Art Ryan was named as one of the "100 Best-Performing CEOs in the World" by *Harvard Business Review* (see Hansen, et al., 2010). To read more about OPX, consult the following references: Economist Intelligence Unit, 1999; Barbian, 2002; and McKnight, 2002a & 2002b.

Six Prescriptions for Increasing Business Literacy

Arguably, there are dozens of creative ways to inform employees about a strategy, its importance, and what has to be accomplished. Below are some principles that underlie successful business literacy efforts, drawn from our experiences with many clients.

1. Remember the basics of learning.

A cliché well known to training and development professionals bears repeating, because many of our clients have never heard it: "What I hear I forget. What I see I remember. What I do, I know." Build your business literacy effort around this truth and you'll succeed. Use involving, active processes. Don't "PowerPoint" people into a stupor. Most people don't learn well through numbers-laden decks of slides. They learn as they interact with the material.

2. Connect business literacy to the strategy.

Think of business literacy as a means, not an end. Widespread understanding of the strategy is essential if you're concerned about strategy implementation. It will help the cause if you think of your business literacy effort as a *strategy implementation* exercise, not as a *training* exercise. Think big and you will help employees find the connection between the overall strategy and their specific assignments.

3.   Employ multiple-way vs. one-way communication processes.

Many internal communication efforts rely on newsletters, videos, and manager briefings to "get employees on-board." In fact, these vehicles just don't go far enough because they're one-way. Employees tune them out. Intensive dialogue processes are vastly more effective because they move people toward alignment as they share their perspectives and best practices. They also create a feeling of "We're all in this together."

4.   Ask people to say what they're learning.

People learn best when they put into words what they're learning. In educational circles, this principle goes by the rather dated-sounding term, "recitation." This is another one of the reasons why those slick PowerPoint presentations don't work: employees aren't saying what they're learning and, therefore, they quickly forget it. This technique is used extensively in all educational settings because it works. Group discussions, even debates, force people to put to words what they're learning. Asking people to tell one another what they've heard a speaker say does the same thing.

5.   Repeat. Then repeat again—in a different way.

Just because you've identified some effective teaching methods and used them well once doesn't mean you've won the business literacy battle. Knowledge decays rapidly when there is no reinforcement of the initial learning. Employees exposed to a stream of varied learning experiences grasp and retain info better than do others who only hear or experience something once. Odds are that the companies in your industry you most admire continually educate their employees using a variety of mechanisms.

6.   Use measurement data to guide the business literacy effort.

If successful execution of your strategy requires that employees understand the strategy, find out if they *do* understand it and take action if they don't. How? By asking them what they know. There are lots of ways to do so without coming off like a cranky schoolteacher. Consider using anonymous surveys or, even better, focus groups in which you ask employees which areas of the strategy are least clear to them.

Action Learning

No one can execute a strategy they don't understand. Increasing the business literacy of your employee population is the foundational ingredient of the strategy implementation process. Getting a workforce up to speed quickly on a new strategy may seem daunting, especially when that workforce has been in the dark for a long time. But any manager, executive, communications professional, or HR specialist, can do this if each bears in mind sound principles about how learning occurs. One good test of progress comes in the form of two questions that employee surveys and other methods can easily assess: "Are our employees acquiring business acumen?" and "Are they having fun in the learning process?" The odds are high that if the answer to the second question is positive, so is the first.

Exercise 1: Evaluate current job one efforts.

Either alone, or preferably with a group of others mixed by level, answer the following questions:

- What mechanisms do we currently use for communicating our strategy to employees?

- How well do those mechanisms work?

- How do we know—are we guessing or do we have data? If we're guessing, how could we get data on this?

Exercise 2: Establish job one content.

- With respect to our strategy, what do our employees need to know? Consult the list on page 67 in answering.

- Do they have this knowledge?
- What information do we need to make a special effort to communicate?

Exercise 3: Assess knowledge of the strategy.

Walk through your company in the next week and ask several people to describe the company's strategy. Don't come off like a cranky professor but as a humble student. Say something like, "I'm not sure we're doing enough to enable our employees to understand the company's strategy. What is your view of that? What could *I* do to make it clearer?"

Once you get this conversation going, slip in the question, "Are you aware of what the company's strategic objectives are, and if so, what are they?" Then ask, "How about our part of the organization: What do we have to accomplish in order to support the overall objectives?"

This exercise will be especially powerful if you and all of your direct reports do it and then gather to compare notes on what you learned.

Exercise 4: Try the approach starting on page 73.

The approach described there entails a means of communicating strategic content to a group of employees. Find or create an opportunity to employ this process. Arrange for someone to observe and critique you afterwards, someone who will be honest with you about your effectiveness.

Chapter Five

Job Two:
Winning Hearts

*...in teaching, in acting and the other arts,
in oratory and in that humbler branch of persuasion
called salesmanship...it is **feeling** which serves as the bridge
between one human being and another.*
—Isabel Briggs Myers

O NE OF US WAS EMPLOYED for a time at a firm owned by a world-renowned and highly admired company. Because the parent company was so well regarded, you can imagine why we couldn't make sense of an email sent to all employees from the Chairman. The subject line said: *"[Name of company], one of the world's most admired."*

To be honored is a good thing, we thought, so the Chairman's communication was confusing. Paraphrasing, this was the message:

I hope you will join me in being disgusted that we won second place in the recent competition for recognition in our industry. We are better than this. I feel let down and I hope I never have to write a similar email again. We are not seen as number one but we should be. None of us should ever accept a disgrace like this again.

Let's see—second place is a disgrace. Hmm... Because we were far down in the corporate hierarchy, we did not have a chance to tell the Chairman what effect his communiqué had on us and our colleagues. But you can count on this: It certainly did not make us feel inclined to go the extra mile to get that firm into the #1 slot the following year!

Employee feelings about their work and subsequent productivity are related. But which causes which? Do enthusiasm and high spirits *produce* or *result from* business success? In other words, does employee morale follow financial performance or does it create those results? A study done in 2003 answered this question.

Practice What You Preach

The study was conducted by David Maister, former Harvard Business School professor and one of the world's leading authorities on conditions leading to success in professional service firms. He conducted a study that asked, "Are employee attitudes correlated with financial success?" To answer the question, he assembled data from 29 firms in 15 countries across 15 lines of business. The results were published in his book, *Practice What you Preach: What Managers Must do to Create a High Achievement Culture* (Maister, 2003).

Maister found that not only are employee attitudes correlated with success, those attitudes can *cause* financial success. Maister found that when employees perceive that their company holds them in high regard, when management creates conditions leading to trust, and engenders a feeling of partnership with employees in a collaborative effort, "a demonstrable, measurable improvement in financial performance (including growth as well as profits)" follows. The financial results that Maister tracked in this study were revenue and profit growth over two years, profit margin, and profit per employee, all of which grow as employees' trust grows.

Maister joins many other critics of modern business leaders when he says, "Of all the goals that businesses say they have (make money, please clients, attract and develop talented staff), the least well done are those related to managing people." Still, among the companies he studied, he found many managers who were very capable in this realm, concluding that "where trust and respect between management and employees are high, financial performance predictably goes up." He also noted that, "...success in management is less a property of firms (the system of the business as a whole) but, instead, is mostly about the personality of the individual manager within the operating unit. Success is about personalities, not policies."

These results should not surprise us. After all, preceding Maister's study, similar results were reported in *The Service Profit Chain* by Heskett, et al. (1997), and *Built to Last: Successful Habits of Visionary Companies,* by Jim Collins and Jerry I. Porras (2004). The book *Good to Great: Why Some Companies Make the Leap... and Others Don't,* by Jim Collins (2001), which followed Maister's study, also corroborates the findings. (As do studies conducted by the Hay Group, and Gallup. The Watson Wyatt Worldwide *Human Capital Index* study also found that effective human resources practices lead to positive financial outcomes.)

A Productive Workplace is Where the Heart is

If a workplace can feel like a home for our spirits, what would that be like? We ask because we believe if you do all the things we advocate, this will be the result. Yes, you will execute your strategy and will very likely achieve financial success, but you will also have contributed significantly to the well-being of your employees.

If you could get inside the skin of employees in the most productive workplaces, here is what you would find. See how many you can say are true for you in *your* workplace.

❑ *In my workplace, I regularly feel important, significant, and valued.*

❑ *In my workplace, I regularly feel competent and capable.*

❑ *In my workplace, I regularly feel worthy, likeable, and good.*

❑ *In my workplace, I regularly and meaningfully contribute to a socially beneficial cause that I feel passionately committed to.*

Those who are familiar with a psychological instrument called

FIRO-F (Fundamental Interpersonal Relations Orientation-Feelings), these descriptions will seem familiar: They parallel what psychologist Will Schutz (1994), its developer, long ago defined as "fundamental interpersonal needs." Schutz observed that when these needs are fulfilled, people are often exceptionally productive.

If you are able to check off all of the statements above, you probably want to pinch yourself you're so happy with your work experience. You probably feel like jumping up and down with gladness and exultation. *Gladness and exultation.* Few other words capture it. It's thrilling to work in a place that make you feel valued and important and involved.

We like the phrase "spirited workplace." To most people, "workplace" and "spirit" is a strange juxtaposition of terms. According to a friend who speaks Hebrew, the word *avodah* means both "work" and "worship." While syntactically kindred in Hebrew, however, the two ideas have always seemed miles apart in most workplaces.

Attending to the human spirit is good business. We say so, in part, due to *Fortune* magazine's annual "Best Companies to Work For" survey. As you probably know, every year *Fortune* chooses the "100 Best" from a pool of candidates that ask to be on their list. The score is derived from employee responses to the *Great Place to Work Trust Index,* a survey assessing the company's culture as well as on-site visits and interviews with employees and managers.

What distinguishes "The Best to Work For" companies? Five things, all listed below (money.cnn.com, 2010). Read them slowly and check off any that are true of your organization:

❑ *Management is competent and is perceived to have integrity.*

❑ *Management supports, cares about, and collaborates with employees.*

❑ *Workers see the workplace as equitable, impartial, and just.*

❑ *Employees feel proud of their jobs, team, work group, and the company as a whole.*

❑ *The workplace is hospitable and "intimate;" it feels like a community.*

A cynic might say, "All this is nice, but I care far less about how employees perceive the company than how the company performs in the marketplace." Fair enough. So, how do those "Best Companies to Work For" stack up in quantitative terms compared to others that don't make the cut? They stand out in at least seven ways. They...

- Receive more qualified job applications for open positions

- Experience a lower level of turnover

- Experience reductions in health care costs

- Enjoy higher levels of customer satisfaction and customer loyalty

- Foster greater innovation, creativity and risk taking

- Benefit from higher productivity and profitability

- Consistently outperform major stock indices ($1,000 invested in the "Best Companies" ten years ago returned $8,188 vs. $3,976 for "non-Best" companies when invested in the Russell 3000)

Winning Hearts—in Action

Winning hearts is an aspect of leadership, a topic that business-people never seem to tire of thinking and reading about. The world continues to be fascinated by the topic of leadership, we believe, because it's elusive: Despite all the books, videos, seminars, and consultants focusing on leadership, it's one of the most mysterious of skills.

We had an in-depth experience a few years ago, that illuminated what good leadership looks like more than anything we've ever read on the subject. We touched on it in the last chapter: the Prudential turnaround project. In the process of that engagement, over 200 times we had the opportunity to watch top executives step before groups of up to 300 people and attempt to educate employees about the company's strategy and enlist them as partners in the company's turnaround.

We were asked to systematically collect data on what those leaders did well and what they didn't do so well. Below is a summary. If you want to have a daunting experience as a leader, do what they did: strap on a microphone and address several hundred people, trying to inspire them while knowing that they hold you responsible for letting their company go down the drain and firing hundreds of their co-workers!

In those meetings, as participants became aware of the challenges their company was facing and were encouraged to say how they felt about it, many spoke out vociferously and critically. Here is a typical exchange between a participant and an executive leader in one of those meetings. Put yourself into the shoes of the executive leading the discussion. What would you say to this employee that would "win hearts"?

> A woman in the back of the room stood with a microphone in her hand and said to the executive and nearly 300 other employees, "Through this meeting, I am learning that the company is in trouble. There are probably many reasons, but one thing is sure: This company has not been managed very well. The result is poor company performance. It seems like this meeting is designed to rouse up the employees to do what's necessary to pull the company out of its troubles."

> Many others in the room felt the same way. We knew this because we heard something like this in each of the meetings we facilitated. The entire room was tensely silent as the employees waited for the executive leader of the meeting to respond, a person who had been with the company for several years.

> The executive responded magnificently: "I want to say two things," she began. "First, I want to acknowledge the courage required to stand up and say what you just said." Turning to the audience, she then said, "If you admire the speaker's courage like I do, join with me in applauding her." The audience cheered their coworker. Then, the executive said, "The other thing I want to say is that I agree with you: The leaders of this company *didn't* manage the company well enough. And I am one of them. And you're right in thinking that these meetings are intended to get you to join with management in turning the company around. I know it's a lot to ask, but that is exactly what I am asking you to do."

The executive, skilled after having conducted a number of these meetings, then asked the audience: "I suspect this speaker is stimulating thoughts for others in the room. Who else would like to share their perspective?" Many hands went up. The next employee said, "We could sit around all day placing blame, but this won't solve a single problem. I say let's stop blaming and start fixing." The room broke out in spontaneous applause.

This executive could make a skillful response, in part, because she was a remarkable person, but she also received a good deal of coaching before the meeting began. Those meetings were intended to elicit truthful reactions and the truth was that many employees felt angry, anxious, and troubled, i.e., precisely the way this participant felt. The night before each meeting, the consulting team would meet with the executives who would be up front to help them get ready for the meeting. The consultants would say something like, "About 10:30 a.m. tomorrow morning, if we're successful, someone will stand up and say they believe the company is tanking and it's your fault. How do you intend to respond?" We role-played various responses.

Leaders develop their skills fastest during practical, task-related activities. The learning derived from just one successful exchange like this tops days of classroom time spent "studying" leadership. The key here is to work with executives in their "natural habitat" to design and lead inspiring and engaging meetings. Doing so kills two birds with one stone: They learn to lead *and* they connect employees with the strategy.

A leader does not have to have an audience of 300 to make a meaningful impact in a company. The truth is that whether your organization has a thousand employees, or just a dozen, or only two, those people probably *want* you to lead, influence them, and draw them into a state of partnership. What if you're the only leader in your company who wants to engage employee's hearts? Answer: you will feel better and employees in your area will appreciate it, and many will say so. It will feel good to all concerned and it will pay off handsomely in terms of the goals you all are trying to reach.

Winning Hearts During/After a Downsizing

Sometimes, strategy execution is accompanied by downsizing. Far from inspiring and motivating people, the decline of focus, energy and goodwill that occurs during and after downsizing distracts and immobilizes people. If you can win hearts at a time like this, you're skilled, indeed. Let's look closely at this circumstance to see if there might be lessons applicable to those and less challenging times.

Figure 5-1: An employee drawing of what it's like NOW to work at their company

We once had the opportunity to work with the employees of a large manufacturing plant that was closing. There were rumors of product sabotage due to the hostility employees felt over losing their jobs. We conducted many voluntary, day-long sessions in which we drew that hostility—and the sadness, fear, and anxiety—to the surface, providing a safe place to express and deal with it. During those sessions, we asked the participants to create drawings displaying their feelings about how they felt about the plant closing. Needless to say, the pictures weren't pretty. Figure 5-1 shows an example of the kind of images that showed up on those drawings. Look closely: This is what stressful employee feelings *look* like. It is the job of the leader to develop the skills required to deal constructively with such feelings. Notice the rain clouds, the executives jumping off the building with their golden parachutes, and employees jumping to their deaths on the right.

One classic study on the subject of employee feelings during a downsizing should give any organizational leader hope. It was conducted by business professor Charles Heckscher of Rutgers University and reported in his book, *White Collar Blues: Management Loyalties in an Age of Corporate Restructuring* (1995).

One of his discoveries was that during downsizing, if people can define to any degree what is needed to turn things around, they will tend to put forth increased effort and energy, not less. Sadly, most leaders in Heckscher's study did not provide this clarity. The implication for leaders is:

> *Tell employees what part they can play in the organization's change, and why it's important that they do so. Associates want to help, to dig in and do something. Tell them what that is!*

Heckscher also found that goodwill, energy, and commitment depend on the sense that the company is moving forward, and that the current trauma is somehow necessary to its success. Where this view exists—and he found that most people will be predisposed to see it this way—hard work follows; where it does not, there will be only despair. The implication for leaders is:

> *Tell associates about what's working while being honest with them about what still needs repair.*

> *Let them know there's a plan to repair what's still broken.*

> *Reassure people that while the pain is not over, and won't be for some time, things are steadily changing for the better. Give examples.*

A third finding was that a powerful force will tend to intervene between individuals' trauma and their responses. According to Heckscher, this force can be described as a desire for meaning, and more specifically a desire to draw meaning from contribution to a *group effort*. Those who cannot find meaning in the downsizing are the most distressed and disoriented. The implication for leaders is:

> *Acknowledge the pain that people in the room are surely feeling about downsizing (and other organizational changes).*

> *Keep reassuring associates that deliverance lies in everyone working together, solving problems* **collectively**.

> *Remind associates that the current pain, as difficult as it might be, is probably necessary to get us where we all want to go: success and restored pride.*

Bring out the Navigators

We have observed that during change, people tend to respond in one of three ways: as a powerless *Victim*, a grasping and clinging *Survivor,* or as an empowered *Navigator* who makes the best of change (McKnight, 2010). The guidelines above are powerful in helping people move into the *"Navigator zone."*

When they are kept in the dark, not allowed to give voice to their fears and concerns, and especially when they have no say over how change unfolds, employees become highly stressed and some react to their circumstances by means of fight or flight. This is the *Victim* mode. Others, the *Survivors,* go into self-protective mode and hunker down, saying yes when they mean no and hoping to avoid notice. Either way, productivity plummets. The drawing in Figure 5-1 depicts the *Victim* mode.

One way to think of the tasks associated with winning hearts is to give enough hope to people that they can begin functioning in *Navigator* mode during change. When in *Navigator* mode, people pitch in and try to help achieve what needs to be accomplished. They can astonish even themselves with their resilience and creativity.

Here is a story about a *Navigator*. A few years ago, we were working with a group of employees who were especially bitter about the changes occurring in their organization, because those changes entailed the layoffs of hundreds of their coworkers. As we were facilitating a discussion that was tapping into the feelings in the room, our client, one of the executives who made the decision leading to those layoffs, was getting visibly nervous. On a break, he said, "I think we should cut off this discussion. It is serving no useful purpose." We pushed for another ten minutes after the break to turn the conversation into a "teachable moment."

When we reassembled, we told the group that we wanted to attempt to paraphrase and summarize everything we had heard before the break. We went on for about five minutes. At the end, we asked, "What would you add to what we just said that would make this summary complete?"

A man in the back of the room said something we had never heard before or since, something that got nearly every head in the room to nod in agreement. It was the voice of a person in *Navigator* mode: "I think it is important to remember," he said, "that today is the past that someone in the future longs to return to." We asked a few of the people who seemed to be in agreement what they took his statement to mean. They all got it: When disruptive change occurs, we tend to idealize the past, but the past wasn't ideal; it was just the past.

To the extent that an organization is undergoing change, i.e., when its future is going to look very different from its present and past, employees will tend to struggle with change. It is the work of leaders to enable to see the benefits of that anticipated future. But sometimes the best way to free people so they can see that future is to first support them a bit in idealizing the past. That picture in Figure 5-1 with the people falling off the roof? Sometimes, this is what it takes to enable people to let go. Almost always, if a leader chides people for their "negative" feelings, those feelings intensify, they don't go away.

Resistance to Change

We have spoken a lot in the past few pages about how leaders can get people to open up to change as if people generally *resist* change. Superficial knowledge about organizational psychology leads many executives to the view that "people *always* resist change" or worse, that "people in *our* organization always resist change."

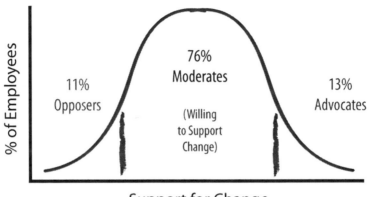

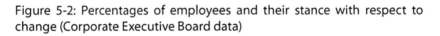

Figure 5-2: Percentages of employees and their stance with respect to change (Corporate Executive Board data)

What percentage of employees are highly resistant to change? What percentage is likely to be highly supportive of change? Fix those guesses in your mind. Now look at Figure 5-2 where the actual results are displayed. Although we use different labels than they do, these data come from research conducted by the Corporate Executive Board (2008).

If you're like most people, you had no idea that the percentage of people in the middle, i.e., those who are willing to support change if the conditions are right, was this high. Yes, some people do resist change under certain circumstances.

Figure 5-3 shows a list of reasons why employees might resist the changes required by your company's strategy. We've listed the cause on one side and the antidote on the other.

Psychologists tell a wry joke: How many therapists does it take to change a light bulb? Answer: Only one, but the light bulb must really *want* to change. It's the work of leaders to cause employees to want to change. As a leader, your task—at least in part—is to attract people to the unfinished work. And this job is made much easier when the benefits to them of doing so are made clear to those whose support you need.

Why Employees Might Resist Change	Antidote
The reason for the change is low, or vague; the cost of change seems to be higher than its payoff.	Clarify it. Then ask them what they heard. Then clarify some more. Ask them what they heard you say.
Past change efforts have not gone well.	Thoroughly explore what didn't work and bend every effort to avoid past mistakes
There is low perceived need for the change. The cost of change seems to be higher than the payoff for change.	Sell the purpose for the change. Educate. Inform. Then listen to what people heard.
The odds of succeeding are low.	Explore the barriers to success and engage employees in problem-solving focused on increasing success.
Those who have to carry out the change do not feel they are involved in the change effort.	Involve them. Give them a role. Consider them your partners in success and tell them so. Ask them what the best way is to involve them.
Those who are asked to change are invested in the status quo.	Explore their investment in the way things are. Bend over backwards to honor the past and their contribution to it. Help them respectfully to let go of the past through celebrations or ceremonies.

Figure 5-3: Reasons employees might resist change and some related antidotes

Quite often, organizational leaders contribute to resistance. One of the sure ways to foment antipathy to your vision is to disparage peoples' pasts. We have seen this many times as new leaders come in with enthusiasm for change, saying things like, "Our systems and processes are antiquated. We are going to turn this company around." What can get overlooked is that most employees probably see the existing processes as pretty good the way they are. Why wouldn't they? They *created* those processes. Employees see the insensitive leader who disparages "the way we do things" as not only inconsiderate but also as callous and perhaps cruel. Who wants to open themselves to the influence of a person like that?

Let's peer into two exchanges that we witnessed between a manager and a participant in two different town meetings. In both cases, the resistance to change was real. The leaders thus had an opportunity to *use* the resistance to inspire and motivate. In each case, the issue at hand was a consequential software migration that was to take 18-24 months and change most business processes.

Here is an exchange that took place between a frontline employee and an executive who had responsibility for the success of the project. The executive had called for questions from the audience.

Meeting participant:	"If we install the new customer service package, won't we confuse our customers? I mean, with all the additional questions we're going to have to ask with each customer call, won't they be turned off and likely to go to another company?"
Executive:	"There will be problems, sure, but this software is state of the art. Look, we all need to get on board because we all stand to gain if we do—and so do our customers. And guess what: The boat is leaving the dock."

In this example, the executive gets points for acknowledging that there might be something to the speaker's perception that the new software might be off-putting to customers, but to say the least, the leader missed an opportunity to inspire. This was one of those meetings in which there was very little participation from the audience, and no wonder: The executive leading the meeting clearly wasn't listening to what was being said. We don't know of course because we are not mind readers, but here is what we guess was the employee's internal reaction to this leader:

*"Here we go again. This is the third software change in two years. Sir, **you** don't have to listen to the complaints of our customers when we ask all these questions. We do. This will be a real turnoff for our best customers."*

In this next example, the executive took an active listening stance and made considerably more headway. This leader validated the speaker's concerns and turned a potential confrontation into a useful dialogue in less than 30 seconds. He cleared the way for the employee to apply his constructive energies to the task at hand and bought enormous credibility with everyone else in the room.

Meeting participant:	[Complaining about a systems design process that left frontline people out] "I've been with this company for 10 years and I've been hearing for 10 years what our customers want and need. But no one has ever asked me or my colleagues what *we* think our customers need."
Executive:	"I get a couple of things from what you said. For one thing, I pick up frustration. More importantly, I pick up that you really want to be involved more. I also pick up courage. This is the kind of candor and fortitude that will make this a useful meeting. You took a risk in speaking out. Thank you."

This executive went on to ask the audience, "How many others here want to be involved more in addressing our customers' needs and making sure they get met?" You won't be surprised that most people raised their hands. Then, the executive created one of the most useful discussions we have ever seen in a Town Hall meeting when he asked, "Let's brainstorm some ways you could be involved.

Put your ideas in the context of our current project. How can we make use of what you know from being on the phone with customers every day as we go forward?" Every idea the executive had in his mind before the meeting about how to involve people was not only mentioned, but several even better ideas surfaced, also.

8 Guidelines For Business Leaders Seeking Buy-In

Compelling leadership stories are simple, consistent, repeated, and memorable. Here's how to make sure you're hitting all four stops. We're writing this book for business leaders, but there is no reason why we can't take a page from that of a good politician. Business leaders, like politicians, are in the influence business and must strive to move people emotionally—to stir the heart—in order to accomplish this. Abraham Lincoln is legendary for his ability to win hearts. Here is his core advice on the subject (quoted in Phillips, 1993):

> *If you would win a man to your cause, first convince him that you are his sincere friend. Therein is a drop of honey that catches his heart, which, say what he will, is the great highroad to his reason, and which, once gained, you will find but little trouble in convincing him of the justice of your cause, if indeed that cause is really a good one.*

1. Choose the feeling you want to induce, and then evoke it.

Writer Maya Angelou, herself a compelling speaker, once remarked, "I've learned that people will forget what you said, people will forget what you did, but people will never forget how you made them feel." Good orators pay as much attention to the emotion they wish to cultivate in their audience as they do in the understanding they intend to convey. How do you want people to be *feeling* when you finish? How might you bring these feelings to the surface?

Barack Obama, running for President in 2008, made his supporters feel confident, important, capable, connected, and righteous. He did so not so much with the memorable phrase but by evoking emotion. On this point, Republican strategist and speech writer, Frank Luntz (inventor of the term "death tax") sees Obama as much more like Ronald Reagan than either JFK or FDR, both of whom relied on eloquence of phrasing to do the same thing. This should make business speakers happy, as most are not especially poetic by nature.

2. Be personal, not institutional. Describe your own experience.

Mark Twain summed it up:

When you fish for love, bait with your heart, not with your brain.

Effective leaders get people to want to do things. They do so in part by letting their audience know that they're human like them. They let their audience know who's speaking to them.

Let others know you're a dad or a mom, or a person who worries, not just a stuffy person who's playing a role.

Let your audience know you aren't perfect, and give them an example that proves the point.

Stop hiding behind those PowerPoint slides. Come down from that platform; get out from behind that lectern. Use people's names. Mingle in the crowd while you're speaking. Reveal some vulnerability.

3. Tell the whole truth; be positive but don't tell fairy tales.

OK, the company is in trouble for the fourth straight quarter and you don't want this news to be a downer. But sometimes people are in denial. Getting people to finally agree that the company is on its knees is not something to jump and down with glee over, but if this is what has to precede action, make it happen.

Keep in mind that you can speak about what is working, in addition to conveying the bad news. And if there is any reason for hope, for heaven's sake say so. Even Lincoln at Gettysburg found a way to be positive: "This nation, under God, shall have a new birth of freedom—and that government of the people, by the people, for the people, shall not perish from the earth."

4. Tell people what's possible if everyone pulls together.

More than just about anything, people want to be part of a winning team. And here is another timeless truth: Among people's deepest longings is getting along in peace and harmony with others. At some fundamental level, it's the ultimate human story—if we work together as members of a cohesive team, we'll be safer, we'll feel better, and we'll be more successful.

The leader who can get people to work together and appreciate one another is a leader with followers.

5. Call people to their higher selves.

People respond to a leader who tells them, either implicitly or explicitly that they can be great and noble and do important things. Writing in *The New York Times,* Roger Cohen, observing candidate Barack Obama, said, "Obama's idea, put simply, was that America can be better than it has been. It can reach beyond post-9/11 anger and fear to embody once more what the world still craves from the American idea: hope" (Cohen, 2008). Business leaders do well to recall that America wasn't built so much by individuals, as by neighbors who were willing to sacrifice their own work to help build the barns of fellow farmers.

We will never forget hearing an expert in business ethics once point out that for most working people, who spend most of their waking hours in workplaces, the biggest influence in their lives from an ethical development standpoint is the nature of the leadership in their companies. If leaders don't urge ethical behavior, their employees aren't apt to display it, either. He went on to say that a great deal of energy derives from feelings of righteousness, energy that can be applied to worthwhile tasks. Most people have generous hearts and want to give to others. Connect with this.

6. Remind listeners that achieving anything worthwhile is hard work and that there will be obstacles.

Screenwriter Robert McKee (see Fryer, 2003) points out that a successful story breaks down along these lines: things are going along well until a problem hits. Despite the best efforts of the hero, the problem got worse. Then, the hero summoned courage and fortitude and found a way to break through. This idea, of course, connects with #5: With hard work, we can be great, but *only* with hard work. Join with the listener's need to hear the truth and hear a great potential ending, but assure them that success will require struggle and effort.

7. Describe the rewards that will follow sacrifice.

Most business leaders can't do what a politician can do: offer everything from tax cuts to health care and, in the case of Obama, even a puppy for his daughters. What if you can't promise anything specific? Offer the pride that comes with trying. Get creative.

8. Tell them what they need to do.

Leadership is about taking people to a better, different place. Throughout the campaign, Obama supporters were asked continually to take action—by Obama, the community organizer. If a person gave a donation, he or she was then asked to attend rallies and call undecided voters. Those who went to the Obama web site were asked to set up their own "my Obama page." If they did that, they were asked to attend local events and share their story on their own "myObama blog." The candidate put it this way: "I'm asking you to believe. Not just in my ability to bring about change. I'm also asking you to believe in yours."

Action Learning

If you wandered through your organization and asked three people at random to describe the company's strategy, would they be able to do it? Suppose they do understand it. If you assured them of anonymity, do you suppose they would each say they are willing to put forth each day discretionary effort in pursuit of that strategy?

Often, when we ask our clients this, they just smile wryly. Winning minds and hearts, the work of Jobs One and Two, is essential to strategy execution. It's no laughing matter.

Exercise 1: Identify the emotional tone of the workplace.

Have a discussion with your direct reports about the hallmarks of an emotionally fulfilling workplace. Explain how these inner experiences lead to greater levels of productivity.

❏ *In my workplace, I regularly feel important, significant, and valued.*

❏ *In my workplace, I regularly feel competent and capable.*

❏ *In my workplace, I regularly feel worthy, likeable, and good.*

❏ *In my workplace, I am able regularly and meaningfully to contribute to a socially beneficial cause that I feel passionately committed to.*

Ask the group to offer their views about the degree to which these needs currently get addressed in your organization. Ask for ideas pertaining to what you as the management team can do to better meet people's fundamental interpersonal needs.

Exercise 2: Read Victim, Survivor, or Navigator.

As a supplement to this chapter, considering reading *Victim, Survivor, or Navigator: Choosing a Response to Workplace Change* (McKnight, 2010). Ask your team to read it a chapter at a time. Have discussions about how to cultivate Navigator behavior among your employees.

Chapter Six

Job Three:
Aligning Local Effort

Nature knows no pause in progress and development,
and attaches her curse on all inaction.
—Johann Wolfgang von Goethe

After enlightenment—the laundry.
—Zen saying

MANAGEMENT THEORIST PETER DRUCKER ONCE observed that when it comes to strategy, most of what we do is talk about it. At some point, he said, "Strategy has to devolve into action." Turning a strategy into real results begins with Job Three. Strategy implementation requires changing not only what business units do, but usually how they go about it, as well. In this chapter, we will tell you how to get strategy fully operational from the top to the lowest levels of your organization—by utilizing resources that all organizations have but that are quite often overlooked and under-utilized: middle-level managers and frontline supervisors.

Before we do so, however, let's ask ourselves why senior organizational leaders would *want* to partner with managers and supervisors and how doing so looks different from the way middle-level managers and supervisors in most organizations are treated today.

Some executives say, whether explicitly or implicitly, "Why should you devote a lot of time and attention to middle- and lower-level employees when it comes to strategy? Shouldn't they just do their jobs? If they just did what was asked, the strategy would get implemented, wouldn't it?"

The short answer to these questions is this: Any meaningful progress towards achieving strategic results would come to a screeching halt in your organization if people only did what they were told. Imagine it: people sitting around waiting for senior executives to tell them what to do to achieve the strategy. Nonsense. For one thing, those executives don't know—they couldn't possibly be able to make the strategy so clear that every employee knew exactly what they should do. For another, while most people want clarity about what's expected of them, it is extremely demotivating to be denied the opportunity for creativity and flexibility in carrying out a job assignment.

But there's more. From a global economic perspective, if employers were to engage employees more as partners in executing strategy, profoundly productive consequences would ensue because fully two-thirds of the world's workforce is in service-delivering jobs. If yours is a service business, for example, like travel, hospitality, banking, insurance, food, logistics, or health care, it is among those that account for over half of World GDP. Companies in these categories employ millions of people who deal directly with customers and the people who manage and supervise them.

Why should we care about this? The behavior of these workers profoundly—and often permanently—affects the perceptions of customers. Everyday, these workers help customers answer questions like "Is this a good company to do business with?" "Will I come back for additional goods and services?" and "What will I tell my friends about this company?" For this reason alone, we feel that they should be included in the work of strategy execution.

Here's a story that illustrates the importance of the issue, one that reveals how frontline managers and supervisors are often treated by senior management. It concerns Melissa, the 30-year-old daughter of one of our colleagues. She oversees the managers of several retail stores and sees her role chiefly as a coach, cheerleader, and mentor. Melissa's company is—or we should say *was*—exceptionally lucky to have her. Her salary is—or we should say *was*—$85,000/year. In return for that sum, and despite being practically ignored by her managers, Melissa worked 14 hours most days and often six days per week. The result was maintaining sales in her region—even in a down economy. Before the chain closed its doors, Melissa's region, as measured by year-on-year sales increases, outperformed every other by large margins. Partly because the chain's management did not recognize the qualities that enabled Melissa to grow sales and therefore did not cultivate those skills in others, the chain fell victim to the economic collapse of 2008. (We're pleased to say that since, she has accepted a very good job from a world-class retailer.)

Melissa's former company is hardly alone in overlooking middle-level and frontline people as key parts of their strategy execution plan. A study by McKinsey & Company (2008) found that frontline managers in most service businesses are so bogged down with administrative duties that they have almost no time to communicate the company's goals and objectives or to coach their direct reports in carrying out their responsibilities creatively. An exceptionally creative person like Melissa will find her way around those constraints, but most managers at her level will not.

The McKinsey study found that supervisors and managers who oversee the work of frontline employees spend far more than half their time in administrative tasks, meetings, filing reports, and travel, all things that compete with coaching and mentoring their direct reports. In the worst cases, these tasks consume 90 percent of the manager's time. Supervisor time spent with frontline workers varies by industry. Many travelers will not be surprised that the airline industry is the worst, where supervisors spend at most only 10-15 percent of the time with frontline employees.

According to the McKinsey study, manager-frontline contact time is highest in the car rental industry at 20-40 percent, but even then, the manager is often solving problems or auditing performance—not coaching or educating workers. Across industries, most frontline managers spend less than 10 minutes per day coaching workers! Our experience corroborates this. Not long ago, we interviewed some line workers in an insurance claims department;. Incredibly, several people didn't even know who their supervisor was! "Oh, Joe is my supervisor?" one said. "I knew he was some kind of manager, but I never see him much. He's always in his office."

The McKinsey study mentioned above is just one of many that show a causal link between supervisory behavior and customer satisfaction, repeat business, and employee engagement. Pivotal to all of this research is the relationship between frontline employees and their supervisors: good relationships lead to good service and vice versa. Similarly, decades of research by the Corporate Executive Board (2008) has shown that in organizations where employees are made part of the strategy creation and execution process, energy is high, commitment to stay with the company is high, and levels of discretionary effort far exceeds those in companies where these conditions do not exist.

What if the employees in your organization do not touch customers directly? Should you involve them in strategy execution? Say we're talking about employees in a manufacturing setting who never see a customer. If reducing waste in a production area is a key strategic goal, this result will remain elusive unless supervisors somehow get line workers to see that change is necessary and get them interested in working more efficiently (Jobs One and Two). The supervisors then have to draw workers into making changes in their area that result in less waste (Job Three).

When supervisors, managers, and frontline employees are overlooked, you can be sure that executive management is failing to make the most of its human resources investment, usually its *biggest* investment. In this chapter, we'll describe some antidotes, articulating strategy execution roles for those at the middle- and frontline-levels.

Strategy Execution: Who Does What?

Depending on where you sit in the organization, the part you play in both strategy making and strategy execution differs. We divide the work of strategy execution into four populations. Figure 6-1 shows them. This chapter will emphasize the work done by managers at the middle level. Chapter Nine focuses in detail on the work of the senior leaders, the Strategy Stewards.

Each employee group has a different role to play in strategy execution.

Figure 6-1: Strategy execution roles are played by all employees

Before defining these roles, we hasten to make a point about nomenclature. The typical practice of referring to people by level, i.e., at the "top," in the "middle," and at the "bottom," can minimize those "lower down" and exaggerate the importance of those "higher up." In fact, everyone is important to strategy execution and should be involved. On a related point, once you begin talking about different hierarchical levels in an organization and what they contribute to strategy making and strategy execution, the question inevitably arises: "Isn't *strategy* constructed at the top and don't those lower down really generate and pursue *tactics?*" Our reply to this is that *what looks tactical to a higher-level group often looks plenty strategic to a lower-level group.* What matters is that everyone at all levels understand the enterprise strategy and generate their response to that strategy by formulating their own initiatives to support it.

For instance, if the senior executives declare an intention to improve competitiveness by introducing three new products in the coming 18 months, the marketing group must find powerful ways to launch them. Are the product launch plans created by the marketing department merely *tactics*—a term with a minimizing connotation? Probably not to those in the marketing department who perceive their plans as strategic! We resolve this issue by avoiding the use of the term tactics altogether, and instead say, "Every work unit needs its own plan by which it will contribute to the organization's strategic imperatives." Most will refer to those plans as strategies.

Strategy Stewards

This is the term we give to the organization's senior executives. These are corporate officers who, by SEC regulation and state law, have the responsibility to (among other things) define the business the organization is in, the organization's vision and objectives for the future, and the means by which that organization will achieve those objectives. The CEO, of course, guides this group. We do not call them Strategy *Leaders*—we reserve this term for those at the next level down—for a reason: to emphasize their roles both as architects and as organizational elders. We use the term "steward" to refer to those with greatest responsibility for building, preserving, and maintaining the organization over time.

Strategy Stewards not only specify the objectives to be achieved, but also oversee their achievement. They function as a group of overseers or elders—or should—and have overall responsibility for the performance and health of the organization. In this role, they guide the evolution of company culture and apportion the resources necessary to build the organizational capabilities called for by the strategy. This includes acquiring and building "hardware"—plants and equipment, for example—and "software"—identifying and grooming talent and evolving a system that nurtures human productivity.

In playing out their role, at times Strategy Stewards are storytellers, narrating the compelling story behind the strategy, while at other times, they interpret the intent of the strategy and resolve disputes about the best way to achieve it. This group establishes goals and objectives and coordinates organization-wide efforts to achieve them, making sure that all units harmonize their efforts.

Strategy Leaders

Workers in this population carry titles such as "director" and "manager." (Depending on the size of the organization, Directors can be in the Strategy Stewards group. The larger the organization, the less this is true.)

These leaders dwell in what is commonly known as the organization's "middle-level." When employees have questions that affect discretionary effort—e.g., "Should I really care about the company's strategy?" and "How real is this need for change I keep hearing about?"—they turn first to these leaders for answers. If the Strategy Leaders are indifferent and unengaged, it is very likely employees who look to them for leadership will be unengaged, too.

When fully engaged, Strategy Leaders interpret and apply the strategy on a day-to-day basis, ensuring that everyone in the work unit understands the strategy and feels some excitement for playing their role in its achievement (Jobs One and Two).

In addition, in organizations where executives take a creative approach to strategy execution, Strategy Leaders also support the daily efforts of their direct reports in pursuit of strategy-relevant goals. Finally, they function as a source of feedback for the Strategy Stewards: what additional support they need to provide.

Frontline Strategists

In organizations where frontline employees see themselves as integral to achieving strategic results, these employees provide crucial feedback that can tell middle-level managers and executives how the strategy is working in the eyes of the customer. These employees collect information on the competitors and the market, relate information on what's working and what's not, and provide information on potential new markets, products, and services. Working cooperatively, they freely cross organizational boundaries while serving customers.

Nonmanagerial Employees

Employees in this category play dozens of roles. They are factory workers, machine operators, order-entry clerks, insurance claims processors, truck drivers, claims adjusters, clerks, social workers, and even doctors. Sometimes they have very little education, sometimes they are highly trained. In many cases, they are the first and only contact your customers have with your organization.

In the last chapter, we observed that during organizational change, employees tend to respond in one of three ways: as a powerless *Victim,* a grasping and clinging *Survivor,* or as an empowered *Navigator.*

Employees functioning in Navigator mode take pride in their work, feel part of something larger than themselves, and put forth discretionary effort. They seek to understand the strategic aims of the organization and shape their efforts to deliver the results the organization most needs.

Nissan of Japan refers to frontline employees as the "nerve endings of the organization" to reflect their importance to the firm in sensing and sending back up to the top sentiments and attitudes of customers. The role of everyone "above" these nonmanagerial employees is to create the conditions that support this and bring out their best effort. The ideas discussed in the remainder of this chapter can go a very long way in doing so.

Break Down Strategies Into Achievable Goals

How does all this look in practice? To illustrate, let's use an example drawn (but disguised) from a client.

Cool-Clear-Water, Inc. (CCW) is a water treatment products and services company, based in the U.S. that does business internationally. The company makes equipment for water filtration and purification and, on a contract basis, operates municipal water treatment plants around the world. Fifteen percent of the current business is in products, the remainder in services.

The CCW Strategy Stewards (the senior officers) committed to an aggressive growth plan calling for a doubling of bottom-line growth in five years. Setting stretch goals like this is not uncommon, of course, in business, but we are always wary when we hear such ambitious objectives: the more ambitious an objective, the more likely the disappointment. And talk, as they say, is cheap. Once schooled by the CEO in the nature of this industry and this specific business, however, we were led to believe the objective was achievable for these reasons:

- The world is facing a growing water crisis (world health and environmental experts predict that existing water supplies will meet only 60 percent of global demand in the next 20 years).

- Municipalities around the world, even in some developing countries, are increasingly committed to water treatment, meaning an expansion in the customer base.

- CCW had, to date, been well managed. For instance, CCW had steadily developed competence in doing business outside the U.S. where the greatest growth would occur, demonstrating a track record of steady growth for many years.

- Finally, CCW would have to grow at this rate—or something close to it—to avoid being acquired in a consolidating industry.

The strategy called for differentiation, which would come principally in the form of intimate service. While CCW equipment was reliable and well regarded, it was not cutting edge, nor was it ever likely to be. Still, doubling growth was possible over five years, the leaders argued, if they could grow the equipment business by 15 percent and the services business by 85 percent. The Strategy Stewards felt that half the gains in the services business would come through acquisition and half through organic growth.

In turn, to meet the services business goals, several things would be imperative, each of which was called out in the strategic plan:

1. Business expansion in existing locations.
2. Business expansion in locations where CCW had no presence at all, mainly overseas (outside the U.S.).
3. More and better salespeople, especially in new locations.
4. Acquisition of services companies, especially outside the U.S. and integrating them quickly into existing operations.
5. Retaining existing clients and extending existing contracts to include add-on services.
6. Enhanced levels of service delivery in existing locations.

These imperatives would place many types of demands on every part of the CCW business, especially Operations, Sales, Finance, and Human Resources.

In this scenario, it is relatively easy to say what the Strategy Stewards must do: Principally, they have to break down the strategy into achievable goals and targets, apportion those accountabilities to the appropriate unit, provide resources, monitor results, and help as needed. What the others lower down in the organization do, however, depends on where they are in the business. If they're in Operations, it means one thing, if in Sales, HR, or Finance, quite another.

Take Operations, for example. Operations has a meaningful part to play in five of the six objectives, above. The only one that does not call for specific contributions from Operations is number 3, more and better salespeople, although Operations could provide valuable input into the *training* of salespeople based on their knowledge of customers' needs. Operations set the following objectives for itself for year one of the growth plan:

Operations' Objectives

1. Support Sales in closing deals in existing locales (provide leads, go on sales calls, gather endorsements, lobby elected

officials). As deals close, create a seamless transition from the prior service provider to CCW operations.

2. Support Sales in closing deals in new locales: Indonesia, Ireland, and the Philippines.

3. Set up Operations in Indonesia, Ireland, and the Philippines: secure local permits to operate/acquire office space, hire heads of Operations.

4. As services companies are acquired, integrate them quickly and seamlessly into existing structures and processes.

5. Retain existing clients by enhancing customer satisfaction by five percent.

6. Extend existing contracts to include add-on services where possible. Reduce contract loss to 2 percent annually.

7. Reduce cost of operating by 5 percent annually.

Notice that many of these objectives are hard to quantify and that achieving some are entirely dependent on the efforts of people in other functions (e.g., Sales and HR). Also notice that not every employee can make a contribution to *every* goal. For example, workers in treatment plants mostly touch goals #5 and #6 (and potentially #1).

Sales' Objectives

Sales has five goals for year one. They are quite different from Operations' goals.

1. Expand business in existing countries by 8 percent.

2. Secure at least one new service contract in Indonesia, one in Ireland, and two in the Philippines.

3. Extend existing contracts to include add-on services: 8 percent growth.

4. Hire and integrate a new head of sales in Indonesia, Ireland, and the Philippines.

5. Select a state-of-the-art sales training provider, and train

all salespeople in the process by year-end.

To achieve the strategy, each of these goals must be broken down into an action plan, the resources required to reach them must be articulated and agreed to, and then they must be communicated to the unit level. In Chapter Eight, we will provide a powerful tool for breaking down these goals in ways that anyone can understand and act upon. The next section tells how the Strategy Stewards can fully engage all implementers.

Empower the Middle- and Frontline-Levels

Once the Strategy Stewards break down the strategy into meaningful goals and accountabilities begin to get assigned, it's time to go to work. Job Three entails making sure that everyone in the organization is fully involved and working cooperatively and enthusiastically with others to get results. This may entail refocusing effort to achieve new targets, effecting process improvements, or simply ceasing off-strategy work.

To fully enlist workers at the middle- and lower-levels, we recommend that the Strategy Stewards take the following steps:

Step One: Senior Leader Session

Engaging the middle-level requires executives to speak proactively and with one voice in anticipation of, and in response to, the five questions employees always have. We call them "The Five Questions Employees have During Change." This step entails a deep dialogue that begins to address those questions.

Most employees want to know:

1. What is our strategy, i.e., what change does it require?
2. What will happen if we don't change?
3. What does all this mean for me?
4. What will you do to support me?
5. What do you want me to do?

In a facilitated session (a half-day is usually sufficient) the senior leaders create a set of concise messages they want managers to convey to their direct reports about the strategy, using the list of five questions as a framework. Most executives find the exercise not only enormously useful but also stimulating, enjoyable, and great personal preparation for carrying the message. By creating these messages together, executives are far more apt to give common answers to the five questions when they hear them. This exercise is not meant to replace what usually goes into an internal communications plan that may already be underway. It supplements and extends those other communications.

We strongly encourage that someone conduct a few focus groups before this session, to learn how ready employees are to engage with leadership in executing strategy and to what extent they already have answers to any of the five questions *now*. With these data, the Strategy Steward discussion goes beyond a theoretical exchange of views as to what employees *might* know to one that addresses what they *do* know.

We have successfully conducted meetings of up to 50 Strategy Stewards to answer those five questions, using the simple meeting design that follows. These meetings are typically very energized and engaging.

1. Present any data from employee focus groups or employee surveys you may have.

2. Post the first question—What is our strategy and what change does it require? Ask the group to call out answers and write them on a flip chart. Don't allow debate at this point. Guide the discussion by asking, "What answer should we be giving to this question?"

3. Once you have filled a flip chart, ask the group, "Of all the things on this list, are there any that are more important than others? What are they and why are they more important?" Get some lively debate going and track the conversation, pulling out the key themes and phrases that a majority of the participants seem to agree with. If no one has broached the subject, ask, "Are there any messages on the flip chart that we

should probably *not* communicate or, if we do, we need to be very careful about how we do so?" Take note of those answers, as well. Don't try to achieve consensus.

4. Post the second question (What will happen if we don't change?). For no more than two minutes, ask the group to call out phrases that might be included in a good answer to this question. You are spending less time here because you just want to "get the juices flowing" and surface any big issues and concerns, not to finish the work; the detailed work will be done in sub-groups.

5. Repeat for questions 3-5.

6. Now, break the group into (minimally) two sub-groups. Assign each group one or more of the questions. Make sure each sub-group takes to their meeting space the relevant flip charts made in the larger group setting in the steps above. Ask each group to take 20 minutes to write out 2-3 simple sentences that answer the question(s). Each group should identify a spokesperson who will share the answer with the larger group. Insist that they write their answer to each question—legibly—on a flip chart.

7. Reassemble the whole group and go question-by-question. Each spokesperson reads the sub-group's answer to their question and then you the facilitator ask the group:

    •   What do you *like* in this answer?

    •   What would you *change,* if anything?

8. As the discussion unfolds, make changes to wording to reflect the consensus.

9. After the meeting, distribute the questions and answers to the Strategy Steward group.

We strongly recommend also using this session as a training opportunity, teaching the executives some basic skills and concepts relating to managing strategic change. If you're following our prescription, you will be providing training programs for managers and supervisors in the next step, who will carry the strategy messages to everyone else in the organization. Most of the Strategy Stewards can profit from the very same training, of course. You could include that training in this session or schedule another.

Step Two: Manager Preparation Programs

Conduct one-day programs for supervisors and managers on how to engage employees as partners in strategy execution. These sessions should be held within businesses and functions.

Best practice is to have someone from the Strategy Stewardship group kick off each of these sessions. They should conduct a 20-minute extemporaneous, give-and-take discussion (i.e., from the heart, no PowerPoint slides) relating to the five questions. The executive should describe the strategy in general terms and then ask, "What part of this strategy do you think we, in [our part of the business] can make the greatest contribution to?"

After this discussion, the senior leader gets back to the five questions and provides the answers the Strategy Stewards have come up with. This person should emphasize that this is not a "script" which managers are expected to recite but rather the core of a dialogue about the importance of everyone working together and why this is important. Participants may think a given answer to one of the questions could be improved. Suggested improvements are discussed and agreed to.

The content of these sessions can and should vary with the organization's circumstances. If the strategy calls for potentially disruptive change and dislocations such as reductions in force, the sales of assets or divisions, more time should be devoted to skill development, i.e., helping employees deal with the stress of change.

Typically, the contents of the training includes:

- **Managing Personal Change.** We tell managers that they have to "Take care of yourself so you can take care of others." Skills in this category equip managers to cope with the personal stress and challenges of change.

- **Building Personal and Organizational Resilience.** Skills in this category help managers build an agile organization and support employees through change.

- **Engaging Employees During Change.** Help managers develop individual action plans to keep employees focused and productive during organizational transition.

- **Conducting Employee Engagement Work Unit Meetings.** Provide managers with a simple agenda/design for the work unit meeting, one that permits give and take: to communicate the messages underlying the five questions and to draw out ideas from the work team as to how to align their work with the strategy.

The last learning topic, "Conducting Employee Engagement Work Unit Meetings," is the most important and, if you're following our logic (the Four Jobs), imperative. This is because the work unit meeting is the principal medium through which the strategy will be articulated and, more importantly, the mechanism by which every work unit will conform its effort to the strategic goals that most relate to them. In the following sections, we will define work unit meetings more fully, tell you how they work, and then we will provide you with details on how you can make this process work in your organization.

CareCorp: The Power of Work Units

Suppose you're the head of operations and services at a large financial services company and have the urgent need to improve the delivery of customer service in the wake of a business downturn. Suppose that for several months, your company has been the subject of negative stories on the front page of every business publication in the country due to a lawsuit the resulted in a $350 million settlement. Suppose, further, that the former head of operations and systems got fired and the CEO and board expects you to bring customer service and efficiency levels up to world class standards in 18 months. Daunting? You bet.

This was the actual situation of Jeff Davidson (not his real name), our client, when he came in from another company to take on this set of challenges. Let's call the company CareCorp, Inc., to reference the property and casualty business they were in. Founded 80 years before as a mom-and-pop insurance business that hired salt-of-the-earth citizens to build business door-to-door, it had grown rapidly, and had left its commitment to neighborliness and personal attention far behind. Having been acquired, sold, and re-sold three times, the company had grown to over 30,000 employees. For Jeff Davidson and his colleagues, turning the company around was do or die. He couldn't do everything, but he could do plenty to help in his 6,500 employee function.

CareCorp was in trouble for several reasons. The lawsuit over illegal sale practices issues demoralized an already downhearted company, generated very bad press, and stripped out needed capital. In addition, CareCorp's products were tired, its salespeople unskilled and unmotivated, and the most recent customer satisfaction numbers were deplorable. Before he agreed to take the job, Jeff knew that the back office was bad, but did not expect to see industry efficiency ratings shortly after he arrived that showed CareCorp as the worst in the industry.

Jeff and his management team set the goals below for the operations and services function for the next 18 months. As we've told this story before, many people have said it would be completely outlandish to set such goals. But Jeff and his team knew that either they would achieve these four goals or the company would probably be acquired and liquidated.

1. Set and achieve world-class operations standards affecting 105 aspects of operations and systems (ranging from underwriting to claims).

2. Increase levels of customer service and satisfaction in the arenas we operate so that CareCorp is in the top three in the industry.

3. Strip out $30 million of cost in the operations and systems function.

4. Increase levels of employee morale, satisfaction, and commitment by 50 percent—even though some layoffs will have to occur as operations are streamlined.

Jeff and his team knew that key to accomplishing the first three goals was accomplishing the fourth goal: increasing employee morale and commitment. The team recognized that if they were going to reach the first three goals, every single employee and every manager and supervisor would have to give it their all.

In working with Jeff, we shared a truism about motivating employees in circumstances like this: while employees in his function might be plenty motivated to work hard so as not to loose their jobs, too much stress and anxiety is not helpful, either. We showed the team the model depicted in Figure 6-2, below, pointing out that stress itself is not a bad thing because as stress increases, so does productivity—up to a point. However, going beyond an optimal level of stress can result in a decrease in productivity. (This is known as the Yerkes-Dodson law. It has been repeatedly validated in human performance studies for over 100 years.)

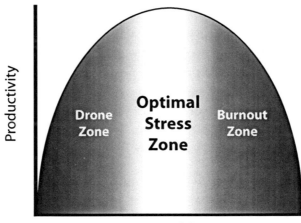

Figure 6-2: Productivity goes up, as does stress, to a point: the point of optimal stress.

The question became, "How can we communicate the urgent need for change in such a way that employees feel excited and energized, not overwhelmed? The short answer was this: by answering the five questions and providing support of various kinds.

Executives had to provide employees in operations and systems with two types of information, and then had to equip them to take action relevant to that information. The information had to do with customer perceptions of the company, and that management saw the employees as crucial to turning these perceptions around. The latter had to come in the form of action, not talk: senior leaders could not just *say* they supported employees; they had to *demonstrate* their support in every way possible.

Following the sequence of creating messages described above, we worked with the top 75 leaders for the better part of two days teaching them how to lead employees in the midst of a turnaround and creating the crisp set of messages that had to be communicated to employees. We proposed a series of meetings for managers and supervisors that could be used to do the work of Jobs One and Two. We also created a 10-minute video of CareCorp customers giving a sober appraisal of the quality of service they were receiving from the company. We would show that video many times over the next few months to groups of CareCorp employees and their managers. At those meetings, employees came away with the following:

- An understanding of the urgent need for change
- A sense of confidence that those change goals could be achieved if everyone worked together
- Tools to use in subsequent work unit meetings where managers and supervisors would address the five questions and would ask and answer these questions:
  1. What do we have to do to align our effort with the strategy?
  2. What work can we start doing to better align with the strategy?
  3. What work can we stop doing?

So equipped, managers and supervisors would begin to conduct work unit meetings. In all, over nearly 650 meetings were held in the first round and at least every quarter thereafter. Employees and managers felt alive and motivated, workers were deeply involved in thinking strategically, and every manager and supervisor, along with their direct reports (our definition of "work unit") began aligning their efforts with the strategy and streamlining their departments. In addition, cross-functional teams were formed to address larger systemic issues. It became difficult to accommodate everyone who wished to be on those teams because so many wanted to help. This is a "problem" every organization should have!

Managers and supervisors were told that they were expected to conduct these meetings often enough to stay current and aligned with the strategy. They were told to determine the frequency for themselves. In some cases, managers held meetings every few weeks, in others, once each quarter. We helped the client make a videotape of a work unit meeting so that no manager could say, "I'm not really sure what I'm supposed to do." The video lacked Hollywood production values, but it worked.

What was the payoff of all this management attention and all these meetings? CareCorp achieved every one of its objectives, including the commitment to becoming world-class on those 105 operational measures. They increased levels of customer satisfaction. Employee morale and commitment rose higher and higher. And boy, did they celebrate!

Work Unit Meetings: How They Function

We have used work unit meetings as the primary processes of employee engagement in diverse settings such as pharmaceutical plants that were transitioning to self-directed work teams, data services companies that were shifting from a products to a services strategy, production lines where FDA infractions had been observed, and hospital settings where new approaches to patient care were being introduced.

Sometimes, senior leaders are skeptical that a systematic process of work unit engagement can lead to strategic results. One CEO where we instituted this practice was thrilled with the results coming out of the meetings but then became suspicious: Could these outcomes actually result from a simple meeting and some follow-up activities? He asked us to do a random survey of managers and supervisors. "Call some of them," he said, "and ask them if they would have gotten the results they're reporting if they had not conducted work unit meetings." We called 50 managers and asked the CEO's question. The answer was almost always the same: first there was a pause and then they said, "Well, we *might* have gotten these results. But we sure wouldn't have gotten them this fast and we would not have gotten them this way." Meaning? They got the results quickly and as a result of a highly participative process that improved morale.

There are several keys to successfully engaging middle-level and frontline managers in pursuit of strategy. We've touched on some of them already. Here are the most important ones:

- Provide simple materials and designs for managers and supervisors to use in the work unit meetings.

- Make it vividly clear why you're doing this and what you expect to come out of it.

- Encourage experimentation and working across the system to achieve those goals.

- Encourage sharing best practices and involve everyone in monitoring progress.

- Use a *JumpStart Assessment* to hold managers accountable (described later in this chapter).

- Don't hold managers and work units accountable for things they can't readily influence, only for things they can control.

- Make the work real, provide support, ensure visibility, reward.

- Debrief

To provide you a glimpse inside a work unit meeting, how they work and what they can produce, let's go back to the Cool-Clear-Water case we worked with earlier in this chapter. You will recall that the strategic plan called for doubling bottom-line growth in five years, and that Operations had responsibility for three goals that could benefit from the direct involvement of frontline employees:

- Retaining existing clients by enhancing customer satisfaction by five percent.

- Extend existing contracts to include add-on services where possible. Reduce contract loss to 2 percent annually.

- Reduce cost of operating by 5 percent annually.

Clearly, even hourly workers in water treatment plants could contribute to these goals. Water treatment services is a fickle business where contractors are changed frequently when customers complain, because among those customers are politicians (mayors, city council members, etc.) and end-users, all of whom are intolerant of water outages. It's also a thin-margin business that is sensitive to price pressure and therefore, must make continual process improvements. If workers and their supervisors pull together, they can streamline operations, operate more reliably and profitably, and in doing so delight customers and users. No customer is going to consider expanding the scope of services they're buying if not satisfied with the current "product."

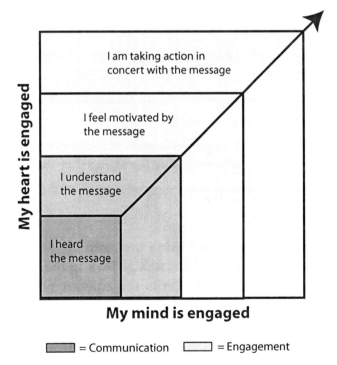

Figure 6-3: Work unit meetings result in both communication and engagement.

CCW's senior management team created a set of messages about the strategy, as described earlier in this chapter, and enlisted

JumpStart Assessment
Employee's Form

1. My work unit created a plan that addresses the change/business challenges we are facing. (Yes/No)

I hear...

2. The message the business leader delivered about the change was logical and compelling.

3. My manager communicated how the change will impact our team.

I understand...

4. I understand the business reasons for our action plan.

5. I know what and when actions are expected of me.

6. Team members know how they need to work together to accomplish this plan.

I am committed...

7. My ideas were considered as we developed the plan.

8. I am personally committed to follow through on the action plan we created.

9. Team members appear committed to follow through on the action plan.

10. Senior management is considering the best interests of all employees as they drive this change.

I can act...

11. Our team has the resources we need to accomplish the plan.

12. Team members have the knowledge, skills, and abilities needed to accomplish the plan.

13. There are no major obstacles in the way of our plan.

14. Accomplishing our plan will have a visible and measurable impact on the business.

Open-ended:

Please tell the leader what was accomplished in this meeting and what your experience was like to be a part of it. As the group has additional meetings like this, what could your manager do to make them more productive and useful?

the support of managers through several regional meetings. Those meetings followed the lines of the sessions previously described. At the meetings, managers were provided with simple meeting designs and materials required to run the work unit meeting, including what we call a *JumpStart Assessment* to ensure compliance and to monitor the outcome of the meetings. (See *"JumpStart Assessment" on page 129.*) The tasks the middle-level managers were asked to complete are summarized in Figure 6-3. (We introduced this concept in Chapter Four.) Note that the work of the manager in such a meeting is twofold, as delineated by Figure 6-3: to both *communicate* and to *engage* employees. Communication, i.e., giving information for the purpose of understanding, is important, obviously. But even if your communication gets through, you've only accomplished so much. Engagement is what you're after when strategy execution is your goal; because engagement leads to action.

While managers are encouraged to innovate in the work unit meeting—as long as they stay true to its purpose and intention—typically the meeting unfolds as described below.

Opening the meeting

The leader introduces the key tasks of the meeting as follows. "The purpose of this meeting is to..."

- Understand our company's changing strategy
- Translate the strategy into terms that specifically relate to our work unit
- Consider all of our work: what's on strategy and what's off? What should we stop doing? Continue doing? Start doing?
- Identify how we can contribute to increased customer satisfaction
- Identify ways can we improve our work processes

Facilitating the discussion

The leader becomes both teacher and facilitator: educating employees about the strategy and facilitating a discussion that accomplishes the objectives cited earlier. The key deliverable from the

Work Unit Meeting Assessment
Manager's Report Form

The purpose of this report is to:

- Support you in capturing your thoughts about the meeting and its results.

- Provide a means for senior management to know the strategic messages are getting through.

- Ensure coordination of action planning across the organization.

- Enable you to tell senior management what support you need going forward.

This report should be completed by [date] and returned to [name] at [email address].

1. Date of meeting?
2. Who attended the meeting?
3. What did you learn in conducting the meeting?
4. What would you do differently next time?
5. Describe your action plan
6. What does senior management need to know about what occurred in the meeting?
7. Whose support do you need to execute your action plan? How will you get it?

meeting is an action plan that states how the work unit will align its effort with the strategy.

Using the *JumpStart Assessment*

Once the meeting is complete, the leader asks participants to complete the *JumpStart Assessment* form (see "JumpStart Assessment" on page 129). The *JumpStart Assessment* is a critical part of the work unit meeting. Essentially, it's a questionnaire, filled out anonymously by the participants that is intended to provide feedback for the manager immediately on the results of the work unit meeting. This is where participants indicate whether or not a plan was actually produced, what they understand the company's strategy to be, and so forth. This plan is returned by the manager to someone (usually in HR) who tabulates the results for the Strategy Stewards. What did employees think the results of the meeting were?

The *JumpStart Assessment* answers:

✓ Did employees understand the key messages?

✓ Did employees feel compelled by and satisfied with those messages?

✓ Are employees committed to taking the necessary action?

✓ Are there any lingering employee concerns relative to implementing the work unit action plans created by their team?

✓ Are there opportunities/needs to coordinate with other work units? What resources are necessary to ensure the plan's success?

The *JumpStart Assessment* survey items are designed to align with the model for communicating change messages referred to in Figure 6-3: 1) employees must first hear the message, then 2) understand the case for change, 3) demonstrate a commitment to the action they now know is needed, and then crucially, 4) to act in accord with the work unit plan for change. Each stage leads to an increasingly higher level of employee engagement. It takes no more than five minutes to complete. The questionnaire is administered anonymously at the conclusion of the work unit meeting.

The manager collects the questionnaires and returns them to a designated person at a designated address. This party tabulates both quantitative and open-ended results via a spreadsheet, noting organizational demographics.

By examining the results of this assessment, the manager can quickly get an impression of the team's level of engagement and pinpoint actions that will lead to a higher level of engagement next time. For example, if survey responses are high for items in the first three sections (hearing, understanding, and committed), but lower for the last section (ready to act), a manager would know to help the team remove obstacles.

When the responses from all work unit meetings are aggregated, senior leaders derive tremendous benefits. For one thing, they can see where in the organization the change message is getting through and where it is not, where commitment is falling short, and so forth. Further, by examining the reports filed by the unit managers—which include the units' action plans—senior leaders might learn that several units are addressing the same systemic organizational issue and thus intervene to ensure coordination of efforts.

Work unit managers are required to file the manager's *Work Unit Meeting Assessment* report, "" on page 131. Filing this report is *not* optional, because, used the right way, it provides a feedback/ control loop that enables senior leaders to know that the strategic messages are getting through, ensures coordination of action planning across the organization, and notifies senior management of what support managers need in what parts of the organization. Unlike the employee report, it is not anonymous. In normal practice, the manager reports are returned to someone in the HR department who compiles them by function or other organizational components (division, business line, and so forth).

In our experience, senior leaders pore over the employee *Jump-Start Assessment* reports and the *Work Unit Meeting Assessments* filed by work unit managers. Why wouldn't they: these are exceptionally rich, actionable glimpses inside the organization.

Other Mechanisms for Involving the Middle

Work-Outs

There are many other mechanisms available to business leaders for involving both middle-level managers and entire work units, including "Work-Outs," action learning teams, task forces, and SWAT teams. Since there are many books written on these methods we will not go into all of them, but given its value over many years, we will describe the Work-Out process, as practiced first at GE and at many companies since. We have used the process, or variations of it, to improve cross-functional collaboration, troubleshoot and revise sales incentive systems, revamp customer services across a 10,000 person call center operation, and enhance collaboration between large departments.

The essence of the Work-Out process is controlled and facilitated collaboration, leading to quick decision-making. The Work-Out process begins with a statement of an issue, problem, or opportunity, and then, through orchestrated step-by-step deliberation, leads to proposals for ways of alleviating the problem or making the best of an opportunity. As practiced at GE (and reflecting Jack Welch's personality), decisions were made on the spot by the senior managers once the proposals were made by participants. We find, however, that flexibility in the decision-making approach is often called for and indeed, even at GE, there were many variations on the "decide now" theme.

Work-Out is an alternative to the typical approach to resolving organizational problems or pursuing opportunities. Typically, managers in the affected areas work out a response among themselves to organizational issues and then announce their decision to those who have to carry it out. There are numerous problems associated with this approach: The leaders miss an opportunity to increase employee engagement, they limit the number of potential ideas and solutions to those that a small number of managers can muster, and because only managers are involved, customer-facing employees cannot provide the customer's perspective.

Work-Outs are vastly more effective than this partly because

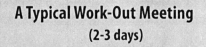

A Typical Work-Out Meeting
(2-3 days)

1. Review purpose of the meeting and the ground rules
2. Provide background info (if necessary)
3. Small group idea generation
4. Share ideas from small groups
5. Employ a nominal voting process (i.e., non-binding) to narrow down the list of ideas
6. Create small groups to formalize recommendations
7. Small groups present recommendations to management for yes/no
8. Decide on next steps

they address one of the most fervent desires most employees have: the opportunity to be involved in a meaningful way in decisions that affect their work. In addition, the Work-Out process accelerates the usual decision-making process which often becomes mired in political machinations.

We find that many senior leaders, when they first contemplate a Work-Out process, fear that the session will turn into a gripe session. In fact, in our experience, Work-Outs almost never turn out this way for three reasons: 1) most employees are so grateful to be involved in meaningful discussions concerning their work, that they come to the session with an inner commitment not to waste the opportunity, 2) we establish ground rules pertaining to "No blaming," "No complaining," and "No whining," and 3) we carefully prepare every participant beforehand with a description of the process and the principles of collaboration and constructive deliberation that underlie it.

The step-by-step process goes like this:

Identify a pressing business problem or opportunity.

Leaders prepare a written document that tells what the issue or opportunity is, the value to the company if addressed successfully, and any other data pertinent to the issue. This document also states the desired outcome of the meeting as precisely as possible.

Identify an executive sponsor of the process.

Make sure this executive is fully cognizant of the opportunity and the principles underlying the Work-Out process. Make sure this person is capable of facilitating dialogue, supporting people as they struggle with issues, and one who can praise and provide redirection in motivating ways.

Design the Work-Out meeting.

Take care to state the desired outcomes and what specific discussions will lead to what results. Identify and select participants for the meeting. Participants should be knowledgeable about the issues, have some passion about the issue, be able to engage in constructive dialogue, and have credibility with peers who are not involved; these people will tell the story afterwards about what occurred in the meeting.

Prepare the participants.

In an ideal world, because you want willing and even eager participation, participants would always be *asked* to participate, in a Work-Out, not told they *must* participate. But sometimes, you need specific individuals to participate whether they are keen to do so or not because they have the specific knowledge and experience the focus of the Work-Out will address. To ensure maximum readiness, participants should be told what the purpose of the meeting is, what outcomes are expected, and what the ground rules and norms will be. The best person to conduct this conversation is the meeting sponsor.

Conduct the meeting.

The box ""A Typical Work-Out Meeting" on page 135, gives a glimpse into a typical Work-Out meeting.

Work-Outs are highly interactive and, when well run, are

highly energizing. After the meeting sponsor outlines the purpose and products of the meeting, facilitators provide any needed background material. Then, participants move into groups for 2-3 hours to create initial recommendations. The potential recommendations will fall into one of the categories in Figure 6-4.

As groups make their presentations on potential solutions, they make clear which category the recommendation falls into. A voting process determines which recommendation the participants in the meeting want to explore further and make final recommendations about. After a second round of deliberation in small groups, recommendations are made to the sponsoring executive(s) who make go/no go decisions on-the-spot.

The Work-Out Payoff Matrix

	Easy to Implement	Hard to Implement
Small payoff	Quick Win	Time Waster
Big payoff	Business Opportunity	Special Effort

Figure 6 4: Work-Out recommendations fall into one of four categories

Take relevant next steps.

At the conclusion of the meeting, the sponsor describes how the Work-Out recommendations will be implemented. Obviously, "Quick Wins" are easiest to implement, whereas "Special Efforts" will require more resources and usually a longer time frame. Participants need to know what will occur and how they will be involved, kept informed of progress, or both.

If you wish to read more about the Work-Out process, two good resources on the subject are Ulrich & Ashkenas (2002) and Slater (1999).

Six Hats

Strategy execution requires changing what people think about, i.e., the objectives of the strategy and why achieving those objectives is important. But arguably, strategy implementers must also change *how* people think and how they think *together*. This is true because the vast bulk of value-adding activity in organizations occurs in small team settings: factory work groups, logistics teams, R&D clusters, and so on. Let those groups employ sloppy or unproductive thinking, and you have troubles.

Researchers who have studied the "emotional intelligence of groups," note that when teams operate in an emotionally intelligent way, the group is more productive because it has evolved mechanisms that allow for both *emotional expression* and *cognitive discipline*. Because groups are so important to strategy execution, some organizations have invested heavily in tools that profoundly enhance the quality and products of their thinking. (Druskat & Wolff, 2001)

Of late, we are particularly impressed with the tools underlying an approach to group work developed by Edward de Bono—and summarized in his exceptionally useful book, *Six Thinking Hats* (1999). de Bono observes that in traditional business settings, the primary modes of thinking consist of analysis, debate, and critique. When these are the only—or even primary—decision-making and innovation tools, ideas that compete with the status quo tend to get beaten down, often at the very time innovative ideas are most needed.

In comes the "Six Hats," a set of behaviors that, when employed thoughtfully, enable people to become noticeably more constructive and creative, within a very short time. Figure 6-5 summarizes the behaviors. There is no mystery about the skills; they are commonplace and any group can make use of them. If there is any magic here, it is the building effect created when everyone in the group engages in the six behaviors *in unison*. As they do so, they align and coordinate their effort. A facilitator keeps everyone "wearing the same hat." Feeling critical of an idea? Great. But express it later when we change to the "Black Hat." Right now, we're wearing the "Green Hat," thank you.

When we wear this HAT	We engage in this BEHAVIOR
YELLOW	Discuss the values and benefits of the potential solution
RED	Share feelings and intuitions about what we're discussing
WHITE	Take stock of what information we have, and what information we need to obtain
BLACK	Identify the cautions, risks, and challenges
BLUE	Plan the focus of the meeting, plan the sequence of "hats," manage next steps
GREEN	Identify ideas and alternatives

Figure 6-5: Six Thinking Hats (illustration © The de Bono Group, LLC)

We recently observed several groups facilitated by our colleague, Pat Carlisle, who was teaching the Six Hats skills. He gave each group the same assignment and 20 minutes to address it using whatever skills that felt most "natural." Then, he taught them the Six Hats process and did the experiment again. Results? In most cases, each group's performance was 20-30 times better after only a few hours of training.

Some companies are introducing the Six Hats tools at the onset of change to give employees a toolkit with which to work through strategic challenges. Managers and employees are often stymied with "where to begin." These thinking tools provide a starting point as well as focus the cognitive and emotional energies of the members.

One company merging two IT departments trained all of its employees to use Hats, so they could design the ways to integrate processes and work better together—two objectives that had been elusive for a long time. An insurance company trained teams in Hats, to speed the time of responding to proposals for new business. Proposal development time dropped from two months to two weeks. A large hospital system in Texas uses the Hats method to drive sessions with frontline employees, for improving care and patient safety. In one application, administrators brought RNs and housekeepers, all trained in Hats, together to solve their ICU bed turnaround time problem. A vice president in this hospital uses Hats to get her busy directors to solve problems together more quickly and effectively.

When managers are given tools like Hats, they are better equipped to facilitate change and experience themselves as an important part of the "action." In settings where there is a shortage of skilled help (e.g., health care), this can also have profound positive retention benefits.

Caveat: Not Everyone Wants Involvement

A key theme of this book is that most employees respond extremely well to systematic efforts to involve them in strategy making and strategy execution. While most employees do want involvement, some—usually 10 percent or less—do not.

We learned this dramatically while working with Prudential. When we started rolling out the expectations to middle-level managers that they had a role to play in turning around the company, some balked. CEO and Chairman Art Ryan made this observation:

When we started preparing our middle-level managers, little by little they would start to realize what was being asked of them. They realized that we were asking them to sit down with their people, educate them about the strategy, and engage them in a discus-

sion about their work. Some of the braver ones would say, "You're asking me to teach people. You're asking me to be a facilitator. I didn't sign up for this." It was really quite remarkable. I had real concerns at that point in time.

If you follow our advice, the vast majority of managers at your company will respond favorably to involvement especially when they experience real support from senior management. Don't be shocked, however, if some managers say they do not want involvement. If you do, our advice is twofold: 1) go the extra mile to hear the concerns of managers who balk; often your supportive attention will be all that's necessary to enable them to work through their anxiety, and 2) where you've gone the extra mile to support reluctant managers and they're still holding out, you're probably looking at a situation where performance improvement plans and other remedies are in order.

Action Learning

The power of Job Three lies in the reality that when employees work cooperatively together to realign their efforts in support of a strategy, they create results that working alone cannot produce. In military terms, getting work units to align their efforts with the strategy is a "force multiplier." When entire functional groups or business units understand the strategy, feel committed to achieving it, and then work collaboratively within their areas of responsibility to improve the business, the organization comes alive with intentionality and focus, individual employees are enlivened, and discretionary, goal-directed activity can escalate to extraordinary levels.

Key to this is involving managers and supervisors at the middle-level, those we have called Strategy Leaders and Frontline Strategists.

Exercise: Assess the degree of involvement.

Ask at least five managers or supervisors to give you their ratings on the assessment tool on the next page. If you lead a large organization, consider making this a system-wide assessment, i.e., ask *all* managers and supervisors to fill out an anonymous survey. If yours is a smaller organization or where this is not practical, approach your most outspoken managers for their answers. First, predict the answers you will get from the managers, then ask them. Compare your predictions with what they actually say.

Use the following scale to answer the questions on the assessment tool:

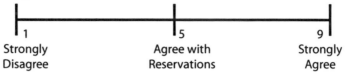

1	5	9
Strongly Disagree	Agree with Reservations	Strongly Agree

Middle-Manager Assessment	
Rating	
	I feel excited by and committed to our company's strategy.
	The people who report to me feel excited by and committed to our company's strategy.
	I know exactly what my own organization has to do to contribute to the company's strategy.
	The people who report to me know exactly what our organization has to do to contribute to the company's strategy.
	I receive all the support I need from upper management to enlist my organization in a pursuit of the company's strategy.
	The additional support I need from upper management to execute our strategy is:

Discussion Questions

1. How did our predictions compare with the actual answers?

2. What did we learn by doing this exercise?

3. What must we start doing, keep doing, do more of, or stop doing in order to support our managers better?

Chapter Seven

Job Four:
Creating Organizational Capabilities

[Most companies] go about managing stability, not change.
Indeed, most of the time senior managers should not be formulating
strategy at all; they should be getting on with making their organizations
as effective as possible in pursuing the strategies they already have.
Like distinguished craftsmen, organizations become distinguished because
they master the details.
—*Henry Mintzberg*

WE SAID BEFORE THAT WHILE all four of the Four Jobs are essential, accomplishing Job Four is considerably more challenging than the three that precede it. Thus, this chapter is the first of two on the subject of Job Four.

Fittingly, this chapter introduces four concepts that can help master the strategy execution work called for by Job Four. The first is *value discipline,* the commitment a senior leadership team makes to the type of competitive advantage it intends to create in its marketplace. We will help you understand the importance of a value discipline in driving strategy and help you choose one that fits your business.

The second is *organizational design criteria,* a term introduced by

Jay R. Galbraith (and described in, among other places, Galbraith, 2001), that articulates the requirements an organization must meet in order to support the execution of a given strategy. We will provide you with many examples of design criteria, show you how and why they vary with value discipline, and how to use them in combination with a third tool, the *Star Model*—a way of conceiving of *organization design*.

This last term, *organization design,* refers to the art and science of fitting the institutional components of the firm—its structure, business processes, and its entire social system—to the strategy. In this chapter, we will show how establishing and using design criteria can aid immeasurably in creating an organization capable of executing its strategy.

But First...

Before we explore those concepts, however, let's summarize where we've been so far.

To this point, we've said that managers and executives need to make sure that every employee who has a part to play in carrying out the strategy understand the strategy. We've said that employees need to understand not only the strategic direction, but also its key elements and the results sought by the strategy. We've said that only when employees understand the rationale behind the strategy can they partner in a meaningful way to fulfill it. We've also said that it's a key job of leaders to enable the employees to think like knowledgeable businesspeople. This is a prerequisite for meaningful participation in decision-making pertaining to the strategy. All of this is the work of Job One.

In speaking of Job Two, we've emphasized that while understanding gets the "heads" of employees involved, successful strategy execution also requires that leaders engage employees' "hearts." If leaders are doing their jobs well, employees will feel motivated to do the work called for by the strategy. And because meaningful organizational improvement almost always means giving up something, it is essential to increase employee willingness not only to embrace change but also to create it. We've said employees have to believe that the net result will have been worth the effort and sacrifice they will be required to make in achieving it.

Job Three, the topic of the last chapter, requires leaders to put in place processes that cause work units to reprioritize their efforts with the strategy. We have said that it is not quite time for jubilation when the entire employee population understands the strategy and feels good about it (Jobs One and Two), although these are essential and laudable accomplishments. The whole point of a strategy is to reach a set of desirable business objectives. Doing the work of Jobs One through Three lays down the foundation for—and makes possible—these company-wide capability improvements.

Job Four: Where the Magic is

If we stop at Job Three and fail to do Job Four, however, we leave money on the table—a lot of money. This is because as important as it is that local effort align with the strategy (Job Three), the many small changes this represents will not amount to systematic, widespread change. Job Four entails making such changes.

Here are a few examples that illustrate the work of Job Four:

- Redesigning the structure of the organization to facilitate better decision-making and bringing new products and services to market faster.

- Improving key business processes consistent with the strategy.

- Reconfiguring the reward and performance management system to enable greater collaboration across organizational boundaries in a way called for by the strategy.

- Developing processes for attracting, developing, and retaining key talent segments called for by a strategy.

Some organizational consultants—ourselves included—use the term "organization design" to refer to the practice of developing the organizational capabilities called for by a given strategy. Strategy experts at McKinsey & Company, a firm known more for its emphasis on strategy creation than strategy execution, have recently been advancing the view that the advantages derived from organization design can exceed those stemming from most other types of organizational initiatives. McKinsey consultants Bryan and Joyce (2007) state that, "Redesigning an organization to take advantage of today's sources of wealth creation isn't easy, but there can be no better use of a CEO's time (p. 21)." They go on to say that...

> *Modernizing organization designs for a 21st century business environment can trump the gains generated by other, more traditional strategic initiatives...Strategic-minded executives may not be able to control the weather, but they can design a ship and equip it with a crew that can navigate the ocean under all weather conditions (p. 23).*

We couldn't agree more. Organization design, in essence, *is* the work of Job Four.

As we said in Chapter One, an *executable strategy* is one that states the value discipline to which the organization is committed (i.e., product innovation, operational excellence, or customer intimacy, and how that discipline will create customer value. We also said that it will also specify the steps that need to be taken in four organization design arenas, and how taking those steps will lead to results for customers and thus, for shareholders.

Over 90 percent of the strategies we see fail to meet most of these criteria. Fifty percent of the strategies we see meet only one or two of them. Most strategies say nothing at all about the value discipline to which the organization is committed, even though this clarity permits intelligent organization design-related decisions more than any other single commitment.

Value Discipline and Organization Design

Since it's so crucial to Job Four, let's put a magnifying glass to that term, "value discipline." Let's see how clarity around value discipline can make organization design decisions vastly easier and considerably more systematic.

The term "value discipline" was introduced to the business world by Michael Treacy and Fred Weirsema (1997) in their book, *The Discipline of Market Leaders: Choose Your Customers, Narrow Your Focus, Dominate Your Market.* Treacy and Weirsema defined value discipline as the approach a company takes to creating customer value and gaining competitive advantage. Treacy and Weirsema identified three disciplines. They were the first authors to make the now commonplace observation that the leaders in a given industry will invariably be best at executing on one of those disciplines, noting that those market leaders will—intentionally—be *only good enough* at the other two disciplines. Attempting to pursue all three will scatter resources and create confusion, conflict, and gridlock. The three disciplines are summarized in Figure 7-1.

Value Discipline	Key Value Creation Activity	Examples
Operational Excellence	Create value by packaging cost, quality, and convenience.	Dell, McDonald's, Walmart, IKEA, Swatch
Product Leadership	Create value through cutting-edge products, useful features, and new applications.	3M, Apple, SONY, Lexus, Google, Disney
Customer Intimacy	Create value through customizing for a total solution.	IBM, Boeing, ARAMARK, FedEx, Ritz-Carlton, Singapore Airlines

Figure 7-1: Treacy and Weirsema's three value disciplines

Companies that work through the value discipline exercise declare which one value proposition they will attempt to excel at. In the remaining two areas, they commit to meeting only the market's minimum expectations. Such companies are clear about the following:

• The one unique value that the company can deliver (either now or in the future) to a chosen market better than any of its industry rivals (best product, best solution, best cost).

- Those things at which their company must excel in order to be "unmatchably excellent" and thus win in its market-place. (Product leadership? Customer intimacy? Operational excellence?)

- How their organization design must be tailored and enhanced to fit their value discipline.

Choosing a value discipline is the first task of Job Four. It is the single-most important strategy execution decision senior leaders make because all other organization design decisions flow from it. Before explicating the disciplines fully, however, we hasten to make an important point: while a company should commit itself to *one* discipline at the level of the enterprise, various units may need to pursue a different discipline. For example, while Apple, Inc. (formerly Apple Computer) is clearly in the product innovation business, it's manufacturing division is devoted to the pursuit of operational excellence. This distinction will become clearer as you read the descriptions of each discipline.

Operational Excellence

A company pursuing the operational excellence discipline is, almost without exception, a high volume business that makes a small margin on a large number of transactions. If it leads in its marketplace, this company is succeeding at producing and delivering products or services *more efficiently* than its competitors. Its commitment is to "best total price," i.e., the best product or service for the money given all other considerations. Best total price must be distinguished from lowest cost. In many fields of commerce, even though many firms may compete partly on the basis of cost, the leader in a given industry is often not *the* lowest cost provider of goods or services. Why? Because it is more committed to a *combination* of values, not just to low price.

The products and services of a firm committed to the operational excellence discipline are often unadorned: They are often (but not always) off-the-shelf commodities like refined gasoline, chemicals, or "ordinary" services that many competitors provide.

Thus Walmart, an oil refiner, or a high volume commercial printer will occupy this strategic space as will a third-party logistics provider.

But companies like Swatch and IKEA also play this game, selling up-to-date products with trendy designs. The commonality is that all of these businesses compete on the basis of best total price, which usually means low margin on high volumes. It is not that service is unimportant, as we'll see, but the customer of this business does not usually expect anything other than *passable* service.

Companies committed to the operational excellence value discipline will typically build a centralized organization that emphasizes teamwork, has highly defined, streamlined, and controlled business processes. The most valued employee in such a firm will tend to be one who follows orders, values routine, authority, and tradition, but one who is also committed to making small improvements to operations that enable greater efficiencies and who will use established procedures to do so.

Product Leadership

When companies commit to making goods that are cutting edge, first-to-market, and highly sought after, they are pursuing the product leadership value discipline. Theirs are considered the "must have" products appealing to customers' needs for exclusivity, trendiness, and high quality. In the auto industry, we're talking Audi and Lexus, not Kia or Toyota. In the electronics industry, we're talking Apple, not Dell or Acer.

Companies committed to the product leadership value discipline will build an organization designed to bring the best total product to market quickly. These companies build products for customers that are discriminating; their customers don't want an MP3 player, they want an iPod. They don't want a watch, they want a Rolex. They don't want an MBA; they want a degree from the Harvard Business School or Wharton. They don't want an antacid, they want "the Purple Pill."

Companies pursuing the discipline of product leadership are often populated with individuals with star quality, i.e., high intelligence, superb design skills, and so forth—or should be. These individuals enable the company to bring high-gloss, gee whiz products to market quickly—products that demand the highest price. These employees are not necessarily the best team players like those most valued in operational excellence settings. They are often very competitive individuals. The employee most likely to win the "Employee of the Year Award" in the product leadership firm is likely to be the one who was able to get his or her big idea implemented, despite the competition of his or her peers. And when these firms go looking for talent, they're generally looking for the best, the brightest, the cleverest, the most ambitious.

It is easy to overlook one aspect of companies that diligently and adeptly pursue the product leadership value discipline: they are good at failing! By this, we mean that being on the cutting-edge may mean you succeed, but it also means you take risks and, over time, bring things to market that don't succeed. A good example is Apple, Inc. Apple, of course, is widely admired for its product successes, such as the iMac, iPod, iPad, and iPhone, as well as for software and user interface innovations. But does the name QuickTake ring a bell? This was Apple's digital camera, introduced in 1994, that cost $749 and took a 0.3 mega pixel picture! Or how about the Apple Pippin, a multimedia player introduced by Apple in 1996. In a 2006 article, *PC World Magazine* identified the Pippin as one of the "25 Worst Tech Products of all Time" (Tynan, 2006).

Companies that pursue the product leadership value discipline succeed if and only if they continually bring new products to market, experiment and learn quickly about each product's potential.

And, if alterations in product configuration, features, bundling, and pricing do not lift sales, they jettison the product without fanfare or sentiment and move on to other products with greater potential. (Anyone remember the Macintosh Newton? In introducing it, Apple's then-CEO, John Sculley coined the term "personal digital assistant." The product died, but the term prevails.)

Customer Intimacy

"Intimacy" suggests a meaningful and significant bond with the customer: If we're intimate, I know a great deal about you, your business, and your worries. It's entirely possible that, within my area of expertise, I know even more than you do about your business. I use my specialized knowledge to help you solve your problems and thus, sleep better at night. In fact, if *you* don't sleep well at night, *I* don't either! That's why it's called "intimacy"—your worries are my worries.

The company pursuing a customer intimacy strategy tends to have a far smaller number of customers than do firms pursuing either operational excellence or product leadership. This is because the essential business model is one of "best total solution," i.e., one requiring a deep knowledge of the customer and a great deal of customization to meet the customer's specific needs.

We find that businesspeople often confuse the meaning of "customer intimacy" with "customer satisfaction." Arguably, customer satisfaction is important to *any* company regardless of the discipline it is pursuing. What company is indifferent to the customer experience? But when we speak of value disciplines, customer intimacy means something special. It means having a profound and thorough understanding of your customers' needs so that you can create customized solutions just for them in just their way. The return for this commitment? Deep customer loyalty *and* deep margins.

On the point of customer satisfaction, you might find it interesting to know that Dell, pursuing an *operational excellence* strategy, is widely regarded as providing one of the worst customer service experiences in the retail PC industry, while Apple, pursuing a *product leadership* strategy, is regarded as providing the best. Why is Apple so concerned about customer service? Because its business model requires it! Theirs is not a customer intimacy strategy, but when you are in one of those Apple stores or on the phone with "Apple Care" reps for support, they want you to feel special—at least more special than you would feel if you were speaking to a Dell customer service agent. They never want you to question that you paid a premium for their product! Apple is the leader in its industry at customer service and is consistently rated among the top three in customer service across all industries (Moren, 2010). But be clear: Apple's goal is to be *only good enough* at delighting customers. Apple is *not* pursuing a customer intimacy strategy.

Figure 7-2: To which discipline is each company committed?

Here's a question that sharpens the point: Whose customer gets the better "customer service"—Apple's or IBM's? Clearly, the IBM customer gets the better service. Why? Because IBM is pursuing a customer intimacy strategy. If you own Apple products and call the customer support line, you may appreciate the service. But if you are an IBM customer, someone who knows your business, your aspirations, and your objectives will strive to call *you* with a creative solution before you even know you have a problem. And for this, you pay!

An executive team building an organization to pursue a customer intimacy strategy will put in place a decentralized organization—one close to the customer—that supports its employees in staying continually up to date with the specialized knowledge the firm requires to create customized solutions. And the "Employee of the Year" in a customer-intimacy organization? The one who thrilled the customer and, as a result, caused the *next* sale to that customer.

Test Yourself

Here's a question to illustrate how crucial clarity about value discipline is to a firm's success: to which value discipline are the organizations in Figure 7-2 committed? Operational excellence? Product leadership? Customer intimacy? If the question leaves you scratching your head, that's our point: In all of these cases, the company's value discipline is vague, which explains why many of them are struggling in the marketplace.

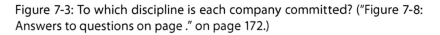

Figure 7-3: To which discipline is each company committed? ("Figure 7-8: Answers to questions on page ." on page 172.)

Let's turn the coin over. How about the group in Figure 7-3? To which value discipline does each belong? Each, of course, is a leading brand.

When senior leaders are clear about the organization's value proposition—and only then—they can make informed decisions about the organization's design and build or improve the capabilities the organization's strategy requires. Without this clarity, systematic organizational improvement is impossible.

Cognitax: A Cautionary Value Discipline Case Study

The following is a story of how failure to choose a value discipline nearly led to a business disaster. The case tells the story of a real firm, but it disguised to protect the client's identity. We'll diagnose the organization and analyze where this company derailed—or nearly did.

Cognitax is the leader in its industry: corporate tax software products, primarily sales and use tax products, but also some income and VAT (European) tax products. The company's hundreds of customers pay an average of $400K for a software product that ties into SAP, Oracle, and other Enterprise Resource Planning (ERP) software packages. Additionally, those customers pay an average annuity of $75K for software updates that reflect ongoing changes in EU, U.S. state and U.S. Federal tax codes. Annual revenues, growing every year for 18 years, are nearing $2B.

Cognitax bundles its tax software with what it considers to be very responsive customer support. The company's literature states, "The combination of product excellence and customer service produces superiority." Recent discussions at the senior level concerning the possibility of outsourcing the customer service function was rejected because management did not feel it could take the risk of loosening its tight quality control over this function. Management did permit some outsourcing of software engineering tasks to Indian contractors, however.

Cognitax is organized along functional lines, at least in its U.S. operations. Its London and Frankfurt operations, acquired as small consultancies 12 months earlier, are organized primarily along consulting practice lines (tax advisory and tax operations)—but there are now customer support functions and small technical groups in each European location.

In addition to being respected for its products, Cognitax has been an employer of choice, at least in its U.S. operations. The U.S. operation has been known for its culture of measured risk-taking, good salaries, and remarkable employee perks and benefits, including free coffee and soda, fitness facilities, and encouragement to leave before 6:00 p.m. each day. Four years ago, for two years running, Cognitax was named a "Best Place to Work" in its home state. The European operations were another matter. Largely made up of the former employees of two small consulting firms, employees in London and Frankfurt experienced the culture as hard driving and high-risk. U.S. employees regarded their European colleagues as quaint but stern, distant relatives. The Europeans regarded the U.S. leadership as entitled and unfocused.

The U.S.-based senior executive team had been in the process of updating Cognitax's strategic intent over the past three years, noting the rapid increase in demand by customers for consulting services relating to the installation of its software. In the U.S., due to Sarbanes-Oxley, some firms had dropped out of this consulting market. Eighteen months ago, the company built temporary teams both in London and the U.S. devoted to delivering these services, work that had—previous to Sarbanes-Oxley—been provided by some of the bigger accounting firms. Redeploying some of its best technical staff to participate on these teams, the resulting one-year revenue from consulting topped $6M in the U.S. and $1M in Europe.

This success prompted the executive team to conclude, "While tax software has been our core business, in the future we intend to balance software revenues with fees derived from consulting services. Our customers need several kinds of consulting help: installation support, tax operations advisory, and tax preparation. We will provide those services."

The EVP of Product Development was at once excited and troubled by the strategic redirection. She liked the spirit of adventure she saw growing, but often, she was the lone voice in senior team meetings who cautioned about setting the revenue objectives for consulting at an unattainable level.

This executive said, "In our first year, we've done amazingly well pursuing consulting dollars. But we hardly know our customers and their real needs at all. Yes, we're responsive when they call our support line, but we don't really know their needs. And selling consulting services requires us to deal with a totally different buyer—the senior tax official in those companies. Today, we're selling to a very junior person." She went on to say that, "Yes, we are tax experts, but let's not get distracted. Our core business is software, yet our last software release was not only late, it was also extremely hard for customers to use."

An internal study of Cognitax's culture, commissioned in response to poor results on a recent employee survey, uncovered some sobering information. Among other things, the study showed that:

- The company had two very different company cultures (U.S. and Europe), neither of which fully engaged employees.

- Middle-level managers in all locations seemed more concerned with fighting for turf than with strategic pursuits.

- Nearly no one had much faith in leadership capabilities of senior management. While the top leaders were perceived to be strong individuals, the report quoted an employee as saying, "They are not a team. They are a collection of egos."

- Perhaps this was why 63 percent of all nonmanagerial employees said they did not understand the strategy, and 49 percent of managers said the same!

- The Cognitax culture seemed to foster a sense of entitlement in which no one felt much of a sense of urgency.

- Employee involvement, while vocally embraced by senior management, did not match employee perceptions.

- Turnover was low at U.S. Cognitax (moderate in Europe), but this was considered by some to be a problem since the company both tolerated poor performers and could not seem to part company with employees whose skills were outdated. One U.S. executive said, "This is a dangerous place. You can get lulled into complacency here. Then, you lose your edge."

Despite these challenges, the most recent sales numbers in both tax software and consulting again showed strong percentage gains. In celebration, the U.S. executives gave a day off and sponsored a company picnic at the U.S. location to celebrate the quarter's success.

Analysis

This case illustrates how even very successful companies, when they do not think through strategic options clearly, can make—or, in this case, *nearly* make disastrous mistakes. Further, it illustrates how clarity about value discipline can support effective strategic decision-making.

Cognitax is flirting with the pursuit of two value disciplines at the same time: product leadership (packaged, off-the-shelf software), which it now excels at, and customer intimacy (expert consulting in a variety of areas), which is, while important, basically a sideline business.

This is dangerous because attempting to do everything well— even two things—is not sustainable. Again, the message from research is, "Do one thing superbly well, be only good enough at the other two."

Cognitax does not really understand its customers' needs well enough to deliver the value a customer intimacy strategy requires, especially one that purports to deliver tax operations advice and even tax preparation, arenas in which Cognitax would be pitting itself against major accounting and management consulting firms, should it enter the contest.

Cognitax's "Corporate DNA" does not support a radical shift in value discipline. In fact, most companies' DNA does not. No company should undertake such a shift without a *lot* of hesitation, study, and advice. Existing organizational systems and processes, even while imperfectly designed, are rigged to deliver a different kind of customer value. While shifting value disciplines can work (IBM went from product-centric to service-centric), doing this successfully requires radical system redesign, unflagging commitment by a coordinated senior team (in itself a rarity), and usually entails sustaining a deep, though possibly temporary productivity dip.

Cognitax's consulting trial outcome is very misleading. The consulting dollars delivered through the one-year trial program represent little more than a windfall. A close look reveals that revenue derived from software installation services was primarily due to other firms abandoning this market in the wake of recent

U.S. legislation (Sarbanes-Oxley). Thus, the revenue from this line would be largely tied to—and limited by—software sales: fewer sales would mean fewer installation consulting dollars. The revenues delivered by the U.S. group in the first year trial ($6M) were significantly greater than that delivered by the European offices ($1M). The Europeans are presumably better at consulting—their historical business—but are not familiar with the software or how to install it.

Employees at Cognitax are disengaged and relatively underproductive. The recent employee survey showed that an alarming percentage (63 percent) of employees do not understand the strategy. Many managers don't, either (49 percent).

An executive describes the company as a "dangerous place," a comment on complacency. The employee population is just coasting, not fully energized and productive. Management ideas about the best way to treat employees have more to do with being supportive than with productivity.

Finally, let's look at the lack of cultural integration of U.S. and European operations. Excited by the deep margins of consulting, the executive team acquired two small European consultancies. These have a very different culture from the U.S. operation, have a very different consulting expertise than do their American counterparts, and have not been successfully integrated either culturally or operationally. Probably the best thing would be for the company to sell these assets or manage them as a stand-alone services business.

We have used this case in leadership development settings many times, and the question always comes up: Why couldn't Cognitax pursue the consulting dollars even though this is not its core business? Our answer is this: Chasing revenue opportunistically is fine as long as it does not unproductively divert resources that could be better applied to pursuing one's core value proposition. In this case, the company's core competency is product innovation, not consulting, i.e., product leadership vs. customer-intimacy. Ultimately, the Cognitax executives scaled back their pursuit of consulting dollars unrelated to the installation of their own software. They did so because they realized that the hunt for these dollars would seriously distract from the business at hand: building best-in-class software products. The capital and executive talent required to form a stand-alone tax advisory and tax operations business, they decided, could be much more productively employed in the existing business. Ultimately, they sold the European operations.

The Star Model of Organization Design

Our approach to organization design has been profoundly shaped by the work of Jay Galbraith, Diane Downey, and Amy Kates. In their important books, *Designing Dynamic Organizations* (Galbraith, et al., 2001) and *Designing Your Organization* (Kates & Galbraith, 2007), they define organization design as follows:

> *Organization design is the deliberate process of configuring structures, processes, reward systems, and people practices to create an effective organization capable of achieving its business strategy.*

Galbraith and Kates use a five-pointed star diagram to show the five elements of organization design. Our version of the Star is in Figure 7-4.

A difference: We place the term "Aligned Leadership" in the center of the Star to emphasize that none of this occurs without the thoughtful guidance of an aligned team at the top and managers at every level that are working in concert with that group. Chapter Nine is devoted to alignment of the top team and how that group can position itself to guide strategy execution.

This model has three different kinds of value for organizational designers: It is a *descriptive* device that tells what a strategy-capable organization looks like; it's also *prescriptive*, telling the user what has to be in place in order to execute on strategy; and finally, it is a *diagnostic* tool, pinpointing where strategy implementation is getting off track.

This is a dynamic model; to get anywhere, the top team has to embark on a journey. Like any adventure, a strategy execution effort will require revisiting points on the Star, and the journey is almost never linear: although you have to begin with strategy formulation you don't usually proceed then in lockstep to creating vertical structure, then lateral processes, etc.

Figure 7-4: The Star Model (adapted from Jay R. Galbraith)

In this chapter, we will describe the work involved in organization design. We will do so in two ways: through a description of the various elements of organization design (structure, reward systems, etc.) and by showing how concepts of organization design, in combination with another tool called a "strategy map," can delineate and define a strategy execution plan understandable by anyone in the organization. Then, in Chapter Nine, we will tell you how we use both tools as we consult to senior teams and support them in creating their strategy implementation agenda.

Strategy

Strategy is at the top position (we think of it as True North), because organizational capability is meaningless without a strategy. To us, organization design is the activity of creating the strategy-capable organization. A clear, thoughtfully created strategy is an absolute business essential, and is among the foremost tasks of a top team. (Others are defining the business the organization is in, what markets it will do business in, and what its mission and values are.)

Strategy defines the goals to be achieved and the work required to achieve it. Any lack of alignment here gets magnified as time elapses, just as happens when a party navigating in the wilderness is off by even one degree from the correct bearing; over time and distance, navigational errors compound.

Structure

Every element of the organization's design must be compatible with the chosen value proposition, contributing something to the organization's capability to create value. This includes structure, which is at the upper right on the Star Model (Figure 7-4).

Structure refers to how budgetary and decision-making power is distributed in the organization. It's the "lines and boxes" that give hierarchical and conceptual shape to the organization. This is what most people think of when they hear the term "organization design" but, as we're discussing, there is far more to design than just structure.

Organizational structure defines the key relationships among the various units of the organization. The terms "matrix organization," "functional organization," "product line organization," all refer to types of organizational structures. Strong top teams are thoughtful in the structures they put in place, knowing that every organizational form has its drawbacks. Making a decision about organizational structure is, in our view, the most consequential organizational design determination a group of senior leaders can make because it will impact every aspect of organizational life: from the speed and quality of decision making to employee morale.

It is far beyond the scope of this book to review, compare, and contrast the various forms of organizational structure. For this information, we refer you to the two books by Galbraith, Downey, and Kates referenced earlier.

Business Processes

The term Business Processes refers to the specific steps a company takes to create customer value. While strategy defines *what* work needs to be done, business processes define *how* that work is done. Ideally, information technology both shapes and is shaped by business processes.

Of all the elements of organization design depicted in the Star Model, business processes are by far the most impacting when it comes to creating customer value. They affect the buying experience, the experience of using the company's product or service, and the after-sale experience. Most of the other organization design elements (structure, reward systems, etc.) are largely invisible to customers, but this is not so for business processes. Other design elements may indirectly affect customers, but the methods, procedures, and employee actions dictated and shaped by a business process affect customers directly and often profoundly.

Part of the work of Job Four is getting business processes right so that they're efficient, customer-friendly, and customer-centric. If you have a brilliant strategy but cannot build processes that deliver the customer value called for it, you have big problems.

Reward Systems (Including Performance Tracking Systems)

Reward systems do three things: 1) they define the performance objectives called for by the strategy, 2) reinforce the competencies the organization values most, and 3) focus the attention and effort of the workforce on what results are needed.

The performance and reward system is comprised of several components. These components comprise the performance management system which, in turn, specifies the work called for by the business strategy, reinforces and leverages core competencies of the company, measures performance and results, and allocates reward for performance.

- Goal cascading processes
- Division, group and individual performance objectives and targets
- Performance review processes
- Compensation, incentives and recognition programs

We put performance-tracking systems like the Balanced Score-card in this category, as well.

People Processes

This term refers to the capability of the organization to attract, select, develop, motivate, and retain people, and to the mechanisms by which employees are connected to the work of strategy execution. Any process or intervention that aids in bringing talented people into the organization and enabling them to make their best contribution falls into this category.

Regardless of the value discipline it is pursuing, an essential capability of any organization is to connect employees cognitively, emotionally, and behaviorally to the organization's strategy. This, of course, is the work of Jobs One and Two. That work falls into the people processes category.

When strategies change, systems and processes also have to change. We counsel teams to use the Star model to assess the current functioning of their organization along each dimension of capability and to create design teams to address changes called for by new strategies.

Assess Your Organization's Design

Once a leadership group clarifies the firm's value discipline and puts in place the required organization design elements, an organization is vastly more capable than before of creating the customer value that leads to financial results.

How do you tell if your organization is due for a retrofit of design to strategy? Use the "Organization Design Assessment Scheme" in Figure 7-5. It will tell you whether or not your organization as currently designed is going to struggle to achieve its strategy due to organization design issues and, if so, where the difficulty lies. We employ this questionnaire in every organization design project we undertake. Note the scale: It goes from 1–*Strongly Disagree* to 9–*Strongly Agree*. In the middle is 5, signifying *Agree*

With Reservations.

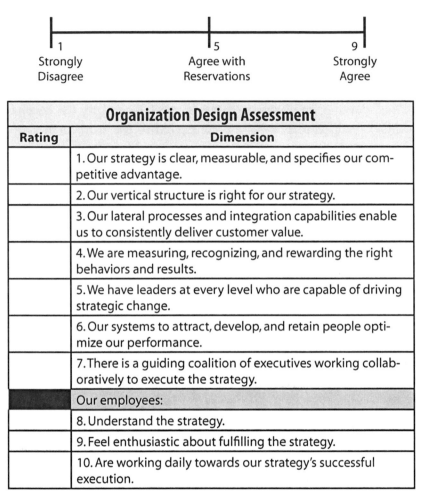

Organization Design Assessment	
Rating	**Dimension**
	1. Our strategy is clear, measurable, and specifies our competitive advantage.
	2. Our vertical structure is right for our strategy.
	3. Our lateral processes and integration capabilities enable us to consistently deliver customer value.
	4. We are measuring, recognizing, and rewarding the right behaviors and results.
	5. We have leaders at every level who are capable of driving strategic change.
	6. Our systems to attract, develop, and retain people optimize our performance.
	7. There is a guiding coalition of executives working collaboratively to execute the strategy.
	Our employees:
	8. Understand the strategy.
	9. Feel enthusiastic about fulfilling the strategy.
	10. Are working daily towards our strategy's successful execution.

Figure 7-5: Organization Design Assessment Scheme

While the actual ratings are important, the discussion the team has that explores them is far more valuable. We collect this information in an interview setting and we always say, "Give us a number and then tell us why you gave that number." Typically when reporting back these data, we calculate frequency responses and standard deviations, not just averages because we think exploring the variability in answers across an executive group can be very revealing.

Remember Cool-Clear-Water (CCW) from the last chapter?

We conducted an assessment very much like this with the top 13 executives after they committed to their plan to double revenue in five years. Figure 7-6 shows their scores on the first five items.

Executive	Q1 Strategy clear	Q2 Struc. right for strategy	Q3 Work processes	Q4 Meas'g, recog, reward'g	Q5 Abundance of leaders
1 MFG	9	8	6	8.5	3
2	6	7	3	5	2
3	7	4	8	8	5
4 SALES	7	1	5	1	5
5 CFO	9	6	6	8	6.5
6	7	5	7	4	2
7	7	7	7.5	4	2
8	7	7	9	5	6
9	7	6	7	6	3
10	5	7	4	4	4
11 PROD	4	3	5	5	4
12	7	3.5	5	4	4
13 CEO	9	5	7.5	5	5
Av	7.00	5.35	6.15	5.19	3.96
SD	1.47	2.01	1.71	2.06	1.51

Figure 7-6: Assessment data from the Cool-Clear-Water executives

Several things stand out in this data set:

- The lowest overall area is Q5, "We have an abundance of leaders at every level who are capable of driving strategic change." This item has the lowest average, which means that the executive group does not believe managers are ready to tackle the company's ambitious growth goals. This item also has a low standard deviation, indicating that most of the executives see the situation the same way.

- On the other hand, the highest scores are in answer to Q1, "Our strategy is clear, measurable, and specifies our competitive advantage." The executives are in substantial agreement on this item as well. This executive team had worked long and hard on the strategy and developed the most thorough strategy document we had seen in some time. The executives worked collaboratively to create the document. No wonder they were in agreement. But notice executive #11: he is an outlier. What does he see that the others do not? This is the head of the Products Division. (This executive was seriously out of step with the CEO and was later terminated.

- The next highest area of agreement concerns the lateral business processes, Q3: "Our lateral processes and integration capabilities enable us to deliver consistent customer value." The variance begins to creep up here. Discussion among the executives made clear to all that, in some cases, they were kidding themselves about the quality of their processes, many of which needed improvement.

- As we mentioned in Chapter Six, the presenting problem of the CEO when we started working with CCW was his suspicion that the structure was not right given the new strategy. Q2, "Our vertical structure is right for our strategy," reveals an area of concern: the range of responses goes from 1-8 (out of nine) with an standard deviation of 2.01, i.e., high variability. Depending on where you sit in the organization, structure is just fine (Operations) or inadequate (Sales).

- Score set #13 belongs to the CEO. We would expect his assessment regarding the adequacy of the structure and strategy to be relative low, because this is why he reached out to us in the first place. And once we got to know him as a very people-oriented person committed to high levels of employee engagement, we could understand his concerns about the people processes reflected in Q4 and Q5.

In the next chapter, we'll tell you how to use these data in an orchestrated, efficient process of bringing organizational design into alignment with the strategy. And in that chapter, we will pull the whole Job Four story into focus with our treatment of the strategy map tool.

Organization Design Criteria

Earlier, we quoted Kates and Galbraith (2007) as saying, "Different strategies require different organizational capabilities and therefore different organizational designs." This statement bears repeating because it sums up the work of fitting the organization to the strategy. The link between strategy and organization design comes in the form of design criteria. Galbraith and Kates define organizational design criteria as follows:

> *Organization design criteria specify and describe the organizational capabilities that your business or unit needs to have in order to deliver on the strategy (Kates & Galbraith, 2007, p. 216).*

The payoff that derives from establishing design criteria lies in their ability to enable organizational leaders to test organizational design decisions (structure, business processes, etc.) for efficacy. With design criteria in hand, leaders can answer questions like these:

- Which competing version of an organizational chart is optimal given our strategy?

- Which business processes have to change to enable us to deliver consistent customer value?

- What specific leadership capabilities do we have to have to successfully execute on our strategy?

- What types of employees must we attract, develop, and retain in order to optimize our performance?

- What must our employees be able to do at world-class levels to execute the strategy?

As we've been stating in this chapter, the first question an organizational designer needs to answer is, "What business game are we playing, i.e., by which model do we choose to compete?" In answering this, it's immensely helpful to have the model of competitive advantage in hand that we explored earlier (operational excellence, etc.). If the answer is product leadership, the organization design will look one way whereas if the answer is operational excellence, it will look quite another way, and so on.

Once a senior leadership team creates a set of organizational design criteria, they are in a position to focus the organization's attention on those critical few objectives that will lead to winning in the marketplace.

In most cases, an organization needs only 4-5 design criteria to sum up the capabilities called for by a given strategy. Figure 7-7 provides some examples of design criteria that have come out of deliberations by top teams we've worked with, broken down by value discipline. Note that useful design criteria begin with a verb; they tell what action the organization will take.

Use the Assessment, Create Design Criteria

Our work with executives very often begins with a request for help in assessing the adequacy of the fit between an organizational structure (lines and boxes) with a strategy that has recently changed or a set of organizational circumstances that are changing. Those requests have sounded like this:

- "We've just modified our strategy. Thus, we are not sure our organizational structure is right for the results we need to get."

- [If it's the head of a division or large support function] "The organization has declared that we must be more aligned with the strategy. We are pretty sure our structure will need to change but we don't know where to start."

- [If it's the head of HR] "My CEO has asked me to look for consulting expertise relating to organizational structure because our strategy is changing," or "Our strategy is changing and we know we have to change everything. I'm being expected to lead the charge, but frankly, I don't know where to start."

Value Discipline	Design Criteria
Product Leadership	• Create new products faster than our competitors • Produce cutting-edge products • Convert customer information and knowledge quickly into market-leading products and services • Create cutting-edge products faster than competitors • Deliver high levels of customer satisfaction
Operational Excellence	• Become a low cost producer of goods and services • Continually increase process efficiency • Exploit multiple distribution channels • Make the customer buying and product-using experience rewarding and hassle-free • Deliver high levels of customer satisfaction
Customer Intimacy	• Customize products at a customer's request • Create alliances with other organizations in order to deliver comprehensive solutions • Function as trusted partners, both within our organization and with external partners and users. • Deliver end-to-end (pre-and post sale) customer service that enhances the value of products • Deliver high levels of customer satisfaction

Figure 7-7: Organizational design criteria by value discipline

In all such instances, we tell the client what we urge *you* to say if your CEO makes such a statement: "The *structure* may need to change, but you can't change structure in isolation. If the structure needs to change, there is very a good chance that other aspects of the organization's design need to change too, e.g., business or people processes. You need to look at *all* aspects of the organization's design."

"But that's *my* job!"

We sometimes encounter executives who recoil from the idea that their direct reports should have a say in creating design criteria, believing that making organizational design decisions is what senior managers get paid for. We have also heard senior leaders say, "And besides, I don't respect the opinions of some of the people on my team so why would I ask them to create design criteria?" Or they may say, "I am thinking about changing some of the people on the team soon, so I'll make those decisions myself."

We usually encourage the leader to pursue a participatory process anyhow, advocating for an approach that allows the senior-most executive to retain decision-making rights (and responsibilities).

That process is simple. It's a sequence that begins with 90-minute interviews conducted by a consultant with each member of the senior team. The consultant should be armed with the assessment "Organization Design Assessment" on page 164. Following the interviews a day-long meeting with the executives should take place, during which there should be a series of facilitated organizational design deliberations. We describe the process in Chapter 9, "Aligning the Senior Team."

Action Learning

This chapter described the work of Job Four, the most challenging of all the tasks of strategy execution. This work involves choosing a value discipline, designing an organization that can deliver on the promise embedded in that value discipline, and actually bringing that organization into existence. This is hard work, but there is no escape from the effort if you wish to come anywhere close to being a leader in your marketplace. If there is a shortcut to winning (there isn't), this long road is it.

In this chapter, we introduced the Star Model, a summary of the organization design work required for strategy execution. We described this as a prescriptive model, a diagnostic tool, and an action planning device. In the next chapter, we will tell you how a senior team can use that model to redesign their organization.

Exercise 1: Identify your value discipline.

Schedule two, half-day meetings of your leadership team. During the first one, introduce the three value disciplines and lead a discussion that answers to the following questions. Seriously consider engaging a professional facilitator to help lead the discussions, one familiar with the three value disciplines.

- Which value discipline(s) is our organization pursuing?
- Which one *should* we be pursuing?

During the second session, put a stake in the ground by forging a consensus around the one value discipline your organization will pursue.

Exercise 2: Assess your organization.

At an additional half-day session, use the assessment form "Organization Design Assessment" on page 164 to determine where your organization is strategy-capable and where it is not. Thoroughly explore all answers. If at all possible, ask each leader to fill out the survey ahead of the meeting and tabulate both means and standard deviations before the meeting. Again, consider using a professional facilitator; these discussions get very animated.

Exercise 3: Develop design criteria.

In a fourth half-day session, work as a leadership group to identify 4-5 design criteria. Remember, the definition of design criteria is, "The organizational capabilities that your business or unit needs to have in order to deliver on the strategy." Be sure that the criteria you select correspond to your chosen value discipline and that they start with a verb; design criteria tell what your organization needs to be superbly capable of doing.

Exercise 4: Pull it all together.

Once you've completed Exercises 1-3, pull your work together in the form of a brief narrative of one or two pages. Vet this document with your organization's key stakeholders: your boss, perhaps his or her boss, your key customers, middle managers, HR business partner(s), and at least a sampling of your key nonmanagerial personnel.

Figure 7-8: Answers to questions"Figure 7-3: To which discipline is each company committed? ("Figure 7-8: Answers to questions on page ." on page .)" on page 153.

Chapter Eight

Strategy Maps:
The Strategy Execution Flight Plan

Strong reasons make strong actions.
—William Shakespeare

W<small>E HAVE SAID THAT DOING</small> the work of Jobs One-Four is not usually sequential. In fact, building a strategy map, which is central to Job Four, can make doing Jobs One-Three far easier.

When we work with clients, helping them build a strategy map is among the earliest things we do. After conducting an audit of the adequacy of the client's strategy (asking and answering the question: "Is this strategy executable?") and examining the fit of that strategy with their current organization, we then help the leadership team begin building the strategy map. Between this chapter and Chapter Nine, we will tell you how we do both.

Creating a strategy map helps senior teams turn what otherwise can be aimless discussions about the faults of the organization or theoretical discussions about how to fix the organization, into practical plans for executing their strategy. We find that as senior teams build strategy maps, they come into unparalleled alignment about priorities, initiatives, and results. Further, the exchange of views almost always improves the quality of the strategy itself.

The strategy map concept is not a new tool; it was introduced by Kaplan and Norton (1996) in their book, *The Balanced Score-card: Translating Strategy into Action.* In that volume and in each subsequent book on the Balanced Scorecard, Kaplan and Norton have discussed strategy maps. Their book, entitled *Strategy Maps: Converting Intangible Assets into Tangible Outcomes* (2004), is de-voted to the topic. In that book, Kaplan and Norton write, "The strategy map has turned out to be as important an innovation as the original Balanced Scorecard itself." (Kaplan & Norton, 2004, page xiii). (If you plan to read just one book on the Balanced Score-card and strategy maps, we advise you to read *Strategy Maps.*)

Despite the credibility, validity, and appeal of the Balanced Scorecard, we find that relatively few companies employ the con-cept diligently and fewer still even know of the concept of strategy mapping. Too bad; both are exceedingly useful tools. Most of our clients have heard of the Balanced Scorecard, but we usually see blank stares when we mention strategy maps.

The Balanced Scorecard addresses organizational performance in four areas as illustrated in Figure 8-1. Note that the Balanced Scorecard is a scheme that articulates a strategy as a set of inter-locking actions which, in combination, produce results. Figure 8-1 illustrates how the organization's intangible assets make tangible business outcomes possible. The arrows indicate causation. Figure 8-1 articulates how the lower, intangible set leads to the upper, tan-gible results.

The theory behind the Balanced Scorecard begins with the ob-servation that businesses exist to generate a profit, a tangible result, but profit flows only because a business has created value of some kind for a set of customers, usually tangible in nature. But those results flow, in turn, from other organizational results that are far more *in*tangible in nature. Those results have to do with business processes and organizational arrangements such as structure, re-ward systems, and so forth, that drive the tangible results.

Thus, financial outcomes and customer results are both lagging measures: They tell what overall results the organization gets after when all is said and done. The leading measures that organizational leaders must attend to are those associated with business processes and organizational capabilities.

You can read the Balanced Scorecard from the bottom up or the top down. From the bottom up, the story unfolds like this: When we put in place certain carefully chosen organizational capabilities, we will have the ability to employ our business processes. Those business processes, when thoughtfully designed and carried out, will create the value our customers desire from us. In turn, this will lead to financial results.

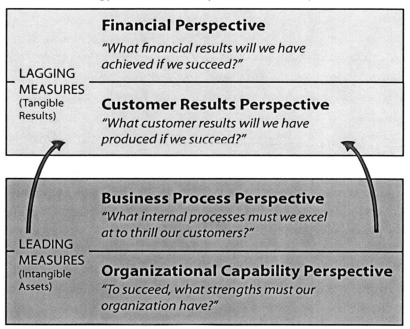

The Balanced Scorecard
A Strategy Must Tell a Story From Four Perspectives

LAGGING MEASURES
(Tangible Results)

Financial Perspective

"What financial results will we have achieved if we succeed?"

Customer Results Perspective

"What customer results will we have produced if we succeed?"

LEADING MEASURES
(Intangible Assets)

Business Process Perspective

"What internal processes must we excel at to thrill our customers?"

Organizational Capability Perspective

"To succeed, what strengths must our organization have?"

Figure 8-1: The Balanced Scorecard is a causal model of how a strategy produces results.

What is a Strategy Map?

A strategy map is a graphic portrayal of an organization's strategy showing how various strategic initiatives will lead to customer results and, in turn, to financial results. A strategy map can depict the aims and intentions of an entire corporation or the plans of just one part of the organization. Organizations derive the maximum value of a strategy map when the senior-most executives create the enterprise strategy map and then the units create theirs. In that way, a strategy map becomes a kind of hologram—or should: Each unit map reflects and aligns with the overall enterprise map.

Figure 8-2 is a simplified strategy map. It depicts how Southwest Airlines (SWA) creates value. Please note that in our use of the language of strategy maps, we use slightly different wording than do Kaplan and Norton. Most specifically, we use the term "Organizational Capability" rather than their term "Learning and Growth," because we think it more clearly communicates what this dimension is all about. (If we have a criticism of the Balanced Scorecard literature, it lies in its lack of guidance for strategy implementers in how to think through and make decisions about initiatives in this arena. Our motivation in writing this book came, in part, from this frustration.)

Reading from the bottom up, we see that the key organizational capability that SWA requires for success is ground crew alignment. When that is in place, the key SWA business process—fast ground turnaround—is fully supported. In turn, this enables the key customer results called for by the strategy: on-time flights and low prices. When all those conditions exist, internal costs go down, revenue increases, and then profitability grows.

In actuality, a good strategy map has considerably more detail than you see here; this is just schematic. For instance, a detailed strategy map document (on subsequent pages) will include initiatives associated with each strategy element and relevant metrics associated with them. Employees at SWA would also tell you that "ground crew alignment" is a very simplistic summary of a sophisticated set of interlocking organizational capabilities (including rigorous pre-employment screening, regular training, innovative compensation systems, etc.). Similarly, "fast ground turnaround" sums up a host of key sub-processes, each of which are highly detailed in operating procedures. Later in this chapter we'll show you how we help clients create and use this additional detail.

Strategy maps function like a kind of Swiss Army Knife for strategists. Using one tool, you can articulate how you will build an organization that is strategy-capable, show how these capabilities enable and support the key business processes, and trace the logical linkage between these initiatives and subsequent customer and financial results. In addition, when finished, you have a very powerful aid for telling the story of strategy execution in your organization.

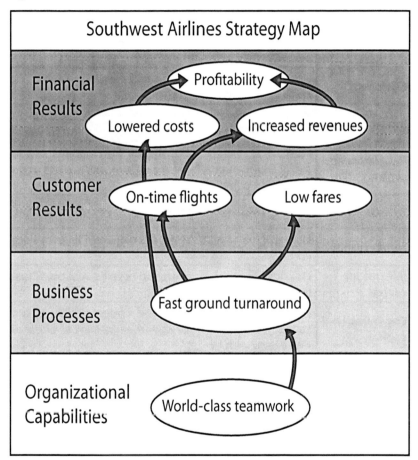

Figure 8-2: Southwest Airlines Strategy Map

Figure 8-3 provides more detail as to what should be considered in the Business Processes and Organizational Capabilities dimensions. While the attention that must be paid to regulatory requirements varies across industries, every business must attend to key stakeholder relationships in their social contexts.

Does answering all of these questions seem daunting? No one

said that strategy execution was easy! Merely reflecting on the difficulty inherent in answering these questions adequately itself makes clear why most companies struggle to execute on their strategies: it's hard work! But this work will help you separate yourself from your competitors.

Internal Processes Must Address Four Questions	
Operations	How will we manage our supply chain, i.e., how we plan, source, make and deliver?
Customer	How will we create, cultivate, and manage relationships with our customers?
Innovation	How will we leverage our core competencies to develop and bring to market new products and services?
Regulatory and social	How will we ensure conformance with regulations and social expectations, how we ensure that we are good "corporate citizens"?
Organizational Capabilities Must Address Three Questions	
Human capital	How will we attract, retain, develop, and leverage our employees' talents and skills?
Information capital	How will we build, manage, and keep current our IT systems and infrastructure?
Organizational capital	How will we ensure employee understanding of our strategy, enthusiasm for it, and alignment of effort at every level with it?

Figure 8-3: Questions that must be considered when strategy mapping

Cool-Clear-Water: Enterprise Strategy Map

On page 180 is a detailed strategy map we helped a client create. We're showing you the full detail of a company whose strategy *and* strategy map, because it has three relatively distinct business lines, is quite complex. Good news: yours will probably be considerably simpler than this one.

The company is in the business of producing water treatment and purification products and running municipal water treatment facilities, but also has a water analysis business. We introduced you to this company in Chapter Six. CCW is a leader in its industry. Theirs is a mixed portfolio involving a hybrid of two value disciplines. On the one hand, the organization requires some of the capabilities called for by a product leadership model (its Products business), and on the other hand, their organization requires some of the capabilities of a customer intimacy model (its Services business). Given that CCW's products are often designed and built—or at least modified—to each individual customer's specifications, the executive team came to the conclusion that, overall, their value proposition was essentially customer intimacy. (It was somewhat different in the Analytical Services business due to the commodity nature of these services.)

Working with this client, we employed a process that we describe in Chapter Nine that began with interviews designed to assess the adequacy of the strategy and the fit of the organization design with that strategy.

As is often the case with our initial encounters with the client, the presenting issue was the CEO's belief that the company's vertical structure was at odds with its growth objectives—in this case, to double revenue in five years. Our assessment confirmed this impression, but also revealed the following:

- While the executive team and board were enthusiastic about the new strategy, managers below the top level were largely unaware of it and unequipped to execute it.

- The company's vision with respect to environmental/green objectives was vague and ill-formed. This was true despite a strategic commitment to building a reputation in this area.

- Executing the strategy called for sales and delivery capabilities in far-flung environments where the company had not operated before, making talent acquisition a key priority, yet the company had no plan in place to address these hiring and on-boarding challenges.

- The strategy called for growth through acquisition, but the company had little experience in acquiring and successfully integrating companies.

CCW Strategy Map

Financial Results	Profit (BIT) $480M	Revenues $5.0	ROIC 10% or above

These **Financial Results** — *Deliver on our promise*

Water Purification — **Operating Services** — **Analytical Services**

These **Customer Results** — *Drive financial results*

- Saves me $ over time
- Provides solutions
- Customer Intimacy*
- Preferred Vendor/Operator
- Quality products & services for $
- Continuous service; no disruptions
- Full regulatory compliance
- Best operational efficiency
- Ethical practices

These **Internal Processes** — *deliver customer value*

- Continuous product improvement
- Adapt prod's to meet local needs
- Develop & refine product range
- Strengthen & expand our intl dist. network
- Develop lower cost products for global markets
- Best in Class Project Management
- Health, Environment & Safety Best Practices
- Effective crisis mgt
- Expand geographical footprint
- Streamline contract renewal/negotiation process
- Full regulatory compliance
- Develop on-site testing
- Standardize policies & processes
- Find efficiencies to improve margins & provide continuous service

These **Organizational Capabilities** — *Enable our internal processes*

- Maintain a powerful Health & Safety program
- Bring organization structure fully into alignment with growth plan
- Identify behaviors required for high performance & cust. intimacy & train all EEs in those skills
- Build a world-class recruitment process that reflects our Value Prop.
- Train sales & managers cust. intimacy
- Fit the reward System to the growth plan
- Create and communicate a vision that fosters and embeds values & drives the cust. intimacy culture

* Do what we say; on-time delivery; Deep knowledge & expertise; Problem empathy; Knowledge-based sales; Easy to work with

- While doubling growth would require unprecedented levels of collaboration among the units, each of the CCW businesses functioned almost completely independently of one another.

Beginning with a two-day off-site, followed by intensive work later, we helped the leaders develop a strategy map. The exercise clarified for team members their need to build organizational capabilities for each of the three lines of business (operating plants, selling products, and providing analytical services) that delivered customer intimacy, even though the customers for each business were different and had different needs.

The executives, who formerly had a very myopic view of the business, came into a high level of alignment while developing the map, realizing that they had to work far more interdependently than ever before in order to reach the growth goals. Reflecting on the process of creating the map, one executive said, "We have never worked this well together before. I am feeling more confident about our future now."

Using the map, the executives were able to tell the following story about their strategy:

Financial results:

We are pursuing a five-year plan that will double our top line growth.

Customer results:

We will achieve this goal as we build intimacy with our customers in the services businesses and in our products business. As we do so, our customers will see us as the preferred vendor (products) and operator (treatment), the provider who best understands their needs and problems, and provides the best overall solution for the cost.

Business processes:

Each of our businesses will have to create some new capabilities, especially those leading to growth in new markets. For instance, our Products Business will have to adapt its products to new markets, and we will have to grow and expand our international vendor/

distributor network in those markets. In our Analytical Services business, we will have to standardize policies and processes to achieve efficiencies and meet regulatory requirements, and in Operating Services, we will have to expand our geographical footprint.

Organizational capabilities:

We will build the organizational capabilities required to deliver on our objectives, including identifying behaviors required for high performance. We will train all employees in those skills as well as build a world-class recruitment process that reflects our commitment to customer intimacy.

Overall Objective	Initiative
Build an organization capable of supporting our key business processes	Create and communicate a vision that fosters and embeds values and drives the needed culture
	Identify behaviors required for high performance & customer intimacy (competency model)
	Train all employees in customer intimacy skills
	Build a world-class recruitment process that reflects our customer intimacy value

Figure 8-4: Detail from CCW Organizational Capability

Once the CCW executives agreed on the strategy map, they formed ad hoc teams to detail each dimension of the strategy map. Those teams identified key initiatives, named people to guide those efforts and established benchmarks and metrics for each one. The CEO named an executive sponsor for each initiative. Figure 8-4 shows what this detail looked like in the organizational capability dimension.

Working out these details is hard work and sometimes tedious, but doing it knits a leadership team into a cohesive and coordinated whole. And who appreciates this the most? The CEO who begins to sleep better at night and who can tell at a glance, which members of the senior team are fully on-board and which are not.

The CCW illustration tells how a strategy map can be invaluable to document and drive an enterprise-wide strategy, but a strategy map can be *as* useful at the unit level, whether an enterprise map exists or not. In the CCW case, the strategy mapping exercise did not stop at the senior level; each member of the senior team, worked with his or her directs reports to create a strategy map for their part of the business, one that coordinated and was congruent with the enterprise map.

IT at Fix-a-Bone, Inc.

Here's an example showing how we've used strategy mapping in a large staff department where there was no enterprise map.

Our client, the head of a large, global IT function in a medical devices company, asked for our help in addressing the growing demands by the company's business lines that IT provide more support in the realm of product development. The company, pursuing a product leadership strategy, was increasingly dependent on IT to speed new products to market.

While the vision of the IT function—"To be a trusted business partner by providing innovative solutions/technologies and superior services to each business line"—was aligned with the company's strategy, our organizational assessment revealed that the function was effective in only the first two of three areas:

- *Provide reliable, cost-effective IT service and support on a day-to-day basis.*

- *Execute ad hoc IT projects as requested in an efficient and effective way (Usually improvements to existing systems).*

- *Provide innovative solutions and services in a proactive fashion to support product development.*

Like many of our clients do, the IT VP seized upon organizational structure as both the cause of department performance problems and its sole antidote. While he was not wrong that the structure was an impediment, his analysis of the overall problem was only partly right: There were *several* aspects of the organizational design that needed attention. Working with him and his team to modify an existing strategy map helped enormously to formulate the road map for strategy execution in all three domains. Figure 8-5 shows the resulting map (highly simplified).

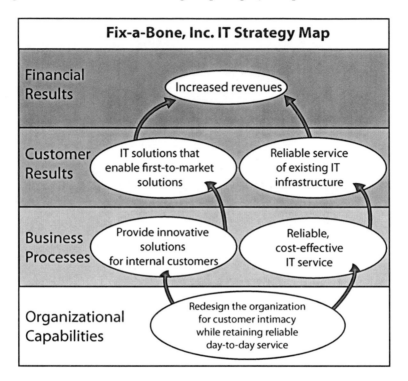

Figure 8-5: Strategy Map for an IT department, medical devices company

When reading from the top down, this map permits the users to tell the following story:

Financial results:

IT exists to support our end-users, i.e., each of the business lines. The primary task of the end-user is to develop cutting-edge medical solutions and bring them to market first. As we enable them to do this, company revenues increase.

Customer results:

The business lines, our customers, want three things from us, each of which is essential to achieving their goals: trouble-free provision of day-to-day IT services and support (e.g., access to the Internet, e-mail, Help Desk support, database management, IT security, etc.), ongoing help in upgrading and improving existing systems, and IT solutions that support them in developing cutting-edge products and bringing them to market before competitors.

Business processes:

To achieve these results, the IT function must build processes that effectively and efficiently address innovation support, infrastructure maintenance, and continuous improvement.

Organizational capability:

*To continue to operate in an efficient way **and** to do a better job of supporting our customers in product development, we have to make various kinds of changes to our skills and organizational structure so that we're closer to the customer, understand their needs better, and have the skills to be able to build the IT systems they need.*

The top tier of the strategy map, of course, mirrors the company's objectives. The Customer Results dimension, on the other hand, states what *IT's* customers are looking for, not the company's customers. In creating the map, those Customer Results were spelled out in detail and associated metrics were assigned. Similarly, the Business Processes dimension of the strategy map was detailed. Figure 8-6 shows the key initiatives in the Organizational Capabilities dimension of the map. Each of those initiatives, in turn, were assigned a delivery date, an associated set of metrics, and a sponsor.

While the end result might look simple, the process of building a strategy map, even for a support organization like IT, is anything but simple. In the process of creating the strategy map with this client, an instructive conversation ensued when the client said to us, "Wait a minute. You are saying that on our strategy map, the Customer Results should be those of the three Fix-a-Bone businesses we support, not IT's own results?"

At first, we didn't understand. We said, "IT is a support organization: your 'customers' *are* the businesses you support." The CIO then said, "But isn't this presumptuous to tell them what their results need to be?" We replied by saying, "Yes, it *would* be presumptuous to tell the businesses you support what results they're after. But you are not going to do this. For now, you are going to make your best guess based on your knowledge of their strategy, and then you are going to vet your strategy map with the head of each of those businesses, asking if you are comprehending their needs accurately. Depending on what they say, you may modify your map."

Organizational Capability Initiative
Redesign the organization for customer intimacy (while maintaining operational excellence). Do so in a highly participative way, one that includes customer input, HR input, and full participation of those who have to carry out the redesign.
Develop a customer intimacy competency model.
Assess all managers against the customer intimacy competency model. Rely heavily on input from customers.
Reassign managers, as needed, to fill roles in the new organization structure.
Develop skills relative to the customer intimacy competencies. (Focus especially on leaders, using a combination of coaching and classroom support, but also cultivate an awareness of the importance of customer intimacy among all employees.)
Develop and carry out a communication process to convey the new focus on innovation and customer intimacy and how departmental structural changes fit into this. Do so in a way that involves all managers in both conceiving and executing the communications plan.
Prepare customers for their participation in the new service delivery model [IT intends to act differently, i.e., more partner-like, therefore the customer will have to act differently, too.]

Figure 8-6: Detail from the Fix-a-Bone IT strategy map

As you can see by this example, creating a strategy map is not just an intellectual exercise created in a vacuum: done right, the process leads to exceptionally useful dialogues both within organizations and with key stakeholders.

Creating a Strategy Map

Going through the exercise of building a strategy map enables the Strategy Steward group to arrive at a level of agreement they probably have never experienced before among themselves. No strategy is static, of course, so a leadership team will modify the strategy—and thus, the strategy map—with some regularity as changes occur in the marketplace and opportunities arise.

There is no one right way to create a strategy map. We've taken the following approaches, all of which have worked in their given circumstances, although the most participatory processes, listed first, produce the highest levels of alignment:

- Begin building the strategy map from the ground up with a senior leadership team during a two-day, off-site meeting. Have a small task force take it to completion.

- Introduce the concept of a strategy map in a leadership development program. Have the participants begin to create the map and prepare them to go back and involve their direct reports in the process that finishes the map.

- Conduct an organization design study and create a draft of a strategy map for leadership review and refinement.

No matter which approach you take, building a strategy map correctly requires—in our view, at least—doing the following first. We like to devote one or more off-site meetings of the senior team to each of these tasks:

- Identify the goals the strategy is intended to achieve, with particular emphasis on customer results and financial results.

- Identify the value discipline to which the organization is committed, i.e., product leadership, operational excellence, or customer intimacy. (This is discussed in Chapter Seven.)

- Identify the design criteria the organization must satisfy.

If the basic strategy is clear at the point the group begins to map it, the financial results segment will usually be easiest to build and may actually already exist. Clarity of other details ranges considerably and usually follows these general lines:

Customer results: Often vague and implicit even in firms where customer intimacy is the value discipline.

Business processes: Often clear in products companies, but very often vague in services/customer intimacy companies.

Organizational capabilities: Very vague and ill-defined in most companies; often executives have no knowledge of or real experience in these matters. The most time will be required here and education and training, as well.

In the next chapter, we will explore how senior team alignment sessions can be used to begin the process of creating a strategy map.

Action Learning

If you were to ask three middle-level managers in your company to name key customer groups, would they all mention the same customers? Would they all say the same thing with respect to the *results* those customers are looking for? What would they say if you asked them to tell you what their department was doing to support each customer segment?

In most cases, you are likely to get a variety of answers to the first two questions, and probably a blank stare in response to the last. This is unfortunate, because it means there is probably a lack of focus in the organization, wasted effort, and misalignment of contribution.

A strategy map is a simple tool that can help rectify this. It clarifies the strategy, shows the causal linkages between its various components, aligns senior leaders, and enables the communication of a compelling story about change. Further, when middle-level managers are equipped to develop their own strategy maps and asked to align them with the enterprise map, unparalleled levels of top-to-bottom coordination can result.

Do the exercises below by yourself. Create a strategy map for your organization. Once you've thought through all the questions, kiss your strategy map goodbye and throw it away. Then, assemble your team for at least three half-day sessions (one each for Customer Results, Business Processes, and Organizational Capabilities), and create a map together. Of course, if they've read this book beforehand (or are otherwise familiar with strategy maps), that task goes a lot more smoothly and efficiently. If not, you may need to add a segment up front, teaching them what a strategy map is and how to use one.

Exercise 1: Establish (or list) your financial measures.

List the key financial measures by which your company—not your own organization unless you are the CEO!—measures its success. Are you sure about this, or are you guessing? Consult the company's strategy statement if there is one, and you have access to it. If you don't, consult other internal documents or at least last year's report to the shareholders. Once you've done so, vet your answers with the CEO and the CFO, or if you don't have access to them, to the highest level person you have access to.

Exercise 2: Define key customer results.

What are the key customer results those financial results in Exercise 1 depend on? Don't guess. Make sure you know. These results can vary by business line, so focus on your part of the business. If you lead a support organization (Legal, Marketing, IT, HR, etc.), make sure you know the results that the *people you support* look to you to help them get. If you support three separate business lines and they're striving for different customer results, you may have one strategy map for each business.

Exercise 3: Define key business processes.

Identify the irreducible few business processes that enable you to create value for your customers. (Your "customers" might be others inside the company if yours is a support organization.) How do these processes deliver value? Are there any missing processes you need to add? Get them on your strategy map!

Exercise 4: Identify crucial organizational capabilities.

Finally, what are the essential organizational capabilities you need to have in place to enable your organization to deliver value? Consider some of things suggested by the Star Model: people practices, such as talent management processes, employee engagement systems, reward systems, and so forth. Of course, the organizational design criteria you established earlier (see Chapter Seven—you did do this, did you not?) will help immeasurably here.

Chapter Nine

Aligning the Senior Team

I am a member of a team,
and I rely on the team,
I defer to it and sacrifice for it,
because the team, not the individual,
is the ultimate champion.
—Mia Hamm

W<small>E HAD THE PLEASURE ONCE</small> of spending an afternoon with Herb Kelleher, former CEO and Chairman of Southwest Airlines. After his informative, and even touching remarks about "how Southwest Airlines expresses love," Kelleher spent a couple of hours fielding questions from the small group. We will never forget his answer to one of the questions because it was so instructive about Southwest's philosophy and approach.

The questioner prefaced his query with the observation that Southwest Airlines had managed to maintain a distinct culture and quarter-on-quarter profit for over 30 years. The questioner asked, "Is setting a company culture in motion a once-and-done thing, or do you have to keep working at it over time?"

Kelleher looked at the man as if he had lost his mind, and said, "You have to work at maintaining a culture every single day!" He went on to describe several actions he had personally taken that month alone to "push back bureaucracy."

Here's something to contemplate: The work of the senior team is, one might argue, to build and maintain a culture—a *strategy-capable* culture—every single day. Yet this possibility presumes that senior team members are working in concert. Research into the functioning of top teams says that a high level of top team alignment is rare.

You will recall that in Chapter Three, we cited research saying that no impediment is more corrosive to an organization's success than a lack of alignment at the top. The study we cited was conducted by professors at Sloane Management School. They found that of a dozen "silent killers" of strategy, top team misalignment was the most deadly (Beer & Eisenstat, 2000). In fact, so crucial is alignment to a company's success that when reviewing a potential buy, most stock analysts will look here—to a company's ability to execute its strategy in a coordinated way—before examining the quality of the strategy itself (Huselid, et al., 2005).

One of the most powerful constraints to teaming at the top is the incentive system, which almost always is built to reward individuals, not teams and are so strategy-misaligned that they literally reward competitive vs. cooperative behavior among executives. A second and related complication is that senior leaders tend to be competitive individuals who have been rewarded for competing, not cooperating. Many executives are effective team leaders but poor team members. Many can foster teamwork among those who report to them, but struggle to cooperate with those at their level.

A third impediment has been identified by Richard Hackman (in Coutu, 2009) and his colleagues at Harvard Business School, one that may surprise you as it did us: Not everyone agrees who is even on the leadership team! When they asked members of 120 top teams who was on the team, only 10 percent agreed on the same names!

Hackman, et al., discovered yet another cause of team ineffectiveness: Senior executive groups often have no clear and agreed upon purpose that would unite their individual strengths into a collective effort. Many bosses prefer to manage on a 1-1 basis and rarely bring the group together for collective work. If the team members have no shared accountability, why should they cooperate? They have no reason to. An example of this is the "Debating

Society," described in the box, "Five Sub-Optimal (But Common) Senior Teams" on page 194. Obviously, it takes no cooperation or thoughtful combining of skills and insights to debate; you achieve this goal by doing the opposite.

But if senior team alignment is so important, exactly what is it? This chapter answers that question in two ways: from the standpoint of agreement on the *content* of the strategy, and from the perspective of *group dynamics*. One might also employ the terms cognitive and interpersonal to refer to the two realms in which team alignment has to occur, the former referring to the intellectual aspects of the team's work, i.e., sifting through strategic options and setting priorities, the latter referring to the group dynamics that affect the work of the team. While there is some overlap between the two, each needs to be addressed and alignment maximized.

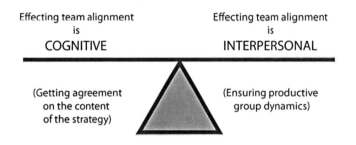

Effecting team alignment is **COGNITIVE**	Effecting team alignment is **INTERPERSONAL**
(Getting agreement on the content of the strategy)	(Ensuring productive group dynamics)

We hasten to point out that alignment, while definable from both standpoints, is never fully realized and is not accomplished once-and-for-all. Alignment ebbs and flows with interpersonal dynamics and across strategic objectives. Alignment in both domains must be managed continuously.

In this chapter, we will identify where "alignment leakage" occurs in both domains, and will offer guidelines and suggestions for achieving accord in the content and group dynamics areas. Because a high level of alignment is necessary for strategy execution, the team leader—and, indeed, the team itself—needs perpetually to monitor and manage it. The good news is that it *is* measurable, hence manageable.

A note on vernacular. The phrase "top team" is common parlance for the group of managers or executives at the highest level of

Five Sub-Optimal (But Common) Senior Teams
Is your team like one of these?

❑ **Information Exchange.** This group gathers principally to provide one another with an update of current activities. When asked to describe their team, the members often say, "Oh, we aren't really a team." And they're right: They don't make decisions or oversee any collective work at all. They are a collection of individuals.

❑ **Debating Society.** A step up from merely exchanging information is a senior group that devotes time to grappling with issues that affect the organization. Driving the debating society is a boss who believes that a vigorous competition of ideas is necessary to promote good thinking. Good news: They're actually attempting to bring their collective brainpower to the challenges at hand. Bad news: Quite often these debates are fruitless or worse—they *reveal* positions, but they also *polarize* positions.

❑ **Royal Court.** The purpose of this group is to pay homage to a central power figure, usually the CEO. In this collective, the boss is often domineering and narcissistic. It's as if the group's sole reason for existence is to listen to the boss expound.

❑ **Commiseration Group.** The team is hapless; it sees itself as unable to engage the next levels in the work of strategy execution. As a result, this group believes the organization is sliding downhill because others won't pull their weight. There is camaraderie in a Commiseration Group, but for the wrong reasons.

❑ **Inquisition Panel.** Some domineering CEOs believe that only when executives from the next level are brought before the senior group and vigorously challenged will they do their best thinking. The meetings held by such a person are a bit like a rude reality show, only instead of the possibility of winning something; the contestants face only the opportunity to escape punishment.

a given business organization. In everyday usage, the term is used whether that group functions in a coordinated, collaborative way, or not, or whether its members are in intellectual agreement with strategic aims, or not. It is tedious and pedantic, we feel, to avoid using the word team except to signify a "good" team, i.e., one that meets these criteria. Thus, we use the term to refer to the senior leadership group regardless of how well it functions. We can and will, however, make distinctions regarding alignment across the two domains and the degree of alignment between and among the members of such groups.

Alignment: A Group Dynamics Perspective

In the market-leading companies, the top team not only creates the organization's business strategy but also executes on that plan in a collaborative way, i.e., it marshals and manages the resources required to achieve those goals. If the organization has a vague formula for winning, employs run-of-the-mill business processes, and cannot make the best use of its talent and other assets, the senior "team" is probably not truly functioning as a team.

From a group dynamics—or process—point of view, here is our four-part definition of an aligned team:

1. A team is aligned when members see its purpose as a stewardship group, i.e., as the organization's caretakers and overseers as well as the primary drivers of its success.

2. Such a team creates and executes strategy which includes identifying and developing the organizational capabilities required to execute the strategy (vertical structure, lateral processes, people processes, etc.).

3. Members see the team as their primary affiliation, not the functional organization that, by title, they oversee (marketing, operations, sales, etc.).

4. The members behave with one another in an open, collaborative, and supportive way. Conflict is seen as not only inevitable but also as potentially desirable and is resolved in a

constructive way.

Most top teams operate quite differently from the description above. The box "Five Sub-Optimal (But Common) Senior Teams" on page 194 lists several common manifestations of leadership teams that we see in our practice—all dysfunctional. Does one of these descriptions fit your team? If so, its functioning undoubtedly handicaps strategy execution in your company.

A Model of Team Development
(Adapted from Drexler-Sibbet)

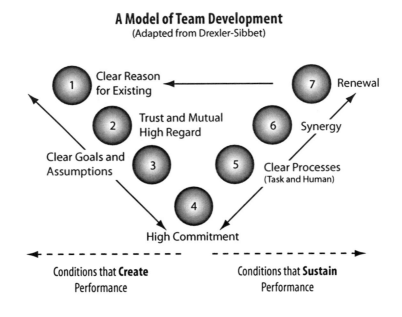

Figure 9-1: The Drexler/Sibbet Team Performance Model

Sometimes top team misalignment shows up in the form of competitiveness—either covert or overt—sometimes in the form of out-of-sync efforts. When powerful people drag their feet instead of actively supporting one another, everyone loses. This is also true when executives appear to agree on strategic objectives, but really don't because they cannot find ways to constructively deal with the differences among them.

Here is an example: In one consulting engagement, serious team misalignment became apparent only after a $300 million project became alarmingly behind schedule. In our initial interviews, we discovered that some of the executives on the top team thought the investment was a waste; they didn't agree with the commitment at all. Others on the team had three different ideas as to what benefits should flow from the investment, and thus each was supporting competing project outcomes!

A common definition of a team is a group of people who need each other to achieve common results, and who work in concert to achieve them. To operate at a high level of teamwork, members must arrive at a state of accord in several areas. Those areas are shown on The Drexler/Sibbet Team Performance Model in Figure 9-1.

Senior Team Assessment		
Yes/No	Arena of Team Functioning	Dimension on Drexler/Sibbet Model
	We function as stewards of our organization, i.e., we define the business we're in, create the organization our strategy requires, and monitor results.	1-Clear reason for existing
	There is a high level of trust, mutual regard, and respect among the members of our group.	2-Trust and mutual high regard
	The members of our team agree on the top five things we need to accomplish to achieve 80-90 percent of our strategic aspirations.	3-Clear goals and assumptions
	The members of our team have a high commitment to the group and its success.	4-High commitment
	We have clear and agreed-upon norms and processes for functioning as a team.	5-Clear processes
	As a team, we work more or less seamlessly together, achieving a high level of results.	6-Synergy
	The members of our team constructively work out disagreements and conflicts as they arise.	NA

Figure 9-2: This simple assessment can be used to gauge team functioning.

This model reflects the dynamic nature of team development: When teams are effective, it is because they have answered questions relating to content, i.e., *what* we do (reason for existing, goals and assumptions, processes), and to process, i.e., *how* we do it (with trust and mutual regard, commitment, and synergy). Answering some questions—chiefly, what is our reason for existing and what must we do to foster trust—produce the conditions that *create* performance, while answering others—e.g., by what processes and norms will we work?—*sustain* performance.

The arrows in Figure 9-1 are meant to show that team development is dynamic and that regressing is as possible as moving towards greater maturity. As circumstances and opportunities change, the functioning of the team can be impacted. Interpersonal alignment must be assessed continuously. In teams, as in marriages, relational depth comes about because the parties resolve the inevitable conflicts that arise, in this case around questions like, "What is this team all about?" "How should we operate?" and "What we are trying to accomplish?"

On the Figure 9-2 assessment, the most aligned teams meet all criteria. Their members have consciously (thoughtfully, openly, deliberately) come into accord in all seven areas. Except for the last item, the statements parallel the elements of the Drexler/Sibbet team model. These criteria set the teamwork bar high. Getting there is hard work. Yet, as we tell our clients, the punishments for lackluster organizational performance are far more painful than the costs associated with meeting the requirements for team success.

Alignment: A Content Perspective

There are three key tasks that the senior leadership teams accomplish from a content perspective. We covered in Chapter Six how this work differs from the tasks accomplished by middle-level managers and frontline employees. The senior team, i.e., the Strategy Stewards...

1. Define the business the organization is in. This includes articulating the organization's:

    •   Mission: Its reason for existing

- Vision: The idealized future the organization intends to create

- Values: The ideals of the organization they will hold dear as they go about fulfilling their mission and vision

2. Develop business strategy to deliver value and show how this will create financial results.

3. Build the organization capabilities required to deliver on the strategy, including developing the talent required to execute on the strategy.

This work, although essentially cognitive in nature, is addressed in a social and psychological context as we've been exploring. Team members are humans, often with vested interests in particular outcomes that favor their own agenda. And even when they cooperate with one another, they can still cripple an organization if they disagree on which goals are worth pursuing, the consequences of pursuing those objectives, and a host of other details. Anyone who has been a part of any meaningful negotiation knows that nearly everyone can agree to a vague, high-level goal; conflict shows up more frequently as the details get worked out and the implications of the agreements become clear.

Early in our careers, we tried to help clients effect top team alignment by focusing almost exclusively on group dynamics. We have since adopted an approach to working with top teams that forges teamwork by focusing on both the interpersonal domain and the cognitive domain. Here are a few facts that will tell you why focusing on both are important. In three recent projects, we found that:

- The 17 core leaders in a for-profit health care setting had 74 separate areas of concern about a new strategy even though there had been superficial agreement on that strategy for three months.

- The executives overseeing a proposed software installation identified 186 concerns among themselves regarding the supposed benefits of the technology despite the commitment of many millions of dollars six weeks earlier.

• Sixteen executives identified 23 ways in which a costly internal service function failed to add value to the business.

None of this is remarkable; every big strategic initiative has its
problems. The key here, however, is this: Those areas of concern,
disagreement, and conflict will kill success and careers in the absence of a process that surfaces and resolves them. A subsequent
section, ""Measuring and Maximizing Strategic Alignment" on
page 202, describes a process for surfacing and addressing these cognitive misalignments.

Aligning a Top Team: Two Glimpses Inside

What goes into effecting top team alignment? As a means of answering, here are two glimpses inside recent top team alignment
projects.

Far-Reaching Strategy Shift

Our client, a CEO, had just received board approval for a far-
reaching strategy shift that would change the very DNA of the
organization. He asked us to help him chart the course for the
organizational transformation the strategy would require. The very
nature of the company would shift from that of a product company (they produce highly technical supply chain standards) to a
service company (expert-driven advisory services for implementing
the standards).

In responding, we conducted 45 interviews with senior executives, customers, and board members. The interviews revealed,
among other things, a dysfunctional senior leadership group and
an organizational structure that was incapable of supporting the
new ambitions.

First, we engaged the group in the task of creating a set of
norms they wished to live by as they went forward; they told us
in no uncertain terms they did not currently function as a team.
Then, we engaged the group in beginning to build a strategy map

(see Chapter Eight). The approach we take to developing strategy maps is highly interactive and involves several rounds of engaging deliberation and idea synthesis. We commissioned small groups to create sections of the map, which they then presented to the other groups for review and critique.

After this, we asked, "What is the nature of the team that has to drive and execute on this strategy?" The output of this segment was a Team Charter stating the purpose of the group, its mission, values and the desired behaviors that relate to the values. They agreed that they needed to function in a considerably different way going forward than they had at any point in the past. At intervals, we called on team members to tell about a time in the past when they were members of effective teams, what these teams were like, and how they operated. This, too, required self-disclosure, but in a safe way.

Toward the end of the meeting, we took the group through an exercise that generated a set of design criteria for the new organization. We then formed follow-up teams to accomplish three tasks: recommend a new organizational structure, finalize the strategy map, and devise a means of engaging employees in a coordinated pursuit of the new strategy. This work took many weeks and was punctuated by regular progress reports in face-to-face settings. Today, team members are collaborative with one another and their meetings are highly productive.

Cats and Dogs

The senior executives of a large department in the research division of a pharmaceutical company spoke ill of one another to colleagues and occasionally would refuse outright to help one another during crunch times. Professional jealousies exacerbated a general lack of interpersonal skill. After many years of unresolved tensions, cooperation at lower levels across organizational boundaries was almost nonexistent as well.

When we came on the scene, the company had just been forced to stop selling a major revenue-producing product due to safety issues. As a result, the company's senior-most executives had asked every organizational unit to find greater departmental efficiencies. Our client, the division head, knew he needed help.

The division executives pointed fingers at one another during the interviews we conducted, making it impossible to determine who had caused what problem. To us, this didn't really matter, though; we weren't there to fix blame, but rather to help them get on with the task at hand. Operating on the principle that most people have far greater appetite for creating a new future than resolving the problems of the present, we took the team off site and helped them create a set of design criteria for the new organization.

Subsequently, acting as process facilitators, we met with the team on four occasions to create recommendations for redesigning the organization. Then, in GE "Work-Out" fashion, members presented their redesign recommendations to the next level of management along with a fresh charter for the team and a set of norms they wished to function by.

While the redesign work was occurring, we arranged for a coach to work with each of the executives, including the boss. Each executive received four, two-hour coaching sessions directed at improving his or her ability to deal with conflict. Each created and implemented a plan by which to repair their relationships with their colleagues. The boss received coaching on how to build a team as well as how, from the leader's position, to manage conflict.

As a result of this intervention, the team began to function more as a cohesive, aligned whole, and found ways to involve the next two levels of management in carrying out the redesign. Two years later, the team functions effectively.

Measuring and Maximizing Strategic Alignment

Because alignment on the content of a strategy is so crucial, especially in enterprise strategies, new software-driven approaches to alignment are emerging. One is the SchellingPoint methodology (SchellingPoint.com). (SchellingPoint is one of our strategic partners.) This methodology is designed to forge leadership concordance around the content of the strategy. The SchellingPoint (SP) process generates a mathematical calculation of like-mindedness, highlighting potential problem areas where strategic interests and perspectives diverge. This methodology employs sophisticated measurement processes, collaboration techniques, and decision-making mechanisms, all of which cultivate deep levels of consensus.

The SP process results in a quantifiable measure of the degree of alignment among executives on a strategy's key drivers, potential derailers, and questionable assumptions. The assessment confirms areas of agreement, but also pinpoints important differences that constrain success.

The term "Schelling point" comes from the work of American economist and 2005 Nobel Prize laureate, Thomas Schelling. It refers to the phenomenon that, in the absence of communication, people will tend to employ a particular solution—they will converge on a point—because it seems "natural" and "right" to them. The objective of the SP process is to create that like-mindedness and thus, strategic alignment.

The SP process is especially useful where there are multiple stakeholders and where the risks of strategy failure are especially consequential, e.g., in R&D applications, merger integrations, ERP installations, and new-product launches. The SP process is designed around the knowledge that alignment breakdowns typically result from a failure to secure agreement—or like-mindedness—in one of four areas:

- Goals: We agree at a high level, but have never discussed specific targets or how to measure our efforts.

- Unintended consequences: We have not thought through all of the implications of what we're setting out to accomplish.

- Barriers: We have not fully considered all of the roadblocks to success, and therefore have not put contingency plans into place to address them.

- Assumptions: We assume we can find venture partners or that we can secure regulatory approvals, but we have not discussed this.

Observing that because most people do not like conflict, SP consultants point out that many strategic discussions center on

204 M<small>C</small>K<small>NIGHT</small> • K<small>ANEY</small> • B<small>REUER</small>

non-controversial subjects (e.g., we need to penetrate new markets), or occur at such a high level that known and tacit perspectives do not get on the table. Unpublished SchellingPoint research
reveals that in most cases, there is no more than 40 percent alignment among top executives about the goals and objectives of their
strategy.

In brief, here is how the SchellingPoint process works:

1. **Interviews.** A sample of outspoken stakeholders who are
   knowledgeable about the issues, identify goals, assumptions,
   barriers, and unintended consequences from their perspective.

2. **Survey.** Interview findings become the basis of a survey which
   is filled out by all stakeholders to quantify alignment.

3. **Analysis.** Specific areas of alignment and misalignment are
   discovered and quantified in the four areas. Areas of agreement and disagreement can be identified across organizational
   units and even individual executives.

4. **Reconciliation.** The results are fed back to the key leadership
   group which reconciles all disparities.

5. **Roadmap.** The group constructs a strategy map, complete
   with goals, measures, owners, and initiatives.

Hallmarks of Teams at the Top

Effective teams spend considerable time together.

We have found that the typical senior executive group spends less
than 12 hours a year formulating strategy, less than one hour per
month! This is simply not enough—and when you consider the
time required to create an implementation plan, it's appalling. On
the other hand, the best teams we've seen spend a lot of time together, at times collectively, at other times working in 2s, 3s, and
4s as team sub-groups. Two or three days a month in team activity
is not excessive if the time is well managed.

Effective teams build in time for asking for help, sharing learning, and celebrating successes.

In the build up to Desert Storm, Lieutenant General William G. Pagonis (2001), Army Director of Logistics, oversaw the massive logistic preparations leading up to delivering 150,000 troops, with their weapons, ammunition, and supplies to forward positions in record time. In most cases, their weapons and ammunition were there before the troops arrived. How did he do it?

For one thing, Gen. Pagonis had two meetings a day with his officers. The first, in the morning, was a stand-up meeting during which each functional officer made a status report. In the afternoon, a sit-down meeting had a different focus: "three up, three down." Each of his reports would talk about three things they had accomplished since the last meeting and three areas they were struggling with. Officers were not punished for talking about struggling; as a result each had a chance to ask for and receive help from the others.

Leaders demand teamwork.

We advise our clients to look each team member in the eye—in the presence of their peers—and ask each if he or she can be counted on to act like a teammate. This may need to occur more than once.

We once worked extensively with a top team of a *Fortune* 50 company in a turnaround situation. The team was considering devoting millions of dollars to a set of interventions that could lead to the organization's transformation. During a two-hour meeting, the CEO listened intently to the presentations and the debate, but said nothing. With only 15 minutes to go in the meeting, he finally spoke. "We have just heard some presentations about what we can do to transform our company. We must decide if it's worth the investment. Personally, I'm not sure it is, i.e., without the most important ingredient: complete and total support by everyone in this room."

He paused. Then he said, "I want to go around the room, hearing from each of you. I want to hear your answer to two questions: 'Can the others in this room count on my complete support for this initiative?' and 'What will that support look like?'" Believe us when we say this: he got buy-in.

Effective teams use coaching help.

Team expert Richard Hackman has discovered that leadership coaching and individual development can work against team skills because these experiences focus on individuals, not teams. Team skills are best learned in the context of team work. When a team coach or consultant is present for the launch and formation of a team and for follow-up sessions to reinforce learning, everyone benefits.

Leaders of teams at the top don't tolerate non-team behavior.

The impact on a team of a high performer/poor team player—someone who gets strong financial results but whose behavior is irksome, competitive, or worse—can be profoundly counterproductive, for both a top team and the entire organization. If you wish your pronouncements on the importance of teamwork to be taken seriously, you must confront anyone on the team whose behavior works against collaboration.

Where to Start

The wise CEO sees an aligned senior team as the epicenter of strategy execution, but also knows that true teamwork comes at a price: becoming a team often requires working through significant conflict. By conflict, we mean a vigorous exchange of ideas about the strategy, the purpose of the team that will execute it, and how that team will operate.

Top team building, at least as we see it, yields benefits of at least two kinds: the *rational* kind, e.g., plans, scorecards, strategies, initiatives, and the like, and the *emotive* kind, e.g., commitments, agreements, and trust. As we've been saying throughout this book, plans are necessary but not sufficient. Also needed are the loyalties and goodwill of the members, individually and collectively, towards team and organizational success.

The path to real teamwork begins with a team charter: who are we and why are we here? What's our work and how do we do it? That discussion has to begin and end with the strategy, but in the middle, there is rich discussion of how that strategy can be rolled out and measured. At every turn, non-team behavior has to be called out and team effort rewarded.

To build a top team, target the following results:

1. Forge agreement on the strategy and direction for the enterprise.

2. Conduct a diagnosis of the current capabilities of the organization, guided by the question, "To what extent can the organization support our strategy?"

3. Compose a charter for the leadership team that specifically calls out their primary role as strategists and strategy implementers.

4. Create a strategy execution plan that includes:

   - What organizational changes need to occur to support the strategy and why they're necessary

   - What business processes, if any, have to be changed or improved

   - An employee engagement strategy that turns employees into partners with management in the strategy execution process

   - A compelling "story line" to use in communicating the strategy

5. Form teams to pursue each aspect of the execution plan.

6. Ensure individual and team commitment to execution throughout the organization and support managers and units in implementing the plan.

Action Learning

Exercise 1: Determine which type of team you are.

Use the assessment tool, "Five Sub-Optimal (But Common) Senior Teams" on page 194, to determine if your team needs to step up its game. Hand out a copy of the assessment at your next team meeting, and ask each person to identify which description fits your team when it's falling short of its potential.

Exercise 2: Assess your team's functioning.

Using the assessment, "Senior Team Assessment" on page 197, pinpoint arenas in which your team fails to function at a high level of performance. Again, hand out a copy of the assessment at your next team meeting, and ask each person to rate how effective the team is in each area.

Exercise 3: Identify which tips are best for you.

Review the "Hallmarks of Teams at the Top" on page 204, and answer the question: Which of the tips in this section are most germane to our team, i.e., what do we have to do to become more adept at driving strategy execution?

Exercise 4: Read about creating a high-performance team.

There are a few good books on this subject. If you have not read one, do so. Don't worry about some of the "old" publication dates: This material is timeless. Listed by author name, some of them are:

Lencioni, P. *The Five Dysfunctions of a Team: A Leadership Fable.* NY: Jossey-Bass, 2002.

A big best-seller, this book teaches through story. It makes the most compelling case we've ever seen made for the top team to be aligned more to their work as a collective than to their work as individual, functional leaders. We feel the title is unfortunate in that it emphasizes dysfunction not high performance, but the overall tone of the book is positive and very instructive.

Hambrick, Donald C., Nadler, David A., & Tushman, Michael
L. *Navigating Change: How CEOs, Top Teams, and Boards Steer
Transformation.* Boston: Harvard Business Press, 1998.

These are some of the top names in organizational consulting. Their advice
is directed mostly to CEO-led teams, but the principles hold for all leadership teams.

Katzenbach, J. R. *Teams at the Top.* Boston: Harvard Business Press,
1998.

A classic, the first of its kind on the modern business scene, this book is still
widely read by CEOs and senior administrators of all types, over 10 years
after first appearing.

Kotter, J. *Leading Change.* Boston: Harvard Business Press, 1996.

This is probably the most widely read book on organizational transformation. Its focus is somewhat broader than just the team, but it has very useful
guidance on how to use a top team to drive change, especially if you're a
CEO driving enterprise-wide change and transformation.

Chapter Ten

HR's Role in Strategy Execution

I believe that HR should be judged by its future
more than be bound by its past.
—Dave Ulrich, 1996

The times may be changing. But HR is not.
—Carroll Lachnit, 2009

WHILE HUMAN CAPITAL IS THE basis for creating value in most organizations, human assets are the least understood by business leaders and therefore, the least effectively managed. Of course, many in Human Resources agree with this, but many of HR's critics have pointed to HR as doing little to solve this problem. Indeed, when McKinsey researchers interviewed over 800 CEOs on the topic not long ago, only 36 percent could agree that, "the strategic plan was meaningfully integrated with human-resources processes—incentive, evaluation, and compensation systems" (Dye, 2008, p. 5).

Many of HR's most strident detractors believe, probably correctly, that line executives will withhold their full endorsement for HR until HR can show—quantitatively—how it contributes to strategically important goals. Several of the most well-known authors in the field of Human Resources have written detailed volumes on how to accomplish this, including Brian Becker and his colleagues (2001) who wrote *The HR Scorecard: Linking People, Strategy, and Performance.*

We are of two minds about this particular book. On the one hand, we recommend it because it spells out more clearly than any other publication we know of how to connect measurement of the organization's human performance to bottom line metrics; it defines the contours of a new and important HR competency—HR strategic measurement. But on the other hand, we have some problems with this book—and much of the related "strategic HR" literature. Appropriately, this book and similar literature urges the reader to adopt the view that HR can and should play "a central role in implementing the firm's strategy." So far, so good. But then the authors put forth the view that "the most potent action HR managers can take to ensure their strategic contribution is to develop a measurement system that convincingly showcases HR's impact on business performance."

Surely HR's "most potent action" with respect to strategy implementation goes beyond proving its own worth!

HR professionals—at least theoretically—are better positioned than anyone in the organization to play a leadership role in the organization's strategy execution effort because:

- HR has an organization-wide purview, i.e., is involved in the business in its entirety.

- Strategy implementation is largely a human capital issue; HR by its very title has meaningful responsibilities in this territory.

- The skill set required for employee engagement and the inclination to use it is more concentrated in HR than anywhere else in the organization.

- HR systems and processes are—or could be—critical drivers and enablers of business strategy.

The term "strategic HR" appears frequently in the literature. Articles and books that use this term generally urge HR professionals to become more active in shaping strategy and function as a partner to line management in running the business. HR has moved admirably in this direction, but there is evidence that HR, as perceived by line management and HR alike, is not moving fast enough or getting involved deeply enough in the organizational change aspects of its role. (More on this to follow). When strategies have to change, organizations have to change. And when organizations have to change, people and processes will need to change. In our view, no one is better positioned than HR to lead these efforts.

Because HR professionals feel pressure to make their organizations more strategy-capable but don't always know how to respond, HR is vulnerable to fads that purport to enhance the capability of the organization but do not. Anyone who has knocked around the corporate world for a long time (or even a short time!), has seen HR-led programs launched to great fanfare that have only the vaguest relationship to the company's strategy. For example, we were asked recently to comment on a client's leadership development plans. Reviewing the five-day (yes!) curriculum that the top 300 leaders in the company would attend, we noted that there was no plan even to mention the company's strategy! Included in the plans we saw were segments on emotional intelligence, group dynamics, culture change, and diversity, all topics worthy of study by any manager. But there was to be no discussion of how these topics would contribute to strategy execution. Promoting context-less training programs is bad HR practice under any circumstances. In hard economic times, it's inexcusable.

As line executives demand more from HR, professionals in the field often have two reactions: They are both pleased and daunted. Implicit in the line's expectation is an indication that HR is needed by the line, and it's nice to be needed. But at the same time, it is not always clear how to meet those expectations. Many of our recent engagements began when the head of HR revealed a lack of familiarity with strategy execution, i.e., what it is, what HR's role should be in it, and how to partner with the line to drive the organizational change called for by their changing strategy.

Lawler and Mohrman (2000) are among many who claim that, "the HR function should be positioned and designed as a strategic business partner that participates in both strategy formulation and implementation." Perhaps we're adding to the pressure that HR professionals feel when we say, as many do, that we believe the word "participates" in the Lawler and Mohrman statement should be changed to "leads." HR function should be positioned as not just a partner, but as a leader in the strategy implementation process.

Yet recent systematic research, conducted by Lawler and Boudreau (2009), and presented in their report, *Achieving Excellence in Human Resources Management: An Assessment of Human Resource Functions,* makes clear that HR is not making a lot of progress. In this 2008 report, they observe the following:

- HR has made almost no progress since 1995 in becoming involved in creating business strategy.

- The amount of time HR spends on rote, administrative activities has not declined significantly since 1995.

- Similarly, HR professionals spend almost no more time today than they did in 1995 functioning as a strategic business partner (up to 26 percent from 23 percent).

Observing that a lot has changed since 1995, HR blogger Carroll Lachnit (2009) was moved to say, "The times may be changing. But HR is not."

The Four Jobs of Strategy Execution model can be useful in helping HR professionals think through their role in strategy implementation. In addressing Job One, HR would support line managers in ensuring that employees understand the strategy. To accomplish Job Two, HR would work with the line to increase employee commitment to the strategy. In accomplishing Job Three, HR would support work units in connecting their efforts to the strategy, eliminating all off-strategy work and beginning new work that is strategy-driven. Finally, for Job Four, HR would help design strategy-capable organizations and effect organizational and cross-functional alignment.

We believe that as HR learns to support the organization in doing these Jobs, it will forever put the question of its value to rest. HR professionals need apologize no longer for not being financial or engineering or marketing geniuses; HR professionals can—and should— be implementation geniuses.

HR as Change Agent

The model in Figure 10-1, below, developed by Dave Ulrich (1996), asks the HR professional—at least the HR function—to play four roles. Like many others in the field of HR, we value this model and agree with it. We also find it formidable: To be expert in four distinct competency areas is a lot to ask of anyone or any function. Many HR professionals—even very good ones—struggle to come close to this ideal.

Figure 10-1: Ulrich's four roles for "HR Champions"

Of the four roles, the research clearly shows that HR plays the bottom two better than the top two—in the view of HR *and* in the view of the line. This is problematic at a time when those HR contributions are being outsourced. HR has always been challenged to prove its worth, but today, the stakes are higher than ever.

According to more recent research conducted by Ulrich and his colleague Wayne Brockbank, where HR is perceived by line executives as making a meaningful contribution to business performance, HR professionals display competence in four areas (Ulrich & Brockbank, 2005). Paraphrasing, those competencies are 1) company culture management (they help define and create it), 2) driving fast organizational change, 3) strategic decision-making, and 4) business literacy.

Since 1987, the Society for Human Resource Management (SHRM) and Dave Ulrich of the Ross School of Business at the

University of Michigan have conducted studies at intervals to define and refine a model of HR competencies of greatest value in business settings.

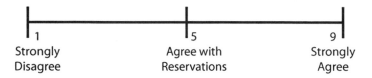

HR AS STRATEGIC PARTNER ASSESSMENT

Rating	Dimension
	1. The input of HR is essential in formulating our business strategy.
	2. HR in my company is expert at driving the organizational change called for by our strategy.
	3. HR is central to efforts that realign our organization's structure, systems, and processes with our strategy.
	4. When line executives need to make changes to the organization (structure, processes, etc.), HR is seen as an indispensable partner and resource.
	5. HR is providing me the support I need to fully engage my employees as partners in the pursuit of our strategic goals.
	6. The HR professionals in my organization function far more as partners, as opposed to cops or enforcers.
	7. The HR professionals who support my business are fully knowledgeable about my business priorities and concerns.
	8. I can rely on HR to help me educate employees about our strategic objectives and to engage employees as partners in pursuit of them.

Figure 10-2: HR strategic partners satisfy the line in several ways.

The 2007 version of this model says that the key to HR effectiveness lies in being a "Credible Activist." Line executives not only listen to such persons, but also see them as business equals. A Credible Activist is proactive, offering a perspective on how to achieve business results and challenges the assumptions of others if necessary. The researchers use the term "HR with an attitude" to describe this individual, referring to the person's assertiveness and advocacy. Competent HR professionals, say the researchers, also possesses several other skills essential to strategy execution:

Talent Manager/Organization Designer

Helps build systems that attract, develop, and retain talent and contributes to the building of organizational structures and processes that are called for by the strategy.

Culture & Change Steward

Helps define and shape the organization's culture consistent with strategic goals.

Strategy Architect

Has a vision for organizational success that is grounded in customer needs and expectations and contributes to achieving it.

We like this model, for a number of reasons. For one thing, we like that organization design skills show up centrally; HR is not just about developing individuals. For another, we think the model applies equally well—at least the three competencies cited do—to those who lead *any* staff position. Whether you are an HR person, the CFO, or the CIO, you need these competencies. SHRM offers what they call an "HR Competency Toolkit" that, for a fee, HR practitioners can use for self-study that reviews the competency study research, explains the six competency areas, and provides what the SHRM site calls "development resources...designed to help you build your competence in the areas you identify as most critical."

As Ulrich and Brockbank put it, "When HR walks into the room...the average 'business IQ' goes up, not down" when HR professionals have the competencies we've been discussing. If you wish to find out if you're perceived this way, ask your business part-ners to give you their most candid answer to the questions in the "HR AS STRATEGIC PARTNER ASSESSMENT" on page 216.

Strategy Land Mines: HR Can Help Materially

Due to organizational inertia if nothing else, every strategy will face some degree of opposition even when everyone in the company agrees that change is completely necessary. The more a new strategy differs from the old one, the more resistance there will be. HR can aid in strategy execution simply by helping the organization antici-pate and address resistance.

In Chapter Three, we reviewed the most common land mines lurking beneath most strategic plans. The HR professional who wishes to be a strategy implementation leader must know which ones are most strategy-threatening for their own business and help line managers and executives identify them, too.

To this end, HR professionals can initiate very useful conversa-tions with line executives by asking these questions:

- "Which of these land mines are most likely to get in our way?"
- "What problems result when these land mines persist?"
- "What measurable business benefits would result from remov-ing or diminishing these land mines?"
- "Which do we absolutely have to address now?"
- "How might we in HR support you in addressing these land mines?"

Execution is Principally a Social System Issue

With few exceptions, the most common impediments to strategy execution are reflections of difficulties or misalignments in the hu-man system, not in technical or financial systems or flaws in the strategy itself. This fact should be, at least in one sense, good news for HR professionals: Where there is trouble in the human system, there are opportunities—and therefore, the need—for HR to show its stuff.

Ultimately, successful strategy implementation requires getting three things right: the social system, the technical system, and the business process system (see Figure 10-3).

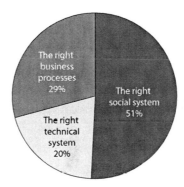

Figure 10-3: Strategy implementation requires getting three things right.

When making strategic shifts in their organizations, most executive teams tend to do a better job of bringing business processes into line with their strategy and identifying the potential benefits of new technology, than they do in aligning the social system with the strategy. This is conspicuously evident in the widespread and well-known failures of enterprise resource planning (ERP) software and other technology installations (SAP, Oracle, and the like). In a famous case, for instance, Nike sued a supply chain management software provider for business losses, claiming the vendor over-promised the merits of the technology. The vendor claimed it was failure of people at Nike to provide needed information. To us, this sounds like a social system issue, not a technology issue.

HR can help effect improvements in both technology and business processes by helping to break down silos and enhance cross-company communication, top-to-bottom, side-to-side. Notice the proportions in the chart in Figure 10-3. The "people issues" are so big that they often overcome otherwise excellent efforts in the other domains.

While these percentages are derived from empirical vs. scientific calculations, our clients have repeatedly validated them. Frequently, we hear it put something like this: "You can get the best technology money can buy and you can identify the ideal process 'blueprint' for your business, but it takes people to wring the value out of the software and to align work with the vision. Without buy-in and cooperation, you're sunk."

Strategy Execution: Where HR Can Start

We have noted that the Four Jobs concept is a systems model of change. It identifies the work that leaders need to do in three arenas of an organization: individuals, work units, and whole organizational systems. This is in contrast to much of the "strategic HR" literature, which quite often focuses on what HR can do to attract and retain *individuals,* motivate and train *individuals,* and enhance the capabilities of *individuals.*

Strategy implementation requires change in all levels of the social system: not just within and between individuals, but in work units, and in cross-functional relationships. As one moves through the Jobs of strategy execution, the work gets more challenging (as in Figure 10-4). It reaches a pinnacle of complexity with Job Four. Why? Because there are more people involved, more organizational systems and processes are affected, and the stakes are higher. We hope this does not seem self-serving, but our advice is to work with a consultant—even behind the scenes—who can guide you through the thicket.

HR professionals can learn—and are learning—to lead the process of strategy execution, but must work in concert with the line to accomplish it.

To illustrate the point, let's imagine the challenges involved if the strategy calls for making shop floor employees in manufacturing part of the sales team like some of our clients are exploring.

Theoretically, by itself HR could accomplish Jobs One and Two without, in any appreciable way, partnering with the line. Traditionally, HR has effectively contributed in this way. HR could, for example, conduct training that enables employees to understand the plan by which they will become instrumental in helping customers choose the right product for them and how to use that product. In addition, HR could help employees learn what will be expected of them in a sales scenario, the rationale behind the shift in role, and even get them excited about playing their part.

It's one thing to get people to learn something; another to cause them to feel motivated to do something with what they learned (Jobs One and Two). It is inconceivable, however, that HR could, by itself, accomplish Jobs Three or Four without the line's full cooperation. To influence how work is done and what work is attempted—the essence of Jobs Three and Four, HR has to have a willing client who wants the help, values partnership with HR, and is willing to at least share the lead.

Easier to accomplish ⬅——————➡ *Harder to accomplish*

Job One	Job Two	Job Three	Job Four
Ensure that employees understand the strategy	Increase employee commitment to the strategy	Align local effort with the strategy	Cause cross-system realignment

HR could do alone ⬅——————➡ *HR must partner with the line to accomplish*

Figure 10-4: The relative difficulty of the Four Jobs

Job Three speaks not only to *individual* change but also to *work units* changing their focus, work habits, and processes. Further, since most strategies require not just one but many work units to make such shifts, Job Three can be a tricky task. To accomplish it well, HR must work intimately with line managers, in settings that HR is not always familiar with, i.e., shop floors, selling environments, laboratories, warehouses, and so forth.

Enterprise-wide systemic change, led from the top by an aligned and deeply committed leadership team is the essence of Job Four. A shift in strategy often requires organizational restructuring, introducing new business and management processes, and other changes. In the present example, if shop floor employees are going to play significant roles in sales, will compensation changes be required? Is the current organizational structure adequate to maximize the expanded role? HR can and should lead the discussions relating to these efforts.

You may recall that in the case of the Cool-Clear-Water example of Chapters Six and Seven, the executive team committed to its board of directors to double its revenue in five years and that the CEO was concerned that the organization's structure was not adequate to support this commitment and asked for our help in making an assessment. Using the Galbraith/Kates Star model to guide our analysis, we were able to help the CEO answer his question about the structure. In the process, we discovered that most of the employee population—those who would be responsible for achieving the aggressive growth targets—did not understand the promise made to the board. Most, in fact, had no idea the commitment was made or why. Those who did know felt little responsibility to play a part in its pursuit. These are problems falling into the realm of our Jobs One & Two.

Immediately, the head of HR volunteered to lead the effort to get employees to understand and commit to the strategic goals. Wisely, however, she also knew that alone, she could not do the work of Jobs Two, Three, or Four. She could not, for example:

- Enable the affected employees to feel energetic about the strategy. This would require full cooperation with managers at the unit level. (Jobs One & Two)

- Align work at the local level with the strategy. Since the strategy called for significant improvements in efficiency, opening new sales offices, and rationalizing product lines, every effected manager would have to engage employees in their area in pursuit of the strategy. (Job Three)

- Finally, that organizational structure would have to change based on decisions only the CEO could make: Job Four. HR and others could provide significant input, but this was a job the senior team had to wrestle with. (Job Four)

HR During Challenging Economic Times

Before we leave the subject of HR's role in strategy execution, let's acknowledge that HR struggles most during times of economic downturns. How can HR make sure it's relevant and contributing?

HR is a favorite whipping boy of many line executives and it gets worse during economic hard times. During downturns, boards and CEOs begin the hunt for cost-cutting targets by painting bull's-eyes on programs that do not have a clear connection with profit-making or cost-containment. Often, HR-initiated development programs are early marks: leadership development, coaching, competency modeling, team building, and so forth. But it is precisely when economic times are tough that HR development is most necessary, especially certain types of it: activities that materially enhance strategy execution.

Making the case for HR development investment when a recession is in full bloom requires you to be on top of your game. HR professionals need to make a strong case showing how development programs contribute to achieving the business objectives most crucial to senior line executives. The best HR response to encroachment is not to get defensive, but to get proactive. The best way to do this—not only during hard times, but at all times—is by showing how development programs contribute to tangible business success.

Here are some guidelines.

Use the Language of Business, not "HR Speak."

When advocating for development programs, use the language most familiar to line executives. During difficult times, boards and CEOs care most about profit: quality of profit, sustainability of profit, volatility of profit. To the extent to which you can show how leadership coaching or another development program addresses these needs, they will be better listeners. Rather than emphasizing how a leadership development program, for example, will address problems identified in the recent employee survey, show how leadership development will enable the business to achieve its profitability targets. If this argument isn't possible, put your energy into something that *does* solve a business problem. Argue for the "scalpel approach" to cost-cutting vs. the across-the-board "hatchet approach."

Starting today, in every one of your conversations with line executives, ask what is keeping them up at night. They are not likely to complain that they lack competency models or wish for a new vision statement. Instead, they will speak of things like retooling time, customer response time, bottlenecks, production costs, efficiency, waste, regulatory issues, and sales slumps. HR will prove its worth as it supports the line in addressing and resolving these issues.

"HR-Speak"	"Line-Speak"
• Leadership training • Competency models • Culture change • 360° feedback • Performance management • Vision statements	• Profit quality • Cost reduction • New product launch • Cost of goods • Customer responsiveness • Regulatory incidents and observations • Sales

Which strategic priorities must HR get involved in? Simple: all those that drive profitability. HR should continually review its initiatives and ask itself questions like this: "We're spending a lot of our energy on leadership development. If the line's biggest problems have to do with reducing cycle time, lowering waste, and forging new financial arrangements with strategic partners, how is our leadership development contributing effort to this—or is it?"

Measure HR's impact—in Terms of *Business* Results, not *HR* Results.

We said earlier that HR professionals need not apologize for not being financial or manufacturing, sales, or marketing geniuses because they can—and should be—*implementation* geniuses. This will happen as HR measures of success are in alignment with the organization's financial measures of success. Please don't be offended if you believe your HR agenda is already in sync with the business agenda. We're simply urging HR professionals to make sure the function truly serves the core purpose for which everyone draws a paycheck.

Arena	HR-Relevant Business Measures
ROI/Workforce Productivity	Revenue per employee and incremental revenue per new hire (If you contract more than 5 percent of your workforce through contingent workers, include those costs in your calculations.)
	Recruitment: Time to fill, opportunity cost of unfilled positions, e.g., lost sales, quality of hire, and diversity hires at various job/organizational levels including senior management
	Performance appraisal: Ratings distributions by job categories and organizational levels; turnover percentage of low and high performers; promotion of top performers
Organizational Climate/ Employee Engagement	Employee engagement, morale, discretionary effort, satisfaction
Retention And Turnover	Retention: Turnover overall; turnover of key players and high potentials/key jobs; diversity turnover; cost of turnover-recruitment costs and lost productivity/sales
Cost And Quality Of HR	Overall financial impact of HR activities over the time period (ROI on human capital employed)
	Internal ratings of HR functions and services
	HR budget as portion of company operating budget—variances and causes
Compensation And Rewards	Compensation and rewards allocation and linkage with performance management process and statistics
	Base and variable compensation allocated per business unit/ function
	Employee satisfaction with compensation
	Competitiveness of compensation in the industry or region

Figure 10-5: HR-relevant business measures

In developing metrics, the key is to identify those critical few measures that senior management needs and wants as part of the overall business dashboard—i.e., those that tie directly into the strategy map if there is one or, if there isn't (typically), that would tie in if there were. At all costs, avoid developing metrics in a vacuum, and provide the decision makers with what they need for guiding the business—and no more. This can be established through front-end consultation with the CEO, COO, and CFO. But be wary of just "filling orders": you want to be responsive, but *your* views matter as well.

We find that senior executives tend to be interested in five categories of HR-related measures. Figure 10-5, "HR-Relevant Business Measures" on page 225, shows these along with more discrete measures that relate to them.

Forge a tight, partner-like relationship with the top line executives.

As the HR function perfects its contribution to strategy execution, it functions less as a cop, expert, or pair-of-hands and far more as a partner. A partnership is one in which both parties are working toward the same goal. Each has "skin in the game." Become exceptionally open to feedback as to how you are aiding or not aiding the line in accomplishing its goals and how the relationship is working/not working. Such a stance is in stark contrast to the disconcertingly frequent HR habit of telling line functions what problems they have, what they have to do to solve them, and how they must do so.

Be a tenacious coalition-builder.

Related to building *partnerships* is building *coalitions*. If a partnership is a dyad that works well together, a coalition is three or more parties synchronizing their efforts in pursuit of a goal. We said earlier that of the four Jobs, Job Four is the most potent because it involves moving big change levers and affecting change at a fundamental level. Doing this work almost always requires coalition-building. Next to the CEO, HR is better positioned than anyone to get three or more powerful people to join forces, but HR professionals are next-best positioned. "I try to find ways to lock them in a room and force them to work things out," one of our HR clients said of key line executives whose cooperation is needed to effect strategic change. By another name, this is coalition-building. John Kotter's book, *Leading Change* (1996) is probably the most widely read book on this topic.

Employ "Action Learning" processes.

Leaders develop best, i.e., fastest and most efficiently, through action learning programs targeted to specific business objectives. If belt-tightening is important, work with line executives to assemble SWAT teams. And get more bang for the buck by using skilled facilitation to drive the deliberations and to get participants to exchange feedback on their effectiveness at intervals. Work with the CEO and line executives to identify projects that will have impact on productivity (cost, margins, and needed innovations). HR gets a lot of "points" by initiating these discussions proactively.

Similarly, focus coaching on helping selected leaders achieve specific business targets. Coaching that focuses directly on helping leaders achieve pressing financial objectives will be seen as more important than coaching that focuses on more general outcomes, e.g., "developing greater executive presence," because it *is* more important.

Don't curtail coaching altogether during challenging times; rather, emphasize it in areas where the business needs to improve performance, providing it to leaders whose efforts will contribute most to these goals. The CEO will want to trim coaching expenditures if he or she cannot see how they contribute to profitability. It is the HR professional's job to show how coaching will help.

Cost-cutting is often associated with reductions in force. In turn, talented younger managers are frequently thrust into assignments with bigger responsibilities than they have ever faced before. Coaching support for these managers can pay off hugely. A skilled coach can help these managers avoid common stumbling blocks that any new manager faces when taking on a new role and can help them think through strategy implementation issues that a more seasoned manager would not miss.

Provide mission-critical support.

Support mission-critical groups of employees in sustaining productivity. If economic hard times generate stress at the top of the organization, they cause even more stress at the middle- and lower-levels, often in the very work units where productivity is most crucial.

The most overlooked organizational asset when it comes to sustaining and increasing productivity is the middle-level manager. You can support your workforce most efficiently by supporting their managers. Training targeted to sustaining engagement and productivity has an obvious ROI. When employee reactions to organizational change threaten productivity, HR can almost be heroic by:

- Helping executives create and communicate a unified message about change

- Sponsoring learning experiences for managers that develop the skills necessary for sustaining productivity during challenging times

- Supporting managers in mission-critical areas as they lead change in their areas

Become more business literate.

Below is a checklist of things you need to know about your business if you wish to lay claim to being deeply business literate. How many can you check off? Where you are not able to check off an item, get the knowledge it speaks to. In our experience, almost without exception line executives who have this knowledge enjoy sharing it. Seek them out. Learn it.

I know...

❏ The annual revenues of our business (and, if relevant, for each of our business lines)

❏ Where our revenue comes from and where it goes (how much to taxes, overhead, etc.) and how much is left in the form of profit

❏ What our market capitalization is (and what this means)

❏ What our price/earnings ratio is (and what this means)

❏ Who our major customers are and on what basis they buy our products and services (i.e., price, solution, ease of use, quality, etc.)

❏ The share of market we enjoy in each segment of our business

❏ The market forces that most impact our business

❏ How HR can help address those forces

❏ What three things are most apt to keep each key line executive awake at night

❏ How HR is helping those executives get more sleep

Become more sophisticated with respect to organizational change.

When HR disappoints the line, it does so because it emphasizes administrative and legal matters over the type of support line managers need in the realms of organization design and change management. If you feel that your weakest competency area is in organization development (OD) and organizational change—as most HR people do—find and take a good course on the subject. You won't regret it.

Some HR professional organizations now offer courses for their members with titles like "OD 101." The OD field offers a variety of methods and tools for enlisting large numbers of employees as partners with management in driving change including Future Search, Open Space, and Appreciative Inquiry. If these terms are foreign to you, sign up for that course ASAP.

Suggestion: Enroll in the learning experience together with the line executive you most need to support. Attending together can create the opportunity for the two of you to build a coordinated approach to strategy execution.

As appropriate, use trustworthy outside partners to support your effort.

At the risk of seeming self-serving, consider reaching to outside partners to help you put together and pursue your approach to helping the organization align itself with its strategy. It does not display inadequacy to do so. In fact, objectivity and creativity may require it. Reflecting the myopia that can result by being a deeply imbedded part of an organization for a long time, Edwards Deming, the famed Quality guru, said, "A system cannot transform itself."

Action Learning

Great opportunities can accompany periods of great challenge, not only to adapt but also to grow. We cannot overemphasize the crucial role that HR can, and must, play in leading during tough times. To do so, HR must be laser-like in its business focus and partner with line leaders to fulfill the business strategy. It's hard work, but in doing this, HR positions itself to get its considerable expertise used, the source of greatest satisfaction for most HR professionals.

Exercise 1: Do the HR Assessment.

If you are the head of HR in your organization, complete the questionnaire, "HR AS STRATEGIC PARTNER ASSESS-MENT" on page 216, in two rounds: first, by yourself then in a meeting of your staff. Discuss the implications for needed change. You will note that this questionnaire does not allow for shades of grey: either HR is delivering the goods, or not. If you are not the head of HR, consider going to that person and, in the most constructive way you can, engage him or her in a conversation about the needs you have of HR that are not being met. Make clear requests about next steps.

Exercise 2: Revisit how HR measures its success.

If you are the head of HR, don't stop with an internal appraisal of your function's effectiveness: get some feedback, preferably from those line leaders whom you most need to support. If you're feeling brave, identify the line executives you most struggle with and start there. Review how your organization measures its success and ask line executives: "Are we measuring the right things?" and "How would you change what we measure?"

Exercise 3: Build your own strategy map.

Based on this feedback, build your own strategy map for HR. Make sure the objectives of the line organization you support are clearly articulated in the Customer Results segment of the map. Go back and review your map with your "customers," i.e., the line executives you support. Ask them, "Are we getting this right?"

Exercise 4: Read Amy Kates' article on HR organization design.

Listed below is the best article we know of on the subject of redesigning HR so that it is more capable of supporting the business. This article has won awards for its usefulness to HR leaders. We urge you to read this article, learn its lessons, and apply them to your own organization.

Kates, Amy. "(Re) Designing the HR Organization." *Human Resource Planning.* 29:2.

Chapter Eleven

Right People, Right Place, Doing the Right Things

*No duty the Executive had to perform
was so trying as to put the right man
in the right place.*
—*Thomas Jefferson*

*We should make war without leaving anything to chance,
and in this especially consists the talent of a general.*
—*Maurice de Saxe*

IN A RECENT INTERVIEW, ERIC Wiseman, CEO of VF Corporation, described an ambitious goal for his organization: Raise revenues from $7B to $11B in the next three years. Wiseman told the interviewer, "If you sit in my office, with a growth plan [like mine] you'll see that I need three things: I need a strong financial lever, I need brands that are winning against the competition, and I need talent. Money and brands don't do me any good if I don't have the talent (in Hansen, 2009)."

Wiseman's perspective is shared by many who have profit and loss responsibility. "If only we had more (fill in the blank: high potentials, super-keepers, fast-track) people. Then we could achieve our goals." It's as if organizational performance is the aggregated effort of the super talented.

Like many others, we believe that talent is crucial to organizational success, which is why we've written this chapter. But we don't believe that a cadre of "super leaders" can, by itself, revitalize a moribund company or make a good company great. Identifying and nurturing outstanding individuals will not—alone—bring your company back from the brink or turn it into a dynamic powerhouse. In fact, if cultivating the talent of high potentials is your *only* approach to talent management, you are apt to demoralize the other 98 percent who do not make it into this elite category.

Develop Everyone, But Not in the Same Way

Let us make explicit a talent management theme that we have been working implicitly throughout this book: Within reasonable limits, *develop everyone*. Throughout this book, we have described numerous instances in which organizations accomplished unexpected results where the real "heroes" were "ordinary" frontline managers and employees, not an elite crop of whiz kids. While strategy execution benefits from segmentation of talent and greater investment in the development of some employees over others—we go into this in greater detail later in this chapter—do your best to support everyone in your organization in playing their part in the strategic drama. As we explored in Chapter Six, involving employees in decisions that affect their work (through work unit meetings), leaves everyone more business savvy and does not require heavy time or dollar investments on anyone's part.

Managing Talent: Some Challenges

When developing a talent management system, it is important to recognize and manage the inherent flaws and pitfalls in *every* process for assessing talent—performance appraisal, talent management and development, or succession planning. Consider this: The ability to identify and develop talent is driven by a firm's recruitment, selection, appraisal, development and rewards processes. Each of these processes is often flawed with inconsistency and bias based on *faulty assumptions,* among them are these:

- Top performers—almost exclusively—are responsible for achieving business results.

- We know how to assess performance and do it well.

- Most people's potential is fixed.

- The rating manager has a broad and objective understanding of an individual's performance and potential.

- This person has the wisdom, sophistication and insight to discern performance and potential across many employees.

- The cultures within various business and work units are identical, and therefore provide a stable context for assessing performance and potential across the organization.

There is no "silver bullet" for resolving these challenges to a talent management system. Over the past twenty years, each of us has witnessed numerous executive teams build faulty performance management and appraisal systems and then, when those systems fail, move on to the next iteration without learning or fixing anything. Don Quixote, anyone?

We are in a new business era where increasing numbers of employees work remotely, in actual or virtual networks, on temporary teams, and in diverse project groups. Additionally, the employee population has become increasingly diversified in age/race/gender mix, ethnicity, skill sets and knowledge specialization. The essential nature of work has shifted from role-bound and hierarchical interactions to fluid collectives of people working together in collaborative networks. For these reasons, it has become much more difficult—but no less important—to accurately observe, measure and assess individual performance.

Fitting Talent Management to Strategy

Once the business strategy is clear, focused and well communicated, attention must turn toward finding and placing the right people in the right roles, specifically those jobs with the greatest potential impact on results and business success. This can be done without creating a nucleus of elites and, as we've said, pains must be taken to avoid doing so.

The best strategy implementers consider talent management holistically, i.e. as a "total systems" approach. In this regard, HR plays—or should play—a key role in designing and leading the process. All of the following processes pertain to—and must integrate with—the talent management process:

- Organization design
- Job design (key jobs)
- Objectives and accountability cascade (e.g., MBO)
- Performance evaluation
- Recruitment and selection
- Rewards management
- Career development
- Succession planning
- Learning and development

Please note that designing and instituting these processes is not "once and done." These processes must be assessed or reassessed in light of new or changing business strategy to ensure their continuing relevance and utility for driving talent development *and* strategy execution.

There are three key tasks to be completed in doing so:

- Clarify the specific performance indicators necessary to guide "people decisions."
- Clarify the roles that are key to driving strategy and the specific competencies each requires for success.
- Ensure that the right people are in those key roles and that they possess the competencies, both operational and behavioral, to deliver results needed.

Based on our experience in managing the boundary between

talent management/development and strategy execution, we have formulated a definition of what we call "key talent." In our view, key talent can be defined as those relatively few individuals who...

- Occupy or who are eligible to occupy key roles within the organization which are critical to strategic success.

- Have proven their ability to consistently perform well above expectations and job requirements.

- Have the capacity and potential to influence key results and business outcomes, including the ability or potential ability to develop other organizational leaders and teams and whose value system is consistent with that of the organization.

As we have been saying, the foundation for identifying, placing and developing key talent is the careful construction of the right organizational structure to fulfill strategy and the design of key jobs/roles within the structure. When these elements of design are absent, the process of identifying and placing the right people in the right roles becomes haphazard, the process often defaulting to specification of existing—and less relevant—accountabilities and competencies which are misaligned with the strategic direction of the firm.

Right People & Right Roles

Just as an organization should segment its customers, it should also segment its employees. While all employees should be engaged, educated about the strategic aims of the company, and meaningfully involved in decisions that affect their work (Jobs One-Three), beyond this a different approach to managing talent is required for each employee population. Given the strategy, some people with certain skills will be more crucial to the organization's success while others will be less so. Attending more to those whose talents are crucial and scarce just makes sense.

Acting on this point means that organizational leaders—ideally guided by the head of HR—will meaningfully differentiate among employees and employee groups *in terms of the strategy.*

One common—but faulty—approach to this is to identify the organization's best performers, perhaps via performance appraisal data or polling among executives, and then to bend over backwards to improve their employment experience. A more strategic approach, in the words of a study conducted by The Conference Board (2006), is "to ensure an organization has the right people in the right places at the right time and at the right price to execute its business strategy."

Managing the Value of Talent

Role Impact (Risk of Skill Shortage)	**CORE Roles*** The "Engine of the Enterprise," unique to the company and core to delivering its products and/or services	**STRATEGIC Roles*** Critical to driving long-term competitive advantage, with specialized skills or knowledge	Roles that *affect* the strategy
	NON-CORE Roles* Talent whose skill sets no longer align with the company's strategic direction	**REQUISITE Roles*** Cannot do without, but whose value could be delivered through alternative staffing strategies (other than full-time headcount)	Roles that are *affected by* the strategy

Skill Complexity (Cost of Talent)

* The names of the roles and the descriptions are drawn from The Conference Board, 2006.

Figure 11-1: A scheme for managing the value of talent

According to the Conference Board study, best practice in talent management engages leaders in discussions that examine the strategy for its workforce implications. By taking a three-to-four year perspective, and segmenting roles based on their importance to the strategy, leaders can agree to investments that align compensation, training and development, selection, and "on-boarding." Once needs have been identified, subsequent work with middle-level managers enables tactical workforce planning.

Consultant Peter Louch introduced us to his concept of Talent Value Management some years ago. Drawing on concepts from supply chain management, Louch uses a two-dimensional matrix to drive talent management discussions. (See Figure 11-1.) We have relabelled the quadrants using terms from The Conference Board study because the terms employed in the latter seem more explanatory.

Going from most crucial to least crucial to strategy execution, those roles can be defined as follows:

Strategic Roles

These are roles the organization needs to maintain its sustainability in the marketplace, its momentum, and its growth. Those occupying these roles carry, guard, and nurture the DNA of the organization and, indeed, create it. If the nature of the organization changes over time, i.e., its value proposition, it is because people in these roles decided a change was necessary. For example, at Fix-a-Bone, Inc., the medical devices company mentioned in Chapter Eight, occupying strategic roles are people with backgrounds in life-sciences who also know how to *bring this knowledge to the marketplace.* Thus, those who have life-sciences backgrounds *and* expertise in product development and marketing in the life-sciences arena are both crucial and rare.

Core Roles

These are roles without which the organization's promise to the marketplace cannot be delivered. Given that Fix-a-Bone specializes in instruments, implants and biomaterials to repair bones and connective tissues, people in this category of talent are biomechanical engineers, materials scientists, and salespeople with deep backgrounds in the life-sciences. Those people must be knowledgeable enough to consult with surgeons as they make decisions about which of the company's devices are applicable in a given circumstance.

People in Strategic and Core roles tend to be scarce and their skills command handsome salaries.

Geoffrey Moore (2005), in his exceptionally clarifying book, *Dealing with Darwin: How Great Companies Innovate at Every Phase of Their Evolution,* observes that if a firm does not innovate, its offerings become a commodity, by which he means that prices stabilize at or below cost. The antidote is innovation, of the kind that creates differentiation. The need for innovation is most obvious in companies that sell cutting-edge products and high-end services. But it is also necessary in those that are playing the commodities game, i.e., those pursuing the operational excellence model. The activity and results of innovation look very different across the value disciplines and the roles required do, too. To quote Moore, to win "you must take your value proposition to such an extreme that competitors either cannot or will not follow."

Requisite Roles

Roles in this category are essential to conducting business, but the contributions made by people in these roles does not vary a lot across companies. For instance, most companies today require deep expertise in information technology, but this does not mean those roles are either Core or Strategic—unless the company is in the business of developing cutting-edge IT products and/or services. Even then, only certain types of skills and competencies in IT could be considered Core or Strategic, i.e., those most figural to the company's value discipline. A good test of whether a role fits into this category or not is to ask two questions: "Do we need these roles to function?" and, if yes, "Could we conceivably get along by *outsourcing* these roles?" If the answer to both is yes, the roles fall into this category.

Non-Core Roles

As firms change over time, especially as their value discipline changes or their product and service lines evolve, what had been Core or Requisite roles can become peripheral. People in these roles are most often transitioned out of the company, although in some cases they are re-trained. Thus, as computer manufacturers and computer users moved away from mainframe computing, many workers who formerly wrote code for and designed these machines were laid off or "re-skilled" so they could play more valuable roles.

Talent Management Term	Definition
Job	A set of responsibilities
Job description	A narrative description of responsibilities along with how and why they are important to the enterprise or function
Competency	Measurable capabilities required to carry out the responsibilities of a given job which includes the skills, qualities, and knowledge required
Skill	The abilities needed to do a job (e.g., a doctor must be able to diagnosis and prescribe)
Qualities/Traits	Personality traits thought to be necessary to performing in a role or job
Knowledge	The information or conceptual mastery a job requires
Competency model	A detailed description stated in behavioral terms of the knowledge, skills, and qualities required in a given role

Figure 11-2: Definitions in common usage for talent management

Detailing the Roles

Once the structure of the organization is in place, leaders must define the key roles within it. Designing specific jobs to ensure alignment of skill, experience and behavioral requirements with strategic objectives can be demanding, a discipline in itself. HR professionals experienced with job design are essential partners in the process. Job design sets a foundation for ensuring that job roles "fit" with strategy. Well-designed role definitions establish a basis for performance objectives, fair and accurate appraisal, employee development, talent management, succession planning, and performance management. Role design should not be an exercise in a bureaucracy, but kept as simple and straightforward as possible.

Role/job design entails three essential tasks:

• Specifying the 4-5 key accountabilities or "deliverables" that the person in the role needs to produce

- Identifying and explicating the competencies, skills and experience requirements of the role

- Defining the behavioral traits and characteristics required for successful job execution

While accountabilities and competencies should be logically and pragmatically aligned with and derived from business strategy, behavioral traits must also be aligned with and supportive of the desired organizational climate and culture. Behaviors of key people in key roles have a powerful influence on shaping culture and setting performance standards throughout the organization. Figure 11-2 provides some useful definitions for doing the work.

Right Behaviors

Key behavioral traits and job competencies need to include both "hard" competencies—more quantifiable, less people-oriented, i.e., "Theory E"—and "soft" competencies—less quantifiable, more people-oriented, i.e., "Theory O." Beyond technical and job-related skills and competencies, the acid-test of talent is the capacity for influencing others, i.e., leadership. Given the difficult economic climate, the boom in technology globalization, and rapid change, the need for leadership has never been more acute. Talent management strategy and processes, therefore, must concentrate on identifying current and future leaders, at all levels, who can take the organization forward.

As organizations downsize, flatten, outsource, globalize and become increasingly virtual in their ways of working, the need for both formal and informal leadership talent becomes crucial. By "formal leaders," we mean employees who occupy positions of positional authority over others, i.e., those who hold managerial or executive roles. As vital as these employees are, the influence of informal leaders should not be overlooked. These are people who, by their behaviors and relationships, positively influence and motivate others without having positional authority. Such people exist at nearly all levels. Best practice calls for identifying and channelling the influence of these people. Some organizations call them "Change Agents," "Change Champions," "Change Advocates," and the like. For guidance about identifying and using them, see Chrusciel (2008).

Leadership Must Focus Less on This...	Than on This...
Compliance	Fostering commitment
Managing	Facilitating/empowering/enabling
Delegation	Coaching/mentoring
Functional/hierarchical focus	Trusted partnership across boundaries
Communicating	Networking and enlisting
Organizing	Aligning
Conforming	Innovating/Pathfinding
Individual accountability	Collective accountability
What *is*	What could be
Leading through position power	Leading through example

Figure 11-3: Leadership behaviors required in the past vs. now

The need for the type of leadership provided by those in roles we have called Strategy Stewards (in Chapter Six) is—or should be—provided by those at the upper levels of the organization. These leaders most greatly influence the performance capability of the firm and also its climate and culture. Therefore, rigorous succession planning must continue to play a key role in the overall talent management strategy and system: Leaders should be identified and a "pipeline" for these and future leaders established and managed.

At the same time, the need for leadership at the lower levels has never been more pressing. Workplaces no longer can function hierarchically with a command-and-control management culture. Today many employees operate in global and virtual collaborative relationships, disparate cross-functional teams, temporary project teams, remote working environments, and often on a 24-7 schedule. Additionally, companies have come to rely on parallel workforces comprised separately of contractors, temporary workers, and consultants. Leadership influence is less command-and-control from the top and more informal leadership from the bottom up. This shift calls for radically new skills, competencies and behaviors than those of traditional management.

What are the "right behaviors" essential for building strategic alignment and extracting discretionary effort in this new era? Figure 11-3 displays a "from-to" summary of behaviors and traits which describe the requisite shift in leadership roles and behaviors.

Our colleague, Karol Wasylyshyn, executive coach and authority on leadership, defines essential leadership behaviors gleaned from her vast experience in clinical psychology and coaching C-suite executives (Wasylyshyn, 2008):

- Emotional fortitude: The ability to utilize self awareness and self management to influence and develop self and others

- Attunement: Empathic understanding of others

- Resilience: Ability to deal effectively with change, ambiguity, pressure and adversity (we like to call it "grace under pressure")

- Emotional intelligence: Awareness of one's own and others' emotional states; thoughtful in responding to others; aware of own impact on others

- Relational capacity: Ability to collaborate and create networks and alliances

As you can detect by glancing at this list, many of these speaks to personality traits and attributes that reflect in behavior but emanate from an inner psychological maturity. On this point, our esteemed colleague, Mark Feck, former EVP, HR for Rohm and Haas Corp., says, "Leadership is an inside out job."

The talent management system must ensure that the new leadership competencies are well defined, articulated in the context of strategy, and become the cornerstone of the firm's core people practices. Senior management must assume primary accountability for defining the requisite behaviors and competencies.

Talent Management in Tough Times

The current economic downturn takes *some* of the urgency away as many companies scale back their workforce and flatten their hierarchies. But these realities only exacerbate other difficulties: they further limit career advancement opportunities and development dollars become scarcer. The financial services and automotive industries are salient examples of this.

When times are tough—and otherwise, for that matter—how much time, focus, and resources should top management commit to the systematic cultivation of talent necessary to fulfill the business strategy? The general answer is, of course, *enough* time, focus, and resources! We aren't trying to be cute: The precise answer varies company by company and strategy by strategy.

Despite today's chaotic environment, companies that seek competitive advantage must continue to develop focused short- and medium-term business strategies and cultivate the talent necessary to execute strategy. In his book, *Winning*, Jack Welch (2005) describes the importance he placed, as CEO of GE, on the evaluation and development of top performers and high potential talent. Similarly, Larry Bossidy, former CEO of Allied Signal, states that he spent from 20 percent up to 40 percent of his time and energy to finding, placing and developing talent and successors for key jobs within the organization (Bossidy & Charan, 2002). That may seem like an inordinate amount of time and attention for a CEO to spend on talent development. But if people, especially strategic leaders, are key to successful strategy execution, then what better use of time is there than for the CEO to carefully select and develop people for key roles?

Action Learning

Senior management often loses sight of the essential fact that strategy can only be accomplished through people and that key people in key leadership and tactical roles need to be positioned as catalysts for driving the results ordained by the strategy. This chapter attempts to define the philosophy, processes and approaches to finding and placing the right people in the right roles in order to produce results consistent with organizational strategies and plans.

Exercise: Segment your talent.

Being strategic includes identifying the key roles called for by your strategy and doing the talent management essential to it. In this regard, the matrix in "Figure 11-1: A scheme for managing the value of talent" on page 238, can be exceptionally useful. In your next strategy-related discussion, ask the questions below:

1. Given our strategy and its related value discipline, what roles go into each category on this matrix?

2. Which roles are in short supply? Which are in abundance?

3. What actions must we take to ensure an adequate supply of talent in the Strategic Roles? Core Roles?

4. Are we managing the bottom tiers as well as we can? What should we be doing differently?

Chapter Twelve

Leading Strategy Execution

There is only one leadership malpractice:
wasting the lives of those we lead.
—*Susan Cramm*
CEO, ValueDance

Leadership involves finding a parade
and getting in front of it.
—*John Nesbitt, futurist*

YOU'VE NOW ACCOMPANIED US FOR eleven chapters. Given that, you are probably a person with high achievement needs, i.e., someone who is committed to getting results and making things happen.

Perhaps you are in your 30s or 40s with ambitions to lead a company or major division some day. Perhaps you are reading this book as part of an MBA program or you're an HR business partner supporting a business and you wish to deepen your skills in helping your business partners execute strategy. Perhaps you're already leading a major business or nonprofit organization. Regardless of your circumstances and ambitions, from a strategy execution standpoint, there are certain things you—and you alone—can and need to do. Partly as a way of summarizing the book, we will tell you what those things are—in as linear and sequential a fashion as we can.

A word about tone. Up to this point, we have attempted to take the voice of the patient, respectful teacher, speaking nondirectively about how others have gone about executing their strategies and what you can learn from them. In this chapter, though, we will speak directly to you in an unvarnished way as if you were a coaching client. We will do so because others are looking to you for leadership and depend on you to do a good job of it. And fair warning: At several points, we are going to urge you to employ a consultant to accomplish certain things. OK, we're biased and given many peoples' experience with consultants, we wouldn't be at all surprised if you were cynical about this bit of advice. Does it help if we tell you to hire a consultant but not to hire *us?* Fine, then.

OK. Let's get going. Time is a'wastin'!

Lead and Manage (Both)

When we begin working with our coaching clients, we review Harvard Business School professor John Kotter's now classic distinctions between management and leadership (1990). Essentially, Kotter defines the task of leadership as producing useful and adaptive change. We like this definition because it implies movement, improvement, conscious and chosen evolution, and intentional transformation. We also like it because it's a muscular, vigorous, and assertive view of leadership: To lead is to make things happen, things that are different, better. Leadership is about taking people, processes, and organizations to a new, better place.

We contrast this with Kotter's definition of management which he essentially defines as getting things done on time and on budget. Like leadership, management is also active, but its action takes place within the constraints of budgetary and other resources. As former New York Governor Mario Cuomo was fond of saying, politicians "campaign in poetry and govern in prose." In a parallel sense, if leadership is poetry, management is prose. The leadership and management tasks of strategy execution, at least as we define them, are listed in Figure 12-1. We will discuss each.

Leadership and Management Tasks Required for Strategy Execution (SE)	
Leadership Tasks (Intrapersonal and interpersonal in nature)	Managerial Tasks (Analytical and sequential in nature)
Make yourself fit to lead Examine—and revise if necessary—your inner narrative about how to motivate others Construct and tell an inspiring story of change Build support for the vision among the stakeholders Celebrate!	Assemble your team and devise a strategy—together Undertake a SWOT analysis Build a strategy map, beginning with the selection of a competitive advantage Develop design criteria then diagnose the fit of your organization with the criteria Begin making organizational design changes Break down the strategy into achievable chunks & enlist the middle Monitor and follow up relentlessly

Figure 12-1: Leadership and Management tasks in strategy execution

We tell our clients, just as we tell you now, that Kotter was right: when it comes to strategy execution, neither leadership nor management is more important than the other; both are necessary. If you wish to become adept at executing strategy, you must improve your leadership game *and* your management game. Both focus effort and generate energy, but they emphasize different things and produce movement of a different nature. Somehow and some way, you have to accomplish the tasks, summarized in Figure 12-1. We'll discuss all of them in this chapter.

Make Yourself Fit to Lead

Many business consultants, scholars, and HR professionals have pointed to leadership as what is required to compete in today's business environment. They note that only through highly skilled leadership can businesses maximize the most expensive and potentially beneficial asset they have: people. As former Herman Miller Chairman, Max DePree (2004) put it, "The signs of outstanding leadership appear primarily among the followers."

This is an appealing formulation, but there is a problem: recent polling data reveals that, as a class, many of today's business leaders are failing. Consider this headline in a report from The Center for Public Leadership (2010): "Business Leaders Are Out for Themselves, Americans Say." According to the underlying study, "In 2005 through last year, Americans' confidence in their leaders marched steadily downward." In 2010, the report says, "Only 10% of Americans believe business leaders generally work for the greater good of society; the majority (52%) believe corporate bosses work mainly to benefit themselves."

Ouch.

Clearly, if you wish to be effective as a leader of strategy execution, you have to induce quite a different perception in the minds of those who look to you for leadership. If there is any good news at all in this study, respondents were speaking of business leaders in general. We know from other studies that when people rate leaders as a group, they are more critical than when they rate their own boss.

Still, if you wish to implement a strategy, and to the extent that your strategy departs from the status quo, you must gain the trust of those whose support you need. Thus, our first requirement for the personal art of strategy execution:

Learn to listen and to reflect.

Most business leaders do not have to work on being more decisive. Rather, becoming more effective entails learning to listen better, a component of trust and respect. In our experience, the higher you go in the organizational hierarchy, the less you're apt to find people—either men or women—who are good listeners. This is a problem for at least two reasons. For one thing, if you don't listen well to others, you can't pick up useful clues about how to influence them. For another, it makes learning more difficult because you overlook feedback about the effects of your own efforts and you think you know it all.

We have stated that strategy execution requires both leading and managing. Each involves getting groups and individuals to want to do things in a particular way and on a given schedule, often to make sacrifices in the pursuit. The leader/manager, therefore, must continually discern the needs of those people and find ways to meet them, if possible, within the realities and limitations of objectives and resources. This is impossible without careful listening.

The closer you get to the top of most organizations, the more you find the psychological profile of a type of leader that is notably deficient at both listening and reflecting. Psychologist David Keirsey, in his classic book, *Please Understand Me*, summed up this type: "If one word were to be used to capture this style, it would be *commandant* [his emphasis]. The basic driving force and need... is to lead, and from an early age they can be observed taking over groups (1978, p. 178)." Noting that this type will strive to reduce inefficiency, ineffectiveness, and confusion, this type of leader is also quite willing to dismiss employees who don't go along. In an update of this book 20 years after the first edition, Keirsey (1998) did not change his view. He said, "For [this type], there must always be a reason for doing anything, and people's feelings usually are not sufficient reason (p. 198)." Question: How can you win the hearts and minds of people if you are indifferent to their feelings? Answer: You can't. (Readers who are familiar with the Myers-Briggs Type Indicator will recognize this as the ENTJ. According to the Myers & Briggs Foundation [2010], less than 2 percent of the general population are of this type while 11 percent of managers, administrators and executives score this way on the MBTI.)

Some people think that doing so is a sign of weakness, that leadership is a matter of making bold decisions in isolation then announcing them. In fact, for most business decisions, "two heads are better than one," i.e., the data required for effective decision making is distributed and a variety of perspectives are beneficial. Good listening skills enable you to get all the data on the table.

Going along with listening, of course, is the companion habit of reflection, i.e., turning over in your own mind what you've heard while all that listening was going on. A reflective person not only hears, but also comprehends and makes sense of what is heard. Reflection is a nonjudgemental process of discernment. To discern is to derive meaning and direction through reflection.

Both listening and reflecting are most difficult when the subject matter is your own behavior, especially when you've been told that your behavior is slowing things down or eroding teamwork. Carefully attending to the concerns and objections of others *about you* is the ultimate test of ego strength. But the reward is learning and the greater potency that comes with it, so stick in there.

Strategy execution can be hard, taxing work—gird yourself.

The good news about having a vision is that life feels exciting, but the bad news is that unless you do everything right, *you* are the only one excited by it! Recently, a client, back in his office with us following a very successful meeting with all of his management staff, look drained. He said, "I'm thrilled at how this meeting went, but, my god, this is hard work." Asked what he was referring to specifically, he said, "To effect change, you have to do everything right and you have to be *patient!* You don't know how many times I had to bite my tongue in that meeting. Holding back is not my strong suit!"

Be credible and trustworthy; be worth following.

In Chapter Five, we summarized the findings of David Maister, whose research showed the causal linkage between acting in accord with a set of values and principles and subsequent financial success in service-delivering firms. The title of the book we cited is, *Practice What You Preach: What Managers Must Do to Create a High Achievement Culture* (Maister, 2003). The essence of his findings was this: when managers show respect and cultivate trust, morale ensues. And higher morale leads to greater financial performance.

We urge you to take a look at this book and learn its lessons.

Bear in mind that one of the reasons why people sometimes drag their feet at the first sign of change is that change begins with an ending. While the leader's own drive to make change happen can be a powerful force, there are countervailing restraining forces. Our counsel is, "Don't be discouraged, but do be prepared."

There are any number of excellent books available today that address the connection between physical fitness and stamina and creativity. Get and keep yourself in good physical shape. If you're over 50, like we are, you might especially enjoy the wise, insightful, and funny book, *Younger Next Year* (Crowley & Lodge, 2007).

Examine—And Revise if Necessary—Your Inner Narrative About How to Motivate Others

Consultant and author Peter Block (1991) once opined that the six most overused words in corporate America are, "People are our most important asset." In truth, very often businesspeople don't have a clue about what motivates others, or if they have that knowledge, don't use it well. We were reminded of this recently when *Harvard Business Review* reprinted a 35-year old article (in 2003) written by Frederick Hertzberg entitled, "One More Time: How Do You Motivate Employees?" According to Wikipedia.com (2010), this article was first published in 1968 and the magazine sold 1.2 million reprints of it by 1987.

The gist of Hertzberg's observation is this: Motivation is determined by internal and external factors. Internal factors have to do with one's experience of work and how those experiences line up with internal drives and needs. Each person is differently and uniquely driven. For example, one person desires a keen sense of achievement, another longs for recognition, a third for responsibility, and still another for a general sense of competence. (Hertzberg called these "motivators.") While these inner motivators are exceptionally powerful, external factors in the work environment (he called them "hygiene factors") are important, too, but tend to mobilize behavior *only when they're absent or out of whack:* pay, advancement, job security, and so on. When present, they don't compel, but take them away and this is all a person wants to focus on. Most people aren't really driven to pursue money, for example, but let pay be at risk and they are plenty "motivated" to secure it.

What is the lesson? Don't expect that everyone will be "motivated" by the promise of future rewards; most aren't. And what "motivates" one person does not necessarily motivate another; you must differentiate among the people you wish to influence and treat them as the individuals they are. Want an instructive learning experience? List the names of your direct reports and write down what you think motivates their best effort. Then go ask them if you got it right. Chances are good that you got some right, but also some wrong.

Before we leave the subject of what motivates others, ask yourself which is the more potent predictor of human behavior: rewards or punishments? Common—but wrong—answer is "punishments." Figure 12-2, "Common Myths About Motivation" on page 255, busts this and several other widely held misnomers about human behavior. If you find that your inner narrative about people and what motivates them is far off the mark of what you see in the "Research" column, seriously consider obtaining the services of a good executive coach to help you look at your leadership approach and its effects.

Assemble Your Team and Devise a Strategy

For a time, a book entitled *The Five Dysfunctions of a Team* (Lencioni, 2002) was very popular among our clients. It is one of those teach-through-fable business books. This one has a powerful message that is rarely heard. In the story, a CEO who's new to her role methodically teaches her team of executives what it means to be a team running a business. The CEO tells her direct reports that their primary allegiance is to the team of which she is the leader, not to their functional organizations. She begins to knit them into a powerful collective that—together—runs and grows the business.

Common Myths About Motivation	
Traditional View	Research
People are motivated mostly by money: the promise of it and the threat of losing it.	People are motivated mostly by inner, intangible rewards. Yes, fear of job loss can also be powerfully motivating—in a negative way. The most powerful motivators are to have an opportunity to do good work and to be a meaningful part of a winning team.
Punishment is a good way to change behavior.	Yes, but chiefly for the worse.
Human behavior is completely baffling; it is nearly impossible to comprehend.	Human behavior is readily shaped if you know what you're doing.
People should just do what they're told.	That and $2.25 will buy you a latte.
Performance appraisals are a pain in the backside, and have almost no positive impact on subsequent performance.	True.
People at work ought to be cooperative, but rarely are.	People at work are fully trustworthy to pursue their own self-interest. Most of human behavior is cooperative because it is in one's interest to be cooperative.

Figure 12-2: Common myths about motivation

It is rather remarkable to us how foreign—and even alien—this idea is to many executives. Widespread is the view that strategy should be created by the senior leader *only*, and that the others are there to execute that strategy. Throughout this book, we have been saying otherwise, pointing out that no one leader is smart enough or powerful enough by him- or herself to do all the strategic thinking for an entire organization.

So, learn to create strategy *with* others. If you're so inclined, create your own view before you pull everyone together, but tuck your preconceptions and conclusions neatly away and engage others in dialogue with an open mind. If the group comes up with something wildly different from what you earlier came up with and you're uncomfortable, say so. Everyone knows you're the boss and no one will fight you if your views make sense. If you include others in creating the strategy, they will feel a sense of ownership and therefore, will support it.

As we said in Chapter Nine, how a top team functions—its process—is as important as is its agreement on the content of the strategy. Pertaining to process, as you work with your team to create strategy, precede, punctuate, and end each session with a reminder: "This is your primary team. Your primary job is to function in a collaborative way with others on this team, in building and growing this business. We do it together." As for the content of the strategy, re-read Chapter One before you gather the team to make sure the strategy you create is *executable*.

Undertake a SWOT Analysis

As part of the strategy-creating sessions (there will be many) do a SWOT analysis. As most businesspeople know, such an analysis focuses on organizational **S**trengths, **W**eaknesses, **O**pportunities, and **T**hreats (see Figure 12-3). The first two (S and W) address internal organizational realities; the second two (O and T) speak to external conditions. It's those "Ss" and "Ws" that concern us most when it comes to strategy execution, because they address organizational capabilities that exist or, because they do not exist, threaten our ability to execute.

In our work with clients, we typically conduct the "Strength-Weakness" portion of the SWOT analysis once the strategy has begun to take shape. (The "O-T" portion has come much earlier in the strategy-creation process.) We position this part of the exercise with the question, "Given the strategic intentions and objectives that you seem to be settling on, what organizational powers, aptitudes, and abilities do you have that support you in achieving them, i.e., what capabilities do you have that you need to maintain as you go forward?" This, of course, addresses the Strengths. We are always cautious about how much time we devote to barriers—although we always scan for and list them—because doing so can suck the energy right out of a planning session.

Once identified, those Strengths and Weaknesses can be very useful in identifying organizational design criteria, i.e., the irreducible capabilities our strategy calls for.

SWOT Analysis

	STRENGTHS	WEAKNESSES
Internal	What do we do well that gives us an advantage relative to our competitors?	What deficiencies render us vulnerable to our competitors?
External	OPPORTUNITIES	THREATS
	What favorable possibilities in the environment make the industry attractive?	What external conditions warn of diminished profitability in our industry?

Figure 12-3: SWOT analysis scheme

Select a Competitive Advantage, Build a Strategy Map

We don't intend to repeat all we said in Chapters Seven and Eight on competitive advantage, value discipline, and strategy maps. But we will say this: If you are still unsure what a value discipline is—and which one your organization is pursuing (or should be pursuing)—don't go a step further without this comprehension. Strategy execution is about accomplishing things. You can't accomplish a thing if you are unclear what that thing is!

After you have identified your competitive advantage, you can begin to build a strategy map. As you now know, a strategy map depicts how you will get results in four arenas: financial, customer, business processes, and organizational capabilities. We recommend that the senior team *begin* the creation of the strategy map, but that you form teams (we call them "Strategy Pursuit Teams") led by senior leaders—but populated by managers from the next level—to finish the map. The debate, discussion, and consensus that ensues can be invaluable in completing a strategy execution roadmap, educating people about the business, and generating commitment.

Develop Design Criteria, Then Diagnose the Fit of Your Organization With the Criteria

Once you have your organization's basic strategy established, it's time to ask, "What must our organization excel at in order to execute this strategy?" In Chapter Seven we called the resulting list "design criteria." We offered the following definition:

> *Organization design criteria specify and describe the organizational capabilities that your business or unit needs to have in order to deliver on the strategy (Kates & Galbraith, 2007, p. 216).*

Once you've created your strategy—even at a high level—we strongly advise you to conduct a diagnosis of your organization for its adequacy in executing it. In Chapter Seven, we provided a questionnaire that can guide this process, but seriously consider taking our advice on this: Secure the services of a consultant to conduct a round of interviews with each member of the Strategy Steward team to collect this information. They should use the nine-point scale we provide in Chapter Seven. After they get each number, they should ask, "Tell me why you give it this rating." In the combination of the ratings and subsequent explanations is a rich story about the organization's capabilities and problems. Do *not* distribute this assessment as an anonymous survey: You will miss a huge source of information.

Once you have the data, convene another senior team meeting to consider it. Since it's based on the Star Model (Chapter Seven), consider each dimension (Structure, Business Processes, etc.). Then, identify 1) what aspects of the organization have to be retained into the future (this is key; don't throw the baby out with the bath water!), and 2) what has to change. Where there is considerable work to do, form Strategy Pursuit Teams to address each arena, e.g., coming up with organizational restructuring suggestions if this aspect of organization redesign seems necessary. Charter each Team with a clear statement of purpose, time lines, and desired objectives. Assign a senior leader to each Team for oversight and support.

Begin Making Organizational Design Changes

If your strategy calls for getting results you have never achieved before, no doubt one or more aspects of your organization are out of whack with the strategy. If you used the Organization Design Assessment in Chapter Seven, you know exactly where the gaps are in the fit of your strategy with the organization design.

This summary chapter is not the place to describe how to tackle a complex organizational restructuring project. But you should know this: Until your organization design changes, your organization is likely to continue producing the results it has always been getting. To get different results, you have to put in place a different structure, change the processes, and/or alter some aspect of the social system.

We find that if the organizational structure fails to align with the strategy, that most people will want to start the redesign here rather than with other elements of the design (e.g., the talent management system or a business process). Given that the structure determines, to a large degree, how resources are allocated and decisions are made, most people can't settle down until decisions pertaining to this come about. To the extent that the structure calls for change, the more attention you will have to pay to the psychological aspects of transition, managing resistance, and dealing with buy-in issues. Keep in mind that no organizational structure is perfect, and be sure to change as little as possible. If your strategy calls for a sweeping organizational structure change, even if you *think* it might, take our advice: Employ the services of a consulting firm that fully understands organizational structure, i.e., when and where different structures are indicated and how to minimize the disruption that most structural changes entail.

As for making other organization design changes, keep in mind that you are creating organizational capabilities, i.e., you are putting into place arrangements that enable your organization to deliver value to customers. As stated earlier, we call them "Strategy Pursuit Teams." Most people come to life when asked to play a meaningful part in making organizational improvements, but only when supported with a clear charter, relevant resources, and effective leadership. We have created Strategy Pursuit Teams to address every conceivable aspect of organization design: reconfiguring sales incentive plans, redesigning the performance management system, devising ways to attract and retain key talent, and of course, reengineering key business processes. With the proper facilitation and support, most employees will astonish you with their wisdom and will delight themselves with their new-found pride in their work.

Construct and Tell an Inspiring Story of Change

If you follow the sequence of inclusive activities we've been describing, at some point in the strategy creation process it will dawn on you: You are forging alignment among your direct reports, but precious few others in the organization know anything at all about the strategy (Job One) or care about it if they do (Job Two).

In Chapter Six, we listed "The Five Questions Employees have During Change." They were:

1. What is our strategy, i.e., what change does it require?

2. What will happen if we don't change?

3. What does all this mean for me?

4. What will you do to support me?

5. What do you want me to do?

We described an exercise in Chapter Six that you can take your leadership team through that will help you answer these questions for others. Importantly, this exercise assures that all of you will answer them the same way. As we've noted repeatedly in this book, it is extremely counterproductive when executives articulate different answers to these questions. The objective here is not to parrot a party line—each leader should develop his or her unique style for answering the questions—but to ensure consistency.

Business leaders, like politicians, are practical people. The only reason either is interested in conveying a message or telling a story is to get people to do things. When a political candidate runs for office, he or she wants people to cast a vote in their favor. Similarly, when a business leader opens his or her mouth in a group of employees, he or she has an opportunity to do three things: enable understanding of the company's (or unit's) strategy, effect commitment to that strategy, and bring about action in support of it.

We have closely watched executives for a long time. Most executives have excellent planning and problem-solving skills, polished analytical abilities, are decisive, and possess a mastery of the fundamentals of their business. But they consistently struggle in a number of areas, all of which are leadership-related: enunciating the story of how the business will create value, empathizing with the concerns of employees who have to carry out that strategy, and engaging associates as partners in strategy execution.

Consider the statements in Figure 12-4, all collected from recent observations of high-level executives in the act of attempting to motivate people. We are not making any of this up.

If Figure 12-4 shows how *not* to do it, what does excellence actually look like? Let's answer this from the perspective of a master storyteller, in this case a screenwriter.

A few years ago, we read an interview with renowned screenwriter Robert McKee (Fryer, 2003). The interview was introduced with this teaser: "Forget about PowerPoint and statistics. To involve people at the deepest level, you need stories. Hollywood's top consultant reveals the secrets of telling them." In the interview, McKee commented that most businesspeople are trained to influence others through exclusively rational means: data, argument, rationale, and lists. But as McKee pointed out, any salesperson knows this is not what compels a person to buy something. A good salesperson connects logic with emotion. Storytelling is the best way to do this.

When we buy products or ideas, or give our allegiance to a cause, we do so not because *the speaker* thinks it's a good idea, but because *we* come to think it's a good idea. And we get there through our feelings. Nothing is more effective than a compelling story for this purpose.

Leader Statement	What's Probably Going Through the Listeners' Minds
"I am going to present my vision so you can move it to the future."	"Why should I move *your* vision to the future? What about *my* vision?" "Why don't you move your own vision?" "Does this have anything to do with me?"
"As I speak, write down questions so we can all get on-board."	"Let's see…'get on-board.' What the heck does that mean? What am I expected to *do*?"
"I want you all committed."	"What's in it for me? This sounds like more work." "Sounds like we're going to a mental hospital."
"Let's go forward with a good, positive attitude about change."	"Who is 'us'?" "Do I have a choice?"

Figure 12-4: Some poorly considered leader statements and their effects

The very best communicators find ways to touch the heart. And in doing so, the audience often comes to the same conclusions the speaker has already come to. Usually, the best device is a simple, heartfelt story.

According to Robert McKee, the narrative that enables people to come to the same conclusions that you've come to follows the basic formula of any compelling drama, whether a movie, a novel, or a play. To help you get the idea, in Figure 12-5, we state the story element on the left and offer a scenario on the right.

Any leader can learn to use this formulation. Gordon Shaw and colleagues (1998) present a similar scheme, noting that, "A good story (and a good strategic plan) defines relationships, a sequence of events, cause and effect, and a priority among items." In other words, a good story conveys a great deal of information in a compact package.

Story Element	Scenario
The story begins with a description of a situation, one in which things are going along smoothly.	"For the past five years, our company has been the leader in the marketplace."
The storyteller then introduces a conflict.	[Drum roll, thunder clap, haunting music] "But today, our marketplace is crowded by new entrants, many of whom can produce products as good as ours at a lower cost. Some of our best customers have already gone over."
He or she tells of the challenges that need to be surmounted.	"To succeed in our changing world, we have to bring new, better products to market and produce them at a cheaper price."
Finally, the storyteller describes a pathway to resolution.	"This can be the most exciting time in the life of our company, if we pull together as one and address all of our challenges. First, we have to...then, we have to...and finally, we have to..."

Figure 12-5: Elements of a story and examples of how it sounds

This schema is as different as water is from ice, compared to the usual way most business leaders attempt to tell the story of change: through bullet points. Shaw and his colleagues note that bullet points have two glaring limitations: they do not describe connections (they're lists, after all), i.e., they don't say what leads to what. What does it really mean when we see a PowerPoint slide like the one in Figure 12-6, one every businessperson has seen umpteen times?

Figure 12-6: Typical inadequate strategy slide (with commentary)

Implicit in a slide like this, to paraphrase these authors, is probably a dynamic and potentially intriguing vision of possibilities for the organization, the market forces impinging on it, and the needs of customers. But a list like this does not tell us how these objectives relate to one another. In fact, many hugely different scenarios could underlie these three bullets. Let's see: Does increasing profitability mean we then can invest in new products, or is it the reverse? This slide does not come close to saying what will lead to success and thus it is impossible for people to meaningfully participate in its pursuit.

Steve Jobs is famous for his skill in telling a business story, particularly during new product introductions, so much so that, although we have not read it, an entire book has been written about it: *The Presentation Secrets of Steve Jobs: How to Be Insanely Great in Front of Any Audience* (Gallo, 2009). Because of Jobs's notoriety in this realm, we made a point of watching his introduction of the iPad in January 2010. Knowing that the average PowerPoint slide has over 40 words, we counted the words on Jobs's slides: The *entire deck* consisted of 78 words! Twenty-one of those words were on one slide alone. Most of his slides contained no words at all.

In a recent leadership development experience, we asked partic-

ipants to tell a compelling story about their vision for their organization. We gave them overnight to prepare, but no special guidance
or instruction. In their remarks the next day, most used heavily
bulleted PowerPoint slides filled with numbers. Their remarks were
almost completely devoid of vitality. The speakers were wooden,
the slides boring. When they were finished, we gathered the chairs
in a circle and spent an hour discussing the power and value of
stories. We introduced Robert McKee's concepts about storytelling
and the importance of emotional engagement. Every person told of
a time when they were moved by a story. Finally, we said, "Reflect
on the stories that were told in this room an hour ago. Did they
connect with you?" They agreed that only one person in the group
had really connected with them. Then, we asked the speakers to
prepare again, using the formulation in Figure 12-5. The results
were strikingly more compelling: The speakers were animated, the
illustrations vivid, there was humor. The reaction of the audience
was palpably more positive.

Anyone can learn to connect with others, even people who
think of themselves as uncreative and introverted. Be yourself,
speak from the heart. People want to hear *you,* not be distracted by
your dazzling slides and numbers.

Break Down the Strategy Into Achievable Chunks & Enlist the Middle

In Chapter Six, we described how several companies break down
the enterprise strategy and how they help work units at the middle-
level interpret the strategy. We illustrated a very powerful mechanism for doing so called "work unit meetings." We said that the
larger enterprise-level strategy should be visible within every work
unit strategy.

It's possible that this kind of talk seems intellectual and institutional. Perhaps you are the plain-spoken type. Then consider
the words of one of the best leaders we've ever had the pleasure of
working with, Art Ryan, recently retired as Chairman of Prudential. When Art was beginning to turn around this company, he

said:

> *My goal is to quickly get to the point that wherever I go in the company, I will be able to see, hear, and feel the strategy. When I talk to a manager, I want them to tell me what they're working on in the context of what we're **all** working on.*

Do your middle-level managers understand the strategy? Are they taking action in their areas to further its achievement? Do you know or are you guessing? If you are making a presentation about the company's strategy and people look glazed over or they ask no questions, they almost certainly do not know how to help achieve it. If you lead a fairly large organization (you're a CEO with 200-300 employees or more), seriously consider training all managers in the art and science of taking a strategy and applying it to their daily work. In classroom settings, teach them how to create and use a strategy map. Then, ask them to go use what they've learned. Build in a follow-up process. Give extra support to those parts of the organization where strategy execution is most crucial.

Build Support for the Vision Among the Stakeholders

Once you have a strategy and know how the organization must change in order to execute it, you should build a stakeholder map—because there are any number of people whose support you will need to execute your plans.

A stakeholder map does not have to be fancy. Just make a list of those people whose support you need to implement your strategy, or otherwise have a "stake" in it. Make sure you consider at least the following categories:

- Higher-ups
- Peers
- Middle-level managers
- Customers
- Vendors

- Human Resources and other staff groups, e.g., IT, Accounting, etc.

To the extent to which your strategy calls for organizational structure changes, you must get the blessing of at least two groups: your higher-ups and Human Resources. Nobody starts changing the lines and boxes without their bosses being comfortable and without HR knowing what is going on. Start with your boss and then go to HR. (If your HR partners are worth their salt and you come to them first, they will send you right back to your boss.)

Identify all the key stakeholders whose support will be required to realize the strategy and develop an approach to moving them in a supportive direction. Share the strategy map. We'll say it again: get HR involved. Even if you feel critical of HR and think everyone in that department is out to lunch, find a way to work with them anyway. You need them, and chances are that your reaching out to them will be just the opportunity they have been looking for to showcase their capabilities.

At some point, you and your team will meet resistance, yet you will need the support of those resistant stakeholders to execute. When it comes to resistance, the toughest nuts to crack are usually those outside your immediate organization, i.e., those who might lose and your organization gains something.

In thinking through issues of building organizational support, we find Peter Block's work on "positive politics" very useful (1991). For one thing, Block defines politics at work in an exceptionally useful way: Politics is the pursuit of self-interest. Block points out that it is nearly impossible, given this definition, to avoid "politics": To do so is self-defeating. Within this, however, Block points out the choices each of us have: 1) to pursue self-interest in a selfish way, or 2) in a way that builds our important relationships with others.

Block draws the contours of the political landscape, along the two dimensions of Trust and Agreement as in Figure 12-7.

The goal of positive political influence, of course, is to move all of your stakeholders into the "Allies" quadrant. That is what the arrows show. While this is never easy and not even always possible, you have to try. One of the most frequent things we hear our clients say—even CEOs whom everyone theoretically has to do the bidding of— is, "My success depends on the cooperation of others. If only they would join with me." The implication is, "Couldn't you also coach *them* and make *them* cooperate so I can get things done?" It's probably not very satisfying, but we tell our coaching clients what we learned many years ago: "Although it takes two to have a relationship, it only takes one to change its quality" (Fisher and Brown, 1989). Since we are only coaching you, not everyone in your world, if someone is going to change, that person is probably going to be you.

Actors in the Political Drama

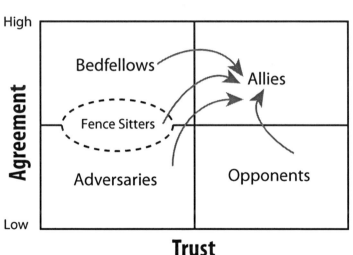

Figure 12-7: New definition of politics: making everyone your ally (Source: Peter Block)

The authors of the world's most widely read book on negotiation (which is *Getting to Yes: Negotiating Agreement Without Giving In,* Fisher, et al., 1991), have made careers of teaching people how to get things done with and through others. In one of their books (Fisher & Brown, 1989), they observe that often, people who need the support of others flee from any type of negotiation when differences arise, posing to themselves—often quite unconsciously—one or another of the following completely artificial dilemmas:

- Should I give in, or sweep my differences with the other party under the rug?

- Where we have real differences, should I sacrifice the relationship to get what I want, or should I sacrifice my interests to preserve the relationship?

- If I want something from the other party, should I give in first, and see if the other party will reciprocate, or should I wait until the other party gives in and then respond in kind?

This list appears to many people to be exclusive: There are no other options. If this seems true for you, hire a coach who can teach you how to improve your influence game.

Monitor and Follow up Relentlessly

Once you create the strategy map and assign action items to it, have at least monthly meetings to review progress against the key initiatives, more often for critical objectives. If deep levels of employee engagement are crucial to your turnaround, devise a way to monitor it and takes steps to shore it up if, and as, it lags. One of our former clients surveyed employee morale and commitment *every quarter for two years!* When we asked the client why she would survey employee engagement every three months, she said, "Employee engagement is crucial to our achieving the strategy. Why wouldn't we frequently assess our efforts to increase it?" We could not argue.

And Finally, CELEBRATE!

Once you've effected organizational change, be sure to acknowledge progress. Do what one of our clients recently did: Close down the plant and put up a tent in the parking lot. Hire a band. Dance. Eat good food. And don't forget to laugh. You deserve it! Best wishes as you move your organization to greatness!

Our web site is filled with resources that support the ideas in this book. Avail yourself of them. Let us know what you're up against, and share your victories. We'd love to hear from you.

www.McKnightKaney.com

References

Barbian, Jeff (2002). "Ensuring Hearts and Minds." *Training*. February.

Becker, Brian E., Huselid, Mark A., & Ulrich, Dave (2001). *The HR Scorecard: Linking People, Strategy, and Performance*. Boston: Harvard Business Press.

Beer, Michael & Eisenstat, Russell A. (2000). "The Silent Killers of Strategy Implementation and Learning." *Sloan Management Review*. Vol. 41, No. 4.

Beer, Michael & Nohria, Nitin (2000). *Breaking the Code of Change: Resolving the Tension between Theory E, and O of Change*. Harvard Business Press.

Block, Peter (1991). *The Empowered Manager: Positive Political Skills at Work*. NY: Jossey-Bass.

Bossidy, Larry & Charan, Ram (2002). *Execution: The Discipline of Getting Things Done*. NY: Crown Business.

Brenman, Jeff, Finch, Karl, & McLeod, Scott (2009). "Did You Know?" Retrieved February 26, from: http://www.chrisrawlinson.com/2009/03/2009-did-you-know-video/.

Bryan, Lowell L. & Joyce, Claudia I. (2007). "Better strategy through organization design: Redesigning an organization to take advantage of today's sources of wealth creation isn't easy, but there can be no better use of a CEO's time." *McKinsey Quarterly*, Number 2.

BusinessWeek (1984). "The New Breed of Strategic Planner." September 17.

BusinessWeek (2002). "25 Ideas for a Changing World," July.

Center for Public Leadership, Harvard (2010): "Business Leaders Are Out for Themselves, Americans Say." Retrieved February 1, from: http://web.hbr.organization/email/archive/dailystat.

php?date=011910.

Challenger Gray & Christmas (2009). "CEO Departures Fall." Retrieved February 27 from: http://challengeratworkblog. blogspot.com/2009/03/ceo-departures-fall-resume-fraud-again.html. Posted 3/12/09.

Chrusciel, Donald (2008). "What motivates the significant/strategic change champion(s)?" *Journal of Organizational Change Management:* 21, 2.

Coakes, Elayne M., Hunter, Gordon, Wenn, Andrew and Clarke, Steve (2002). *Socio-Technical and Human Cognition Elements of Information Systems,* NY: Information Science Publishing.

Cohen, Roger (2008). "Perfecting the Union." *The New York Times,* November 6.

Collins, Jim (2001). *Good to Great: Why Some Companies Make the Leap...and Others Don't.* NY: HarperBusiness.

Collins, Jim & Porras, Jerry I. (2004). *Built to Last: Successful Habits of Visionary Companies.* NY: HarperBusiness.

Conference Board, The (2006). "Strategic Workforce Planning: Forecasting Human Capital Needs to Execute Business Strategy." NY.

Conference Board, The (2010). "U.S. Job Satisfaction at Lowest Level in Two Decades." Retrieved February 25, from: http://www.conference-board.organization/utilities/pressDetail.cfm?press_ID=3820.

Corporate Executive Board (2008). "Improving Employee Performance in the Economic Downturn." Wash., DC.

Coutu, Diane (2009). "Why Teams Don't Work." (Interview with Richard Hackman.) *Harvard Business Review,* May, pp. 98-105.

Cramm, Susan (2010). "Are You Committing Leadership Malpractice?" Retrieved February 25, from: http://blogs.hbr.organization/hbr/cramm/2010/01/are-you-committing-leadership.html.

Crowley, Chris & Lodge, Henry S. (2007). *Younger Next Year: Live Strong, Fit, and Sexy - Until You're 80 and Beyond.* NY: Workman.

de Bono, Edward (1999). *Six Thinking Hats.* NY: Back Bay.

DePree, Max (2004). *Leadership is an Art.* NY: Broadway Business.

Druskat, Vanessa urch & Wolff, Steven (2001). "Building the Emotional Intelligence of Groups." *Harvard Business Review,* March.

Dye, Renee (2008). "How Chief Strategy Officers Think About Their Role." *McKinsey Quarterly,* May.

Economist Intelligence Unit (1999). "Prudential's Learning Project." *Strategic Finance,* June-August.

Fisher, Roger, Ury, William L., & Patton, Bruce (1991). *Getting to Yes: Negotiating Agreement Without Giving In.* NY: Penguin.

Fisher, Roger and Brown, Scott (1989). *Getting Together: Building Relationships As We Negotiate.* NY: Penguin.

Fryer, Bronwyn (2003). "Storytelling That Moves People: An Interview With Screenwriter Robert McKee." *Harvard Business Review,* June.

Galbraith, Jay R. (2001). *Designing Organizations: An Executive Guide to Strategy, Structure, and Process.* NY: Jossey-Bass.

Galbraith, Jay R. Downey, Diane, & Amy Kates (2001). *Designing Dynamic Organizations: A Hands-on Guide for Leaders at All Levels.* NY: Amacom.

Gallo, Carmine (2009). *The Presentation Secrets of Steve Jobs: How to Be Insanely Great in Front of Any Audience.* NY: McGraw-Hill.

Goldsmith, Marshall, Greenberg, Cathy, & Robertson, Alastar (2003). *Global Leadership: The Next Generation.* NY: FT Press.

Hansen, Fay (2009). "What the CEO Wants From HR." *Workforce Management,* July 20.

Hansen, Morten T., Ibarra, Herminia, and Peyer, Urs (2010).

"The 100 Best-Performing CEOs in the World." *Harvard Business Review.* January-February.

Heckscher, Charles (1995). *White Collar Blues: Management Loyalities in an Age of Corporate Restructuring.* NY: Basic Books.

Hertzberg, Frederick (2003). "One More Time: How Do You Motivate Employees?" *Harvard Business Review,* January.

Heskett, James L., Sasser, W. Earl, & Schlesinger, Leonard A. (1997). *The Service Profit Chain.* NY: Free Press.

Huselid, Mark A., Becker, Brian E., & Beatty, Richard W. (2005). *The Workforce Scorecard: Managing Human Capital To Execute Strategy.* Boston: Harvard Business School Press.

Kaplan, Robert S. & Norton, David P. (1996). *The Balanced Scorecard: Translating Strategy into Action.* Boston: Harvard Business Press.

Kaplan, Robert S. & Norton, David P. (2004). *Strategy Maps: Converting Intangible Assets into Tangible Outcomes.* Boston: Harvard Business Press.

Kates, Amy & Galbraith, Jay R. (2007). *Designing Your Organization: Using the STAR Model to Solve 5 Critical Design Challenges.* NY: Jossey-Bass.

Keirsey, David & Bates, Marilyn (1978). *Please Understand Me: Character & Temperament Types.* Del Mar, CA: Prometheus Nemesis Books.

Keirsey, David (1998). *Please Understand Me II: Temperament, Character, Intelligence.* Del Mar, CA: Prometheus Nemesis Books.

Kotter, John (1990). *Force For Change: How Leadership Differs from Management.* NY: Free Press.

Kotter, John (1996). *Leading Change.* Boston: Harvard Business Press.

Lachnit, Carroll (2009). "HR Stagnation." Retrieved June 11, from: workforce.com.

Lawler, Edward E. & Mohrman, Susan A. (2000). "HR As a

Strategic Partner: What Does It Take to Make It Happen?" *Human Resource Planning.* Volume 21: No. 3.

Lawler, Edward E. III & Boudreau, John W. (2009). *Achieving Excellence in Human Resources Management: An Assessment of Human Resource Functions.* Stanford, CA: Stanford University Press.

Lencioni, Patrick M. (2002). *The Five Dysfunctions of a Team: A Leadership Fable,* NY: Jossey-Bass.

London Business School (2010). "CEO challenge 2008: top 10 challenges—financial crisis edition." Retrieved February 25, from: http://lbslibrary.typepad.com/bizresearch/2008/11/ceo-challenge-2008-top-10-challenges-financial-crisis-edition.html.

Maister, David (2003). *Practice What You Preach: What Managers Must Do to Create a High Achievement Culture.* NY: Free Press.

McKinsey & Company (2009). "Unlocking The Potential Of Frontline Managers." *McKinsey Quarterly,* August.

McKnight, Richard (2001). "The Four Jobs of Strategy Implementation." *OD Practitioner,* May.

McKnight, Richard (2002a). "Moving the Rock: Transforming Prudential Through Whole System Change." *Proceedings,* OD Network.

McKnight, Richard (2002b). "One Prudential Exchange: the Insurance Giant's Business Literacy and Alignment Platform." *Human Resource Management Journal,* Fall.

McKnight, Richard (2010). *Victim, Survivor, or Navigator: Choosing a Response to Workplace Change.* Philadelphia: TrueNorth Press.

McLuhan, Marshall (1994). *Understanding Media: The Extensions of Man.* Boston: MIT Press.

Mintzberg, Henry (1994). *The Rise And Fall Of Strategic Planning.* NY: The Free Press.

money.cnn.com (2010). "100 Best Companies To Work For." Retrieved February 25, from: http://money.cnn.com/magazines/

fortune/bestcompanies/2010/.

Moore, Geoffrey A. (2005). *Dealing with Darwin: How Great Companies Innovate at Every Phase of Their Evolution.* NY: Penguin.

Moren, Dan (2010). "Apple Ranks Third in Customer Service Survey." Retrieved February 25, from: http://www.pcworld. com/businesscenter/article/189946/apple_ranks_third_in_ customer_service_survey.html.

Myers & Briggs Foundation (2010). "Type Tables." Retrieved April 1, from: http://www.myersbriggs.org/my-mbti-personal-ity-type/mbti-basics/type-tables.asp.

Nussbaum, Bruce (2002). "Why the World Needs New Think-ing." *BusinessWeek,* August 26.

O'Toole, James & Bennis, Warren (2009). "What's Needed Next: A Culture of Candor." *Harvard Business Review,* June.

Pagonis, William G. (2001). "Leadership in a Combat Zone," Boston: *Harvard Business Review,* December.

Phillips, Donald T. (1993). *Lincoln on Leadership: Executive Strat-egies for Tough Times.* NY: Warner Books.

Schutz, Will (1994). *The Human Element: Productivity, Self-Es-teem, and the Bottom Line.* NY: Jossey Bass.

Shaw, Gordon, Brown, Robert, & Bromiley, Philip (1998). "Strategic Stories: How 3M Is Rewriting Business Planning." *Harvard Business Review,* May.

Slater, Robert (1999). *The GE Way Fieldbook: Jack Welch's Battle Plan for Corporate Revolution.* NY: McGraw-Hill.

Terkel, Studs (1997). *Working: People Talk About What They Do All Day and How They Feel About What They Do.* NY: New Press.

Treacy, Michael & Weirsema, Fred (1997). *The Discipline of Mar-ket Leaders: Choose Your Customers, Narrow Your Focus, Domi-nate Your Market.* NY: Basic Books.

Tynan, Dan (2006). "The 25 Worst Tech Products of All Time."

Name and Subject Index

The Authors

Richard McKnight

Richard (Rick) McKnight, PhD is the author of *Victim, Survivor, or Navigator: Choosing a Response to Workplace Change.* For the five years prior to co-founding McKnight • Kaney, he was VP, Organizational Consulting at Right Management. Before that, he was self-employed for 20 years as a consultant to senior leaders in various Fortune 500 firms.

Tom Kaney

Tom has specialized in the strategic management of Human Resources and organizational change for over 20 years. He has been SVP Human Resources for Medarex, Inc., SVP Human Resources for GlaxoSmithKline NA, and a leader in HR at Subaru of America. Tom is widely acknowledged for his expertise in business strategy formulation and execution.

Shannon Breuer

Shannon is President of The Wiley Group, a Philadelphia-based wealth advisory firm. Shannon has led enterprise-wide HR and communications initiatives in Fortune 100 firms for 20 years. As Director of Corporate HR and Communications for Sunoco, she established new talent management systems that directly link to strategy, created and installed mentoring and networking programs, and launched and managed the company's diversity strategy.

McKnight • Kaney
Strategy Execution

Based in the Philadelphia area, our methodology gets every employee, every leader, and every business line and unit on the same page. We combine eight strands of expertise:

- Organization design
- Strategy mapping
- Senior team alignment
- Employee engagement
- Change management
- Performance management
- Alignment of HR with the strategy
- Executive coaching

You can find out more about us at McKnightKaney.com.

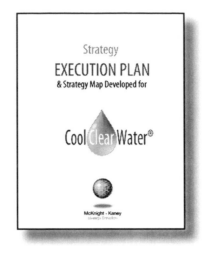

Strategy
EXECUTION PLAN
& Strategy Map Developed for

Cool Clear Water®

McKnight · Kaney

Strategy MAPPING®

An Alignment & Strategy Execution Planning Methodology
for Senior Teams

This process builds an execution plan and an aligned senior team. More than mere team-building, it supports senior leaders in identifying and removing barriers to strategic results while building a sustainable, high performance organizational culture. This methodology positions senior leaders as a coordinated strategy execution team and enables them to enlist all employees as partners in driving for strategic results.

Through this process, senior leaders assess the fit of all aspects of their organization's design—structure, processes, reward systems, people processes—with the strategy and, where there are gaps, create plans to close them.

Executives emerge with a written plan that summarizes actions the senior team will take in six capability areas that correspond to MKB's organizational design model: vertical structure, business processes, reward systems, leadership development, people practices, and top team alignment.

McKnightKaney.com

Inquire About The

Leading Strategy Execution®

In-House Seminar

The Holy Grail of strategy execution for most senior leaders is getting everyone in the organization to understand, feel enthusiastic about, and take action in alignment with the company's strategy. This seminar will help your leaders accomplish this.

In the seminar, participants:
- Create an executable strategy
- Document their strategy in the form of a Strategy Map
- Design and implement an organization capable of delivering on the strategy
- Build an aligned team that will execute the strategy
- Learn how to get all employees on-board
- Cultivate support for the strategy from all stakeholders

McKnightKaney.com

Strategy change means organizational change. Help your employees deal with it.

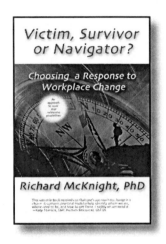

This book is written to help employees make the best of workplace change. It tells how employees can use workplace change as an opportunity to learn and grow despite the turbulence around them.

The book articulates the three choices everyone has during change: to be a Victim who fights or takes flight, a Survivor who deals with change via political maneuvering, or to be a Navigator, one who finds ways to use the upheaval to become a stronger, wiser, more productive person. The book provides detailed guidance for getting out of Victim or Survivor mode and moving into Navigator mode. The final chapter contains checklists, worksheets, and exercises helpful to the reader who wishes to choose a productive response to their current circumstances.